SOUL PSYCHOLOGY & RAJA YOGA

Spiritual Practices for Enlightenment

Leoni Hodgson

All rights reserved.

Copyright © Leoni Hodgson published December 2021.

No part of this publication may be reproduced, stored in a retrieval system, or transmitted in any form or by any means, electronic, mechanical, photocopying, recording or otherwise, without the prior written permission of the author.

ISBN: 978-0-6483012-8-8

About the Author

Leoni Hodgson works professionally as a practitioner and teacher in several specialist areas in the esoteric arts - Astrology (DMNZAS - Diploma Member of the NZ Astrological Society 1982, and the PMAFA - Professional Member of the American Federation of Astrologers 1983), Esoteric Psychology (MA in Esoteric Psychology and Ph.D. in Esoteric Philosophy), Raja Yoga and Esoteric Healing (INEH Certificate).

About this Book

Over the ages, Eastern Teachers have given humanity various systems to facilitate self-understanding and to bring about the evolution of consciousness. Buddhists gave the Noble Eightfold Way, Christianity the Ten Commandments and Patanjali gave us Raja Yoga (to name a few).

Then in the 20th Century, the Tibetan Master Djwhal Khul (DK) gave the world Esoteric Psychology. It draws upon all the previous teachings, adds to the science of Astrology and modern Psychology and introduces the Science of the Seven Rays. This latter science is but a study of the various energies that make up a human being and their intelligent mixing and harmonising and this part of Esoteric Psychology is studied in this book.

Esoteric Psychology is the Science of the Soul. It is the study of soul energy, how it affects human psychology and determines what a man should be. This science studies the evolution of consciousness.

Khul also gave us his interpretation of the Raja Yoga sutras of Patanjali, the study of mind and its development so that enlightenment can be achieved.

The essential points in these two books have been gathered together in this work, in an attempt to simplify what can appear complex.

The goal of this book is to help students gain a clear understanding of consciousness - the developments the soul makes and the problems it faces, as it journeys from ignorance to enlightenment. This information is accompanied with spiritual practices to empower students and so they know what they have to do to intelligently walk the Spiritual Path.

Leoni Hodgson

Acknowledgments

This book is dedicated to the world service work of the Tibetan Master Djwhal Khul; particularly in the field of Esoteric Psychology and the evolution of consciousness.

Loving thanks to my husband Jim Hodgson who supports me so generously in all my endeavours.

Thanks to Dreamstime Buddi-Bodi clipart.

Other Books Written by the Author

Journey of the Soul.
A Handbook for Esoteric Psychology and Astrology.
Published 2018.

Medical Astrology.
Discover the Psychology of Disease using Triangles.
Published February 2018.

Astrology of Spirit, Soul and Body.
A Handbook for Esoteric Astrology.
Published November 2018.

Learn Astrology.
A Guide for Absolute Beginners.
Published February 2020.

The Spiritual Evolution of Nations.
Astrology Eclipses, Stars & Planet Transits.
Published April 2021.

Foreword

Soul Psychology & Raja Yoga: Spiritual Practices for Enlightenment; is a long title for a short truth – that of the soul's development through the gradations of incarnation. What does it mean, where does it go, and what is it for? These then are the eternal questions of the soul's journey from ignorance to awakening bliss. Our soul's journey is one of discovery. The discovery of meaning. Our brother Djwhal Khul talked a lot about the World of Meaning in his many books. This volume by Leoni Hodgson adds to the accumulated knowledge concerning this stupendous feat – from mineralisation through the vortex of time through the soul to the Monad. This book not only adds knowledge, it adds the ingredients of understanding – and it is clearly laid out and easy to read.

In *Chapter 1: Evolution of Consciousness;* the various parts of our nature – personality, soul and spirit are explained. Then the soul's journey from ignorance to enlightenment are examined in "the Three Halls of Spiritual Training" section. Charting the journey from Lemuria, through Atlantis to our Aryan state of being and henceforth through the initiatory gates of passage that we each must tread. This book outlines for us, in readable terms, the ring-pass-not of the soul's incredible functions as it climbs, through many lifetimes, from the mire of illusion to the real.

In *Chapter 2: The Seven Rays & Psychology,* the author has described each of the Seven Rays, how they function and produce seven major psychological types. Readers will also learn how to create their own Personality Profile chart and that of others, and how to read such a chart.

In *Chapter 3: Esoteric Psychology,* Hodgson has taken the essence of these teachings and has placed them within the context of modern psychological thought. This pioneering work was presented to humanity by the Tibetan Master, Djwhal Khul, through the various Alice Bailey books in the early 20th Century. The many problems that beset both the masses and also Mystics and Disciples, are categorised as problems of misaligned energies, which need harmonising and balancing. Hodgson has placed modern psychological problems and thought into the context of this Eastern Wisdom.

In the original manuscript of Alice Bailey's commentary of Patanjali's teachings concerning Raja Yoga, we find this injunction (later included in the book Discipleship in the New Age Vol.1): "Seeking nothing, asking nothing, hoping nothing for the separated self; may we be content to be in the light or in the dark, to be active or passive, to work or to wait, to speak or to be silent, to take praise or reproach, to feel sorrow or joy—our only wish to be what They need as instruments for Their mighty work, and to fill whatever post is vacant in Their household."

In *Chapter 4: Raja Yoga Spiritual Practices*; Hodgson has extracted the important work which we must all apply to progress from darkness to Light, from the unreal to the Real, from death to Immortality – and in the process of doing so, serve in a Master's Ashram.

As we progress, the greatest of all illusions becomes all the more apparent – that of separatism. For there is no greater lie than the falseness of the illusion of temporary existence, or that we are separate from the One Universal Existence. Both Djwhal Khul and Patanjali (the author of the Raja Yoga teachings), highlight these points in their work and the necessary steps to take to reach enlightenment. These problems are clearly highlighted in this book, and the recommended spiritual practices to overcome them.

Welcome to the journey of light which, *Soul Psychology & Raja Yoga: Spiritual Practices for Enlightenment,* sets forth – combining both knowledge and the open hand of friendship. The soul's assent is assured, as are the guiding hands of light that seek you out. One thing is for sure, you will never be alone. Your steps are those that have been trodden before and you light the way for others to follow.

Steven Slava Chernikeef, MSc, MA.
Author: the Esoteric Apprentice, 2025
and the World Teacher and others.

SOUL PSYCHOLOGY & RAJA YOGA

Spiritual Practices for Enlightenment

CONTENTS

CHAPTER 1: EVOLUTION OF CONSCIOUSNESS 1
   I. Spirit, soul & body: The Journey of the Soul. 3
   II. Three Halls of Spiritual Training. 17

CHAPTER 2: THE 7 RAYS & PSYCHOLOGY 29
   I. the 7 Rays & Psychology 31
   II. The 7-Ray Personality Profile Method 47

CHAPTER 3. ESOTERIC PSYCHOLOGY 63
   I. Psychology Problems affecting the masses 73
   II. Problems of Mystics & Disciples 99

CHAPTER 4. RAJA YOGA SPIRITUAL PRACTICES 109
   Book 1 - The Problem of Union 111
   Book 2 - The Steps to Union. 119
   The Eight Means to Yoga 131
       Means I Yama: "The Commandments." 132
       Means 2: Nijama, "The Rules." 139
       Means III: Asana (right poise). 143
       Means IV: Pranayama (BreatH-Control). 145
       Means V: Pratyahara - Abstraction - Detachment. 148
   Book 3: Union and its Results. 155
       Means VI Dharana - Concentration. 155
       Means VII. Dhyana - Meditation 157
       Means VIII Samadhi - Contemplation 173
       Appendix 179
       Index 186

CHAPTER 1: EVOLUTION OF CONSCIOUSNESS

I. SPIRIT, SOUL & BODY: THE JOURNEY OF THE SOUL.

As we grow and evolve, we reach a point where an urge arises within us to better understand what life is all about. We ask ourselves questions about our existence and begin a search to find answers.

"Who am I"?

"Who am I," is the first question that arises with burning and insistent intensity. The query is instigated by our spiritual nature and when it is pursued, unfolds our consciousness. If we are still identified with sexual desire, we might say "I am a passionate and sexual being". If we are still identified with intellectual cleverness, we might answer, "I am intelligent". Or, if we are identified with higher wisdom our response may be "I am a kind and loving soul". We express as much of the inner wisdom and love of the soul that we are able, and we answer the question differently depending upon our level of consciousness and the perspective from which we view life.

"Where do I come from?"

This is often the next question that concerns the searching soul - "Where do I come from?" The spiritual philosophy upon which this book is based is sourced from mystical Biblical teachings, esoteric Buddhism and Vedanta, and the answer they provide is that we are children of a higher supernormal Power. All lives that exist have been inspired into existence by this Power which some call God, and are returning to God. The Bible says the same thing that we exist because of God and our task while on earth is to become like God.

People think of God in many different ways. But esoterically, it is the Source of Light and Life, which resides in the heart of every atom and scrap of life in the universe. Here is an esoteric definition for God that is fundamental to the whole philosophy of this book.

> **God defined.** That sumtotal of manifestation which can be called Nature, or God and which is the aggregate of all the states of consciousness. This is the God to Whom the Christian refers when he says "in Him we live, and move, and have our being"; this is the force, or energy, which the scientist recognises; and this is the universal mind, or the Oversoul of the philosopher. This, again, is the intelligent Will which controls, formulates, binds, constructs, develops, and brings all to an ultimate perfection. This is that Perfection which .. lies hidden at the heart of the atom of chemistry, within the heart of man himself, within the planet, and within the solar system. It is that something which drives

all on toward the goal, and is the force which is gradually bringing order out of chaos; ultimate perfection out of temporary imperfection; good out of seeming evil; and out of darkness and disaster that which we shall someday recognise as beautiful, right, and true. [1]

In a technical sense, God in manifestation is triune, appears as a three-fold energy influence commonly known as "Spirit-Soul-Body" or "Father, Son, Holy Ghost" (Bible). This trinity as it manifests through the human kingdom, is shown in the drawing.

"Why am I here and where am I going?"

Then follows a series of questions about the purpose of existence. Our evolutionary task as a soul, is to continually broaden our perspective of life by living the most creative, fulfilling and productive life that we can manage - to learn, grow in character and expand our psychological understanding of the world. We achieve this through many incarnations, and by passing through all the human departments in the world, from the very lowest to the highest. Consequently, we grow spiritually until in time, consciousness becomes illumined with the radiance and wisdom of our true soul nature.

----

§ **The goal of Soul Psychology & Raja Yoga is to help students gain a clear understanding of consciousness - the developments the soul makes and the problems it faces, as it journeys from ignorance to enlightenment. This information is accompanied with spiritual practices to empower students and so they know what they have to do to intelligently walk the Spiritual Path.**

---

1 Bailey, Alice. The Consciousness of the Atom, 21-22.

The Human Constitution - our Spiritual Nature.

An overview of our spiritual nature is essential in this study of esoteric psychology, because - whether we realise it or not, we are profoundly affected in every aspect of life by the influences streaming in from the soul. Many of the psychological disorders we experience are directly related to this influence. This section will help readers understand these different levels of consciousness.

1. The Monad - Source of Consciousness.

The Monad - also known as a ray or spark of God, is our highest spiritual aspect because it is our direct link with God. The soul is the vehicle of the Monad.

In the '7 Planes of Consciousness' diagram further on, note that the Monad is one level down from God consciousness in the manifesting process. It is too pure to descend any lower. The Monad is the ultimate source of consciousness, the highest aspect in all living entities in the universe. At the birth of a universe, wave after wave of Monadic groups stream out from the central Life (God) to circle through the universe from high to low and then from low to high again; a cycle called the "Cycle of Necessity" [1].

During this cycle, the Monads work through all the kingdoms of nature (via the soul), to experience and learn at all levels. This is a great sacrifice made by the Monads, because by falling into incarnation - and during the aeons they are submerged under the veils of matter, they lose their high intelligence and spirituality. [2] But eventually, when this cycle is complete, this intelligence and spirituality is regained and the enlightened Monad is absorbed back into its Source. Here is a wonderful description of this consummation:

> After the separation between the life-principle and the body takes place, the liberated soul — monad, exultingly rejoins the mother and father spirit. Adam who has completed the circle of necessity is freed from the last vestige of his physical encasement. Henceforth, growing more and more radiant at each step of his upward progress, he mounts the shining path that ends at the point from which he started around the Grand Cycle. [3]

2. The Spiritual Triad of "Spirit".

On the next level down is the Spiritual Triad, the body of expression of the Monad.

When we refer to our spiritual nature or to "spirit", this is the Spiritual Triad. The inclusion of the word "triad" is because it is triple in nature. It is of the nature of atma, buddhi and manas; or spiritual will, spiritual love (or soul), and spiritual mind; or the Will of God, the Love of God and the Mind of God.

In the '7 Planes' diagram, note that the triangle that represents the Triad anchors at the very top of the mental plane, technically on the 1st subplane. This is the highest and finest layer of mental essence. This point of the triangle represents the Mind of God.

During the evolutionary process, the Triad works through the soul (which in turn uses the personality - mind, emotions and physical), to perfect self-consciousness.

---

1 Barborka, Geoffrey; The Divine Plan, 105.
2 The Mahatma Letters to A. P. Sinnett, 94.
3 Blavatsky, Helena; Isis Unveiled 1, 303.

3. The Soul.

Every living thing has a soul, be it an atom, animal, man, planet, galaxy etc. The soul is the middle or mediating factor in the Spirit-Soul-Body trilogy. The soul is the child of Father Spirit and Mother Matter. When God (Spirit) breathed life into matter when the two merged, soul or consciousness arose.

The Universal Life moves through all the kingdoms in nature and there are various levels of "soul". However, although every living thing has a soul - not all souls are equal in consciousness. The group soul in the mineral kingdom is not as developed (in terms of conscious awareness and response) as the oversoul of vegetable life. Likewise, the animal soul is not as advanced as souls in the human kingdom. The great difference between the two latter kingdoms is that animals have a group soul, they all share the same memories. Humans have individualised souls and an individual path in life. Consequently, within the human kingdom some souls are more spiritually advanced than those who are still in the "flesh and devil" stage of life experience.

1. The Human Soul stage.

We began our journey in the human kingdom, when - at the dawn of history, as animal-men, we received the gift of an individualised consciousness/ intelligence/ soul.

Soul, consciousness, intelligence, the psyche, these are all synonymous terms.

Thus, we began to make individual progress towards enlightenment. The primary driver of human evolution, is *pain*. The uses of pain are many, but as the soul incarnates from life to life, pain and the learning experiences associated with it leads the human soul out of darkness into light, out of bondage into liberation, and from agony to peace. Peace, light and liberation within the ordered harmony of the cosmos is the God-given right for all souls.

> Soul is that integrating coherent something which makes the human being *a thinking, feeling and aspiring entity*. The intellect in man is that factor or quality of soul-awareness which enables him to orient himself to his environment during the stages in which his personality is under development. [1]

The nature of the soul is light and love. But while it goes through the human experience it loses its identification with its spiritual origins and identifies with the forms it uses to incarnate through. This is the dark night of the soul experience. In this period, the soul is sometimes called the "human soul."

2. The Spiritual Soul stage.

Then there comes the stage when the soul begins to extend its range of response into the higher levels of the mental plane (where the soul body, the egoic lotus is located), and into the Buddhic plane. Freed from all attachment to forms in the human worlds, consciousness, the soul, comes into its own as identification is made with the Spiritual Soul.

> The soul alone has the power to contact the germ or the principle of Buddhi (in the Christian phraseology, the Christ principle) to be found at the heart of every atom. [2]
>
> Buddhi, is the Universal Soul, the Christ consciousness, also called Universal Mind or Intelligence. *Buddhi, is the spiritual soul in man.*

---
1 Bailey, Alice. Intellect to Intuition, 53-54.
2 Bailey, Alice. Light of the Soul, 19.

3. The Solar Angels and Man.

As their name suggests, the Solar Angels originate from the Sun. They are fire devas of the mental plane and are included in this section because they have an intimate connection with the soul of man. The Solar Angels act as our Spiritual Soul (Buddhi), until we have built the bridge of consciousness (antahkarana) to the Buddhic plane, to our Spiritual Soul.

At the birth of the human kingdom, the Angels came to earth to help primitive animal-man become truly human. To achieve this, they planted in man's higher mental field, the seed of his soul nature, called the egoic lotus or the causal body. At this early stage, this seed was like a closed and colourless lotus bud.

The Solar Angels remain with us through the aeons, hovering over the egoic lotus and helping it to unfold like a flower by fanning its flame. Under this attention, gradually across lives, the spiritual gifts inherent in the lotus develop. The Angels remain with us until we can guide our own destiny wisely.

Unfoldment of the Petals of the Egoic Lotus.

In the egoic lotus are three circles of petals, surrounding an inner ring of three more petals that cover the "jewel in the lotus". When we become spiritually conscious, the Spiritual Triad works through this "jewel" and through the centres of the seven major chakras in the body. Each petal in the lotus represents certain qualities that are latent within the nature and each petal unfolds as its associated quality unfolds.

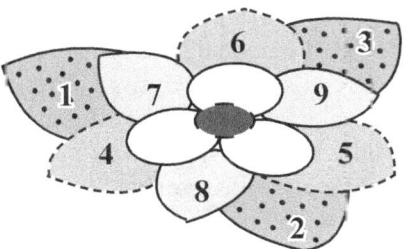

Petals
1. Knowledge-knowledge.
2. Knowledge-love.
3. Knowledge-sacrifice.
4. Love-knowledge.
5. Love-love.
6. Love-sacrifice.
7. Sacrifice-knowledge.
8. Sacrifice-love.
9. Sacrifice-sacrifice.

The 3 inner petals cover the "jewel in the lotus."

a. The Knowledge Petals (1 to 3). They unfold through experience on the physical plane, through the pain we experience as we try to survive, and the rejections and hurts we suffer. As we learn to make better choices to avoid these sufferings and rejections; petals 1 to 3 unfold.

b. The Love Petals (4 to 6). They unfold through experience on the astral plane and through emotional challenges. At this level we are required to transmute selfish love into unconditional love and selfish desire into higher aspiration. As we progress and stabilise ourselves emotionally, love of the Real develops and personal desire is sacrificed for the greater group good. Petals 4 to 6 unfold in this period.

The unfoldment of petal 5 (the love-love petal), is most significant for spiritual growth. It means we have reached the stage when real progress can be made because we are learning to love unselfishly. This is when the Solar Angel gives its full-time attention to our development, and when we step onto the Spiritual Path. [1]

c. The Sacrifice Petals (7 to 9) unfold on the mental plane and mark the first three human initiations. Petal 7, marks the 1st Initiation - control of the physical nature. Petal 8, marks the 2nd Initiation - control of the emotional nature. Petal 9, marks the 3rd and 4th initiations that free us from the human worlds. This is when the Solar Angels leave us and return to the Sun.

---

[1] The Spiritual Path: also called the Path of Spiritual Development or just "the Path", is the search for spiritual knowledge and enlightenment.

The Sutratma, Antahkarana and the Creative Thread.

These 3 threads of light connect man to his soul and spiritual aspects.

1. The Life-Thread, Sutratma, the Silver Cord. The sutratma works from above downwards and is the direct stream of life emanating from God, to the Monad, to the Soul, through the human bodies to the heart where it anchors. This thread carries the life, the will and purpose of the Monad. It vitalises the physical, emotional and mental bodies and forces them to evolve. When it withdraws, the body dies.

2. The Consciousness Thread, the Antahkarana (Bridge of Light, the Rainbow Bridge, the Thread of Continuity, and the Path of Return). It is our conscious response to God, built out of mental essence from below upwards. It inter-weaves with the sutratma as it does so. All the wisdom we gain through our life-experiences, meditative work and the magical creative work of the soul goes into its building. When completed, it spans the gap between the higher and lower divisions of consciousness, from the brain to the spiritual Triad. Through it, information flows between the soul, mind and brain.

First the antahkarana knits together the personality aspects and by the time we are integrated personalities, it has reached from the brain to the concrete mind. Then, as group consciousness develops, it extends to the soul on the higher mental plane. The final link of the antahkarana is built directly from the personality to the Triad (bypassing the soul), then to the Monad. Spiritual awareness is developed in this final stage of building. It gives the initiate who has achieved this, control over the life.

The antahkarana represents all *past* experiences that have led to our current level of *awareness*. The thread withdraws every time we go to sleep or lose consciousness and reconnects as we wake up.

3. The Creative Thread. It is the product of our creative efforts, constructed through the ages. As it is built, it synthesises and interweaves with the life and consciousness threads. In the primitive man stage, progress is virtually nil. But as we truly come alive, from the standpoint of intelligent awareness, and as we go out into life to express ourselves fully and creatively, the building of the thread is more rapid. Anchoring in the throat chakra, the centre of creative activity, it is constructed through our mental and spiritual creative efforts over the centuries.

Ida, Pingala and Sushumna.

In the spinal column are three energy threads known as *Ida, Pingala* and *Sushumna*. They are the externalisations of the antahkarana, the sutratma and the creative thread. Pingala carries the fire of matter which develops the personality. Ida carries solar fire (the fire of mind) and is related to the path of consciousness and soul unfoldment. Sushumna is the path of pure spirit and carries electric fire (spiritual fire or force).

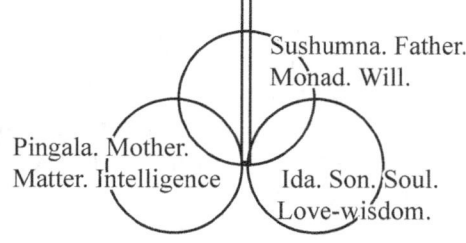

Alice. Bailey, *Esoteric Healing*, 184

As evolution proceeds, Ida and Pingala begin to equilibrise, reflecting the alignment that is taking place between the personality and soul. When a connection is made between the personality and the Monad (via the completed antahkarana), the Monad arouses kundalini from the base centre via the Sushumna path.

The Human Constitution - the lower Nature.

§ **The non-spiritual part of our nature consists of the physical body in its dense and etheric parts, the emotional body and the lower concrete mind body. When the forces of these separate parts integrate into a composite whole (as they do in the developed, intelligent man), the "personality" comes into existence.**

1a. The Dense Physical Body

The soul, our true nature, is a light-being. The physical body gives the soul access to the physical world and this is vital because the ascension of consciousness can only occur through experience on the physical plane.

The physical body is like a robot. It does what it is told to do. If we are emotional people, the body will be used to search for happiness. If we are ambitious, the body will be used to pursue wealth and power. If we seek enlightenment, the body will be used for that. Whatever our life ambition may be, we achieve it only through the medium of the physical body. Therefore, we must look after it and take steps to keep it healthy and strong. Especially when we advance spiritually. Then, the body must keep up with the normal demands of outer life as well as cope with the higher forces pouring through from the soul. The Master said:

> A good server causes the Master no anxiety from physical causes, and may be trusted to guard his physical strength so he is always available for the carrying out of the Master's requests. He does not fail from physical disability. He gets sufficient rest, adequate sleep, rises early and retires at a seemly hour. He relaxes whenever possible, eats wholesome and suitable food. A little food, well-chosen and well masticated, is far better than a heavy meal. He ceases from work when (through accident or the recurrence of inherited physical disability) his body reacts against action and cries out for attention. He then seeks rest, sleep, dietary precautions and necessary medical attention. He obeys all wise instruction, giving time for his recovery. [1]

A problem of many enthusiastic servers, is that they exhaust themselves physically. In the following quote, Master Djwhal Khul told one of his disciples how to vitalise his exhausted body. It is included here so that readers can follow the advice if they wish.

> Etheric vitalisation lies in meditation *where you are concerned* and the bringing in of energy to your physical body through its instrumentality... the main cure for you and the source of success in all your work lies in your persistence in meditation and your contemplative endurance. You have untold reserves upon which to draw and as yet you use them not as you might. You make not adequate use of the meditation period. How to utilise the meditation period so as to benefit from it physically. Visualise the inflow of energy to the centres in the etheric body and the vitalisation, above all, of the heart and the throat centres. This should be carried forward in a rapid and definite manner. [2]

---
1 Bailey, Alice. Letters on Occult Meditation 345-6.
2 Bailey, Alice. Discipleship in the New Age I, 157.

1b. The (Physical) Etheric Body.

The physical body has two levels - the dense physical and the etheric web which most people cannot see.

The etheric web is a golden-coloured network composed of millions of very fine energy lines (nadis), which underlie, support and vitalise the dense physical body. Every form in nature has its own individual etheric web, and each is a tiny link in the overall, universal mother-web that stretches across the entire field of space.

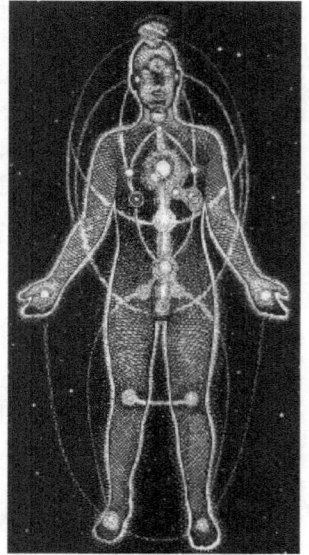

> The field of space is etheric in nature and its vital body is composed of the totality of etheric bodies of all constellations, solar systems and planets which are found therein. Throughout this cosmic golden web there is a constant circulation of energies and forces. [1]

These nadi energy-strands form the channels through which prana flows. Prana is the vitalising energy of life that flows from the Sun. The web has been described as a network, permeated with fire, or as a web, animated with golden light. In the Bible it is called a "golden bowl." (Ecclesiastes 12:5).

Artistic impression of the etheric web, from *'A Thousand Points of Light'*, Malvin Artley.

The etheric web is the energy framework and blueprint upon which the dense physical body is constructed and to which it conforms. The dense body takes on the shape of its web. Underlying and interpenetrating the entire body, the etheric-web gives it energy and life.

All forces that play through the field of space must pass through the etheric web to reach the physical body. The web of the average person draws in life and soul force, and forces from the lower mental plane, the astral plane and prana from the physical plane to vitalise the physical body. The web also picks up energy from the environment we are in and the people we mix with. Those who have made a connection with the soul can also consciously draw in soul and spiritual forces.

The state of our individual etheric web determines our health. A strong, robust etheric is an excellent conductor of vitality and gives excellent health. A poorly strung together web with obstructions and impediments leaves the body impoverished energetically and susceptible to disease and ill health.

The Chakras or Force Centres.

In the web are many force centres (chakras), formed where energy lines cross. They are whirlpools of force that swirl etheric, astral and mental matter into activity of some kind. Because the action is rotary, the result produced in matter is a circular effect that can be seen by the clairvoyant as fiery wheels.

Crown — 960 petals
Ajna — 96 petals
Throat — 16 petals
Heart — 12 petals
Solar Plexus — 10 petals
Sacral — 6 petals
Base — 4 petals

'Radionics and the Subtle Anatomy of Man,' David Tansley.

---

1 Bailey, Alice. *Esoteric Astrology*, 11.

There are seven major chakras - major because they are involved with the development of consciousness. These seven are safely developed through a normal and balanced approach to life and through right-thought. Forced development through intense meditation or breathing practises is dangerous because it draws in excessive pranic and spiritual fire that will inflame an unprepared nervous system.

> The centres in the human being deal fundamentally with the FIRE aspect in man, or with his divine spirit. [1]

Regarding the location of the 5 lower chakras.

> Some consider them to be at the front of the body, which is the involutionary route that carries energy downwards. The esotericist considers them to lie at the back, just outside the spinal column. The spine is the evolutionary route which carries energy upwards. [2]

1. The 3 lower chakras.

a. The Base Chakra. It draws in physical plane energy to vitalise the dense physical body. Individuals with very powerful and selfish lower wills also work through this centre. It is the last one to fully open in the spiritually awakened man, when kundalini power in the base is drawn upwards to the crown.

b. The Sacral Chakra. It governs sex and other physical and material appetites and comforts. It draws in the energy of desire from the astral plane. Those who are still controlled by lower desire work primarily through this centre. When the physical appetites are being balanced (marking the 1st Initiation [3]), sacral energy begins to be raised to the throat centre.

c. The Solar Plexus Chakra. It draws in emotional force from the astral plane. In average man it works closely with the sacral and throat centres. [4] In such people, the desire for happiness, material satisfaction and comfort is compelling and the mind is a slave to that compulsion.

2. The Four Higher Major Centres.

As consciousness rises, the higher chakras come alive.

a. The Throat Chakra. Intelligent people who are not yet creative in a spiritual sense, focus in this centre. It draws in energy from the lower mental plane, from the concrete mind to vitalise the creative life. When this centre comes into activity, it marks the first faint orientation of man towards his spiritual nature.

b. The Heart Chakra. Under soul impulse and as the emotional life is balanced, aspirants begin to awaken this centre. [5] As desire transmutes into spiritual aspiration, the heart chakra draws up the energies of the solar plexus, which are then expressed through the heart. The heart centre relates us to the Buddhic plane and the second divine aspect of love and wisdom. It is the centre of spiritual, unconditional love, just as the solar plexus is the seat of personal, conditional human love.

---

1 Bailey, Alice. A Treatise on Cosmic Fire, 165.
2 Bailey, Alice. Esoteric Psychology II, 589.
3 Initiation is simply an expansion of consciousness, moving up one subplane or plane on the spiritual ladder.
4 Consciousness focuses in 3 chakras and planes at a time.
5 This occurs at the 2nd initiation.

c. The Brow or Ajna Chakra. Advanced intelligent people, aspirants and disciples focus here. As the seat of personality power, the ajna comes alive prior to the Path. Today it is awakening rapidly in many. It gives higher creativity and the ability to understand patterns and greater wholes. But if the ego is still in control of life when it opens, instead of its power being used for the greater good, its force flows down into the lower chakras to feed selfish material interests. The ajna opens fully when enlightenment occurs (at the 3rd initiation).

d. The Crown Chakra. It provides the soul with its point of entry and exit in the body. Disciples are awakening the crown, but it only opens fully to 3rd degree initiates (at enlightenment). At the 4th initiation, the Monad - from the crown chakra, takes control of all the centres and forces in the body. It draws up kundalini (the fire of matter), from the base chakra

> The human being who can do this in full consciousness is therefore an initiate who has left the third initiation behind him. He, and he alone, can safely raise this triple fire from the base of the spine to the head centre. [1]

As kundalini weaves its way up the etheric spinal column, etheric substance separating the various centres burns away. This poses grave physical and psychological danger for the man or woman who - through arrogance or ignorance, raises this fire prematurely.

2. The Astral / Emotional Body.

The emotional body (also called the astral body, the desirous, passionate body), gives expression to emotions ranging from love and compassion to fear and hate. It forms attachments, aspires, attracts, repulses, feels and fears. A great reflector - when unpurified, it takes colour and movement from every passing desire, sound and motion.

- In advanced man the emotional field anchors in the heart centre, giving expression to higher feelings of spiritual love that emanate from the Buddhic nature (spiritual soul) on the Buddhic plane.
- In the average person, it anchors in the solar plexus centre and the desirous sacral centre.

The consciousness of the average person is still focused primarily in the emotional body. This means that in such people, all major life decisions are driven by the wants and needs of the astral body. Such people swing between the opposites of pleasure and pain and life is filled with turmoil, instability and fear. It is the most difficult and painful part of our spiritual journey.

This problem was pointed out by Buddha in his Four Noble Truths when he said, "The cause of all sorrow and woe is desire for that which is material."

The difference between feelings, emotion and desire (passion).

The mind and astral bodies work together to produce feelings, emotion and desire. As we move through our daily life our astral sense constantly "feels" and tests all our experiences. Feelings are generated all the time, but these may not necessarily evolve into an emotion. It is only when the mind engages, that an emotion is generated.

An emotion arises when the mind investigates to discover whether an experience that generated a feeling is "good" or "bad". If the mind determines the experience is good, a positive emotion arises such as "I am happy." If the mind judges the experience to be bad, a negative emotion rises, such as "I am sad." Then, emotion evokes desire.

---
[1] Bailey, Alice. Esoteric Healing, 185.

Desire or passion is the sensuous grasping after that which gives pleasure in the outer life. Most people are caught up in a cycle of desire. They desire, they pursue the desired object, they get the desired object, then after a while as the attraction for that object wanes, the object is discarded. Then the cycle starts again with a new object. Or, if the desired object is denied them, they descend into a period of emotional suffering. And so it goes. In the Raja Yoga sutras, Patanjali said desire is, "an attachment to objects of pleasure." [1] Prolonged desire for something etches it deeply into the emotional brain and an addiction forms. Desired objects can range from the very coarse, to the desire for intellectual pursuits and desire for a god or Master. Lower desire keeps us bound to the Wheel of Rebirth, physical incarnation and a life of suffering.

> It is love of sense perceptions and attraction for all, that brings a man back
> again and again into the condition of physical plane existence. [2]

Buddha also told us how to escape this life of suffering - simply, detach from the desire for material things. It is the toughest but most important challenge and battle we face on the Spiritual Path. This is achieved through detachment training so that the emotional body stops responding or reacting automatically to external stimuli. It trains the astral ocean to become serene and mirror-like. When we achieve this, we have taken a vital step towards liberating ourselves from the world of suffering.

3. The Mental Body.

The mind distinguishes humans from animals. It is the individualising principle that enables us to know that we exist, that we feel and that we know. We spend many lives developing the mind (the 6th sense) and once achieved it is an evolutionary achievement. This development is crucial in the battle to control the astral nature, because only through the will-aspect of the mind can this be done.

> The will, which usually demonstrates itself through a programme or ordered
> plan, originates in the mind. [3]

a. The average human concrete mind is like a computer. It is the thinking, analytical machine that is used to build thoughts, to concentrate, to analyse, to associate, to sort, to compare, to contrast, to deduce, to correlate and to memorise.

Whenever we think, the mind is at work, building our thoughts from mental essence. Everyone makes thoughtforms, but unthinking or dreamy people make vague and ill formed thoughts that dissipate quickly. Strong thinkers produce well thought-out thoughtforms that are sharply defined, which last longer and have a powerful effect on others.

b. Lower mind holds a record of the past. Its contents are a combination of the unconscious and conscious aspects of mind. Every action leaves its impression. Nothing is lost. The records of all our experiences are stored in the subconscious mind. This colours our whole life experience. We are the result of all that we have ever thought, felt and done. When we look at life through the lower concrete mind, we look through a window coloured by all past experiences. When a new image comes into the mind, the existing vibrations modify it. The new thought in turn, modifies the existing mind contents. This is why the mind is called the "slayer of the real". It is impossible to see life clearly, to see reality as it is as long as the

---

[1] Bailey, Alice. Light of the Soul, 135.
[2] Ibid, 67.
[3] Bailey, Alice. Esoteric Psychology II, 419.

unconscious mind is filled with residue from the past. Perception is inaccurate. As a result, so-called free-will is not free at all. Tied to lower mind, we react in accordance with our past. We may aspire to change, to live by higher ideals, but good intentions will be defeated if the contents of the mind are not purified.

c. Kama-manas mind: in the average person the mind seems to be fused with the astral /desire (kama) body. As a result, its natural inclination is to downward look into the lower three worlds. This is why there is an instantaneous emotional-mental reaction when such people see or hear something they do not like, or that they do like. Mind is not free or impartial. It is bound to the astral nature. It is its slave. This type of mind is defensive and fearful. It constantly scans life to identify any dangers or attacks.

> Lower mind is pivotal because it unites either with the soul or with the ego - Gautama Buddha reportedly said that "The mind can make a man a Buddha or a beast".

d. The mind's ultimate function is to be the instrument of the soul. Our job is to learn to detach the mind from its downward gazing tendency and train it to "look upwards" towards the soul, while it still does its job in the outer world. This is what is required.

The Brain, the Switchboard of the Mind.

The brain is a wonderful and delicate instrument that serves the mind. In conjunction with the five senses, it is the medium through which the thinker communicates with the physical world. Djwhal Khul called the brain, "That great receiving plate upon the physical plane." [1]

For a long time, the personality is "the thinker" that controls the brain. But as spiritual disciplines proceed, gradually the soul becomes "the thinker," and it uses the brain as its eye to gaze into the physical world. This is achieved by building the antahkarana, the thread or bridge of consciousness, from the brain to the soul.

4. The Personality.

People are generally referred to as "personalities." But in the early stages there is only a loose arrangement of emotions interspersed with glimpses of intelligence. The mind, emotional and physical bodies all act independently and pull in different directions. Consequently, life is an unregulated and chaotic struggle. As the mind develops, the ego [2] becomes ambitious for things it wants to get in the world. To get these things, it uses mental-will to coordinate and control the emotional and physical forces. This integrates these three bodies and consequently, the "personality"/ ego arises. The personality knows what it wants - and now that it is a coordinated force, has the will and drive to get what it wants.

> **Personality defined.** A personality is a blend of mental energy, of emotional energy and of vital force, and these three are masked, hidden or revealed by the outer physical form. These aspects develop sequentially and progressively and when integrated or unified, constitute that sense of individuality which justifies the use of the word 'I', and which relates all occurrences to a self. Where this central conscious entity exists, utilising the mind, reacting sensuously through the emotional body and energising the dense physical, then one has a personality. It is awareness of identity in relation to other identities. [3]

1 Bailey, Alice. Light of the Soul, 412-413.
2 In modern psychology, the ego refers to a person's sense of self-esteem or self-importance. This is how it is used in this book. Some esoteric writers such as Helena Blavatsky used the term "ego" to signify the indwelling thinker, the soul.
3 Bailey, Alice. A Treatise on White Magic, 391-2.

Chapter 1. Evolution of Consciousness - I. Spirit, Soul & Body: The Journey of the Soul. - 15

At first the personality is separative and selfishly ambitious and fights the soul to control the life. Unspiritualised, this rampant and ambitious ego is a danger to itself and to others. But gradually, as spiritual disciplines are applied, the personality is brought under the control of the soul. When this happens, lower autonomy is eliminated. The "I am I" thinking aspect has been raised into the soul. The personality maintains the traits of the personality ray (whichever ray it should happen to be), but its forces, talents and powers are now extensions of the soul, to be used in the world as service requirements demand.

Diagram - The 7 Planes of Consciousness in the solar system.

Planes			Chakras
1	Logoic plane. *God/ Avatar awareness*	God consciousness in our solar system	Crown
2	Monadic plane. *Christ / Buddha*	MONAD	Crown & Ajna
3	Atmic plane. *Masters of the Wisdom*	Spiritual Triad	Crown & Throat
4	Buddhic plane. The Spiritual Soul. *Arhats, intuitives.*		Heart & Ajna
5 -1	Mental - higher - *adept*	ANTAHKARANA	Heart & Ajna
-2	- *initiate*	Egoic Lotus	
-3	- *disciple*	ANTAHKARANA	
-4	Mental - lower - *aspirant*	Mental Unit	-Throat
-5	*Average intelligent man*	Mind	
-6	subplanes		
-7	subplanes		
6	Astral plane. *Average Emotional Man*	Emotions	Solar plexus/ Sacral
7	Physical-etheric plane. *Unevolved animal man*	Physical-Etheric	Sacral & Base

NB. All planes have 7 subplanes, but they are shown only on the mental plane.

This chart will help readers gain a clearer understanding of the planes and the different levels of consciousness in our solar system. The names of the planes are on the left-hand side and so are the names of those who have reached that level of consciousness.

Each plane represents a combination of spirit and matter.[1] Matter is simply spirit at its most dense; spirit is matter at its finest. The 7th plane is the most dense - the 1st plane is the finest. Through life experience over many incarnations, consciousness ascends through these levels. As a consequence, we become more spiritual and less material.

1st Logoic Plane. The plane of God consciousness.

2nd Monadic Plane. The plane of the Monads - they work through the Spiritual Triad.

3rd Atmic Plane. The Spiritual-Will (or Atma) aspect of the Triad.

4th Buddhic Plane. The Spiritual-Soul (Buddhi) aspect of the Triad.

5th Mental Plane.
a. On the 1st subplane of the mental plane, is the Spiritual Mind aspect of the Triad.

b. On the 3rd subplane is the average egoic lotus (which rises to the 2nd and 1st subplanes as we progress).

c. The antahkarana, the bridge of consciousness, spans the gap between the concrete mind and the soul and from the brain to the Monad, spanning the 3rd, 2nd and 1st subplanes to do this. It interweaves upwards with the sutratma as it progresses.

d. On the 4th subplane is the mental unit, the concrete mind.

6th Astral Plane. The plane of the emotions. Most people function at this level.

7th Physical Plane. The physical-etheric body level.

a. The dotted vertical line represents the sutratma, the life-thread. It stretches through all planes from spirit to form.

b. On the right-hand-side of the chart are the names of the seven major chakras associated with each plane. They each draw in the forces from their planes to be distributed through the physical body.

c. The lower three planes (5 of lower mind, 6 and 7) are the human worlds.

d. The Path of Spiritual Development begins at the soul, on the higher mental plane.

e. Note that the arrows for the Paths of Evolution and Spiritual Development go off the chart at the top. There are six higher universes above ours. We scale them all.

f. A simple way to view the process is like climbing a ladder. We move from one level to the next, from one chakra to a higher one. But in truth, the planes are not stacked one on top of another as the diagram shows. This is for convenience. They are spheroidal and intermeshed.

This concludes this section on the Human Constitution. In the next section, the evolution of consciousness is examined.

---

1 All 7 planes are subdivided again into 7 subplanes. The planes are not stacked as shown, but are spheroidal.

II. THREE HALLS OF SPIRITUAL TRAINING.

In our solar system, we pass through seven expansions of consciousness and as many initiations. This growth occurs in three great Halls of learning, which are equivalent to kindergarten, high school and university. This process is guided by the Solar Angels who "touch" consciousness three times to stimulate evolutionary growth.

INITIATIONS are inner syntheses and fusions that mark specific developments and expansions of consciousness. Each initiation enables us to function consciously on a higher level than before and to express a greater proportion of wisdom. Here is a definition.

> What, therefore, is Initiation? It is first of all the entering into a new and wider dimensional world by the expansion of a man's consciousness so that he can include and encompass that which he now excludes and from which he normally separates himself in his thinking and acts. It is, secondly, the entering into man of those energies which are distinctive of the soul and of the soul alone—the forces of intelligent love and of spiritual will. [1] The following chart lists 9 initiations we take in this solar system. 7 are related to each plane of consciousness. Notice that each initiation gives greater freedoms and interaction with the universe. Initiations 8 and 9 occur also in our solar system, but they are considered more cosmic than systemic.

Nine Initiations in our solar system (Rays and Initiations, 340).

	Initiation Name	Plane	Chakra affected	Candidates	Freedom:
1	Birth	Physical	Sacral	Aspirants	.. from the physical appetites
2	Baptism	Astral	S. Plexus	Disciples	.. from the emotional control
3	Transfiguration	Mental	Ajna	Initiates	.. from the personality
4	Renunciation	Buddhic	Heart	Arhats	.. from the material world
5	Revelation	Atmic	Base	Masters	.. to see the higher worlds
6	Decision	Monadic	Throat	World Saviours	Freedom of choice
7	Resurrection	Logoic	Head		Freedom of the Cosmos
8	Transition	Planetary	Hierarchy	*Beyond Earth life*	
9	Refusal	Systemic	Shamballa		

---

1 Bailey, Alice. Esoteric Psychology II, 12

A. The Hall of Ignorance - development of Human Life.

1. Birth of the Human Kingdom.

Our physical human race began when our souls graduated from the animal kingdom into the human kingdom. This was organised by the Solar Angels, who make two interventions in this hall. The first intervention was at the dawn of human history.

Solar Angel intervention 1--

The Solar Angels are the fire angels or builders of the mental plane. They appropriated an animal-man vehicle to work with and gave it the spark of mind, an individual human soul (egoic lotus). [1] This intervention was called "The Touch of Appropriation," and "individualisation". This was the birth hour of the human soul and the human kingdom. Immediately, the young soul begins training in the Hall of Ignorance.

----

1. Incarnations spent in this Hall: approximately 700. [2]

2. The Goal. To desire and experience all that human, material life has to offer. To live earth life to the fullest, to be self-indulgent and satisfy all lower cravings. By living fully in the "World of the Flesh and the Devil," the mind and personality develop and are used to totally exhaust desire.

3. The experience. In the Hall of Ignorance, consciousness identifies with the phenomenal world. The form controls and the material side predominates. Consciousness is "kama-manasic," or mind heavily influenced by the emotions. This means the emotions and desires control the thought life and life-decisions that are being made. Young souls, [3] who constitute the bulk of the emotional masses labour here. So do educated men and women who are still polarised in the selfish and separative personality.

These influences do their work until the throat chakra is developed and the lower mind controls the emotional and physical impulses. Once the cup of pleasure has been fully drained and the mind recognises this as a fact, then dissatisfaction with all that has been known and experienced rises. This leads to the portals of the Hall of Learning and to the Probationary Path. [4]

2. The first 3 levels of consciousness develop in this Hall.

▲ *Lemurian consciousness - physical man.*

The first physical human root race was called the "Lemurian Race. [5]

Consciousness was dull and inert. This primitive race focused in the sacral and base chakras and lived on a continent called Lemuria. There are still pockets of people with their consciousness at this level hidden away in isolated regions. Aeons of adjustments and developments occurred during which the soul tightened its hold upon the physical body and refined the physical/ sexual appetites.

---

1 Animals have a group soul.
2 Bailey, Alice. A Treatise on Cosmic Fire, 825.
3 Young souls: are those who are still identified with the outer phenomenal world. In most cases, their Monads would have entered into earth-life later than "older" souls.
4 Bailey, Alice. Initiation, Human and Solar, 64.
5 There were two embryonic non-physical races before the Lemurian Race, which can be liked to the gestation period prior to birth.

▲ *Atlantean consciousness - emotional man.*

Gradually over time, racial-consciousness began to rise into the next higher plane of consciousness - the astral plane. The feeling nature came alive and man began to desire. Focus lifted from the sacral chakra to the solar-plexus.

As the consciousness of the race stabilised in the emotional body, the urge for satisfaction became less animal and more emotional. No longer (for instance) was just food adequate, now cooked food and the choicer portions became desirable. Moods and feelings were recognised and the subtler pleasures such as the desire for peace and happiness.

This is the level at which the masses of humanity today are still located. Although part of consciousness may be reaching into the mental plane, the emotional nature still dominates their choices. Such people, the average masses, are still Atlantean in consciousness.

▲ *Aryan consciousness, intelligent man.*

Gradually, the consciousness of the race began to rise into the throat chakra, to pierce through into the lower mental plane, causing the powers of the concrete lower mind to unfold. This is the level of growth that is rapidly taking place today on earth amongst the educated masses.

> Lower mind awareness and intelligence is called "Aryan." It has nothing to do with a physical race or Nazis (who adopted the term), but concerns this mind-level development.

The lower mind develops its power and self-consciousness develops - the ability to view oneself as an "I". The mind, emotional and physical bodies integrate into a composite whole and the personality emerges, a most important development.

a. At first the personality is selfish and separative. It is driven by a sense of personal destiny, by a sense of power, self-love, exalted ambition and a determination to dominate the environment.

b. Then, as a small measure of soul contact is acquired, the personality's methods and motives become a mixture of selfishness and of spiritual vision. Enough is known to aspire to something higher in life, but will-power is lacking. In desperation a call is made to the soul for help. This triggers the second Solar Angel intervention.

Solar Angel intervention 2---

The struggling soul sends out a cry for help and the Solar Angel responds with the "Touch of Acquiescence," a booster-surge of intelligent light energy to strengthen the mind and spiritual will. This touch opens the doorway to the Hall of Learning.

----

§ *Thus the first, the longest and the most difficult part of the Path is completed. The indwelling soul has managed to make major impacts upon the bodies it has to work through while in incarnation, and now the lower nature is relatively sophisticated. Human life in all its depths and heights has been experienced and now, with the soul's passage into the Hall of Learning, spiritual training begins in earnest.*

B. The Hall of Learning or Knowledge - 1st Initiation.

The Acquisition of Knowledge.

1. Incarnations spent in this Hall: approximately 70. [1]

2. The Goal. To take the 1st Initiation and become a self-conscious individual, free "from the control of the physical body and its appetites." [2]

3. The experience. It begins with a sense of satiety and tiredness with things as they have been known and a desire to change life so that it aligns with a new and higher set of values. A search for knowledge brings about an understanding of the soul. There is a recognition of duality in the nature, which needs to be coordinated, and the need to balance and control the physical appetites.

> The evolutionary goal in this hall is to acquire and assimilate "knowledge." This is the product and goal of the Hall of Learning, achieved by utilising the five senses.

We go out into the world and we correlate, we diagnose and we define what we experience through the use of the intellect. All that we are certain about through weighing and measuring, is part of this experience. All that concerns the material side of evolution is part of the experience in the Hall of Learning.

▲ Aspirational Consciousness - the mystic.

Eventually, there comes a stage when interest in the outer, material side of life wanes and in response to increasing light within, the indwelling soul begins to turn inwards. Those who have reached this level are called aspirants (also devotees), because although still basically selfish, they now aspire to finer things in life.

> Aspirants are preoccupied with their own little affairs and with their own small efforts, for their own interpretations of truth and for their pet ideals of peace. All their lives they have fought for an ideal and a dream and they love that more than they love humanity. [3]

The probationary Path of Discipleship has been reached (the 3rd subplane of the mental plane), and the mind is being illumined with the light of the soul. This stage in the life of the aspirant-devotee is a life of struggle.

> The life of aspirants is one of constant movement, changes, differentiations and continuous building and breaking, planning and seeing those plans disrupted. It is a life of ceaseless suffering, of frequent clashing with environing circumstances, of numerous friendships made and [broken], of mutation ceaseless and consequent agony. Ideals are transcended only to be found to be stations on the road to higher; visions are seen, only to be replaced by others; dreams are dreamt only to be realized and discarded; friends are made, to be loved and left behind. [4]

The aspirant's fight to overcome the hindering obstacles of the physical nature leads to the 1st Initiation.

---
1 Bailey, Alice. A Treatise on Cosmic Fire, 827.
2 Bailey, Alice. The Rays and the Initiations, 685.
3 Bailey, Alice. The Externalisation of the Hierarchy, 310.
4 Bailey, Alice. Treatise on White Magic 264.

------------------------- The 1st Initiation -------------------------

1. The goal of the 1st Initiation. This is to bring the animal nature and appetites fully under control. This initiation is represented in the Bible by Jesus' birth at Bethlehem, in the manger surrounded by animals (representing the animal nature).

2. Candidates for the 1st Initiation.
    a. Advanced intelligentsia and aspirants, including mystics and devotees who seek union with God, but who have not yet developed the powers of the mind. The latter being emotional are still subject to glamour.
    b. Those who are beginning to exhaust and deny the demands and desires of the lower nature (food, sex, materialism) and who now aspire to a higher and finer life.
    c. Those who are becoming interested in human welfare, who desire true peace based on right human relations implemented by goodwill and those who are drawn into a new life of group service.
    d. People who are in "revolt against materialistic religion." [1]

3. Advice to help candidates. Because control of the physical appetites is the goal for this 1st Initiation (no one is accepted for training by the Masters whose physical appetites are still in control), encourage a healthy diet, fasting and vegetarianism. The use of physical energy in pastimes and creative activities that develop the mind is helpful and so is participating in personal development and esoteric groups.

4. Chakra Activity. As the life focus moves gradually from sex to higher creative endeavours, the sacral energies rise to the throat centre.

5. Qualities demonstrated when the 1st is taken. Those who have taken the 1st initiation have taken the first step into the spiritual kingdom and have started on the pilgrimage of the Path. A totally new life and mode of living has begun, a new manner of thinking and of perception. There is a new attitude to relationships and although negative attitudes persist, the love of all humanity has taken root in the heart.
    a. There is freedom from the control of the physical appetites [2] and sex has become a natural and balanced appetite.
    b. Mental equipment is growing and the emphasis turns to astral control. [3]
    c. Inner and outer silence are developing. There is less talking and more listening.
    d. There may still be little soul control. [4]

At the 1st initiation we become "accepted disciples" [5] and pass into the Hall of Wisdom. [6]

Having groped his way through the Hall of Ignorance during many ages, and having gone to school in the Hall of Learning, he is now entering into the university, or the Hall of Wisdom. [7]

---

1 Bailey, Alice. Destiny of the Nations, 149.
2 Gathered from AAB. The Rays and the Initiations, 685
3 Bailey, Alice. Initiation, Human and Solar, 84.
4 Gathered from AAB. Esoteric Psychology II, 14.
5 Bailey, Alice. Discipleship in the New Age, I, 728.
6 Bailey, Alice. Initiation, Human and Solar, 84. Accepted Disciple covers the stages of the 1st and 2nd initiations.
7 Bailey, Alice. Initiation, Human and Solar, 10.

C. The Hall of Wisdom - the 2nd & 3rd Initiations.

The Occult Life.

1. Incarnations spent in this Hall: approximately 7. [1]

2. The goal: to control the emotional life so that the 2nd initiation can be taken, and then control the entire lower nature so the 3rd Initiation can be taken.

3. The experience. A further expansion of consciousness occurs as identification is made with the spiritual man. There is a growing capacity to enter deeper into the mind of the Logos [2] and to realise the true inwardness and vast sweep of the great pageantry of the universe.

▲ **Discipleship consciousness - the Occultist.**

The "discipleship" level of consciousness has been reached. Consciousness has risen to the 3rd subplane [3] of the higher mental plane. The personality is coordinated and fusion with the soul increases. The soul is now coming into its spiritual maturity.

Here is a description of a disciple:

> **For what is a disciple?** He is one who seeks to learn a new rhythm, to enter a new field of experience and to follow the steps of that advanced humanity who have trodden ahead of him the path, leading from darkness to light, from the unreal to the real. He has tasted the joys of life in the world of illusion and has learnt their powerlessness to satisfy and hold him. Now he is in a state of transition between the new and the old states of being. His spiritual perception grows slowly and surely as the brain becomes capable of illumination from the soul, via the mind. As the intuition develops, the radius of awareness grows and new fields of knowledge unfold. Frequently then he reaches the position in which Arjuna found himself, confronted by enemies who are those of his own household, confused as to his duty and discouraged as he seeks to balance himself between the pairs of opposites... (continued) ...

This quote ends (below) with an important point being made. The disciple finds and works with a group of like-minded and principled disciples, and with that part of the Spiritual Plan for Humanity that she or he can best contribute to.

> .... As he perseveres and struggles, surmounts his problems and brings his desires and thoughts under control the Master is found; his group of disciples is contacted; the plan for the immediate share of work he must assume is realized and gradually worked out on the physical plane. [4]

The tests of discipleship are severe - this experience is called "the greater burning ground." A pure heart, true unconditional love, mental acuity and a determined orientation towards the light is required to help the disciple move through these life challenges. If any of these do not exist, the disciple will fall. But this too is temporary and part of the overall experience.

---

1 Bailey, Alice. A Treatise on Cosmic Fire, 828.
2 Logos: a cosmic intelligence, the manifested unity at the head of any hierarchy, sometimes referred to as "God."
3 Bailey, Alice. Initiation, Human and Solar, 179.
4 Bailey, Alice. Treatise on White Magic, 58-60.

------------------ **2nd "Atlantean" or Baptism Initiation** ------------------

1. The goal of the 2nd Initiation. To control the astral body. This initiation is represented in the Bible with Jesus' baptism in the River Jordan.

2. Candidates for the 2nd Initiation.
    a. Emotional crises are driving the person to seek relief and inner peace.
    b. There is an ability to think in wider terms and to work in groups.
    c. There is mental flexibility and a lack of fanaticism to any truth or spiritual leader. [1]
    d. The emotional nature is making the transition from personal and conditional love, to unconditional love for all humanity.

3. Advice to help candidates. Explain the goal of the initiation. Encourage intellectual development and spiritual practices such as Raja Yoga, which train the mind to be more responsive to spirit. Encourage a study of the astral plane, the need to apply emotional disciplines, to meditate daily and to join a group espousing high ideals, etc.

4. Chakra Activity. Energies are transferring from the solar plexus to the heart. Sacral energies continue to move to the throat centre, via the heart, giving an aspiration to serve. The ajna centre is coming alive and the battle is on between the personality and the soul to see who "sits in the driver's seat," (the ajna).

5. Qualities Demonstrated when the 2nd Initiation is taken.
    a. Aspiration and longing to serve is so strong, rapid development occurs.
    b. Desire is being transmuted into love, [2] and humility is being demonstrated.
    c. Emotions may still powerful but the mind is now able to control them.
    d. The determination to think in wider and more inclusive terms is demonstrated by voicing the fact that all men are divine. [3]
    e. There is a growing sense of unity with all that breathes and with the One Life. This leads to expressed brotherhood - the goal of the Aquarian Age. [4]
    f. People who seek mental polarisation, who aspire to think and to know and who are demonstrating control of the physical appetites, they "have taken the second, or are on the verge of so doing." [5]

Disciples who have taken the 2nd initiation are regarded as "probationary initiates." Only when the 3rd is taken are they truly initiate. Once the 2nd has been taken and the desire nature is under control, the Path is travelled with increased speed and sometimes the 3rd and 4th are taken in the same or next life. [6]

Danger on the Path.
Until the third initiation is taken and pride is overcome, there is still danger that the disciple may mistake the spurious for the real, succumb to glamour and take the left-hand path of Black Magic - use soul-force for selfish, material use. But once the 3rd initiation is taken this is not possible.

---

1 Gathered from AAB. The Rays and the Initiations, 127.
2 Gathered from Bailey, Alice. Esoteric Healing, 156.
3 Bailey, Alice. The Rays and the Initiations, 679
4 Gathered from Bailey, Alice. The Destiny of the Nations, 138.
5 Bailey, Alice. Rays and Initiations, 667.
6 Bailey, Alice. Initiation Human and Solar, 84-85.

---------- The 3rd Transfiguration-Enlightenment [1] Initiation ----------

1. The goal of the 3rd Initiation. Soul control of the personality. This leads to the battle fought between the Dweller on the Threshold and the Angel of the Presence.

The Dweller on the Threshold. It is a vitalised thoughtform, the sumtotal of lifetimes of persistent and unregenerated attachments and selfish bad habits still deeply ingrained in the nature and that stand like an imposing wall between the disciple and enlightenment. Always present, the Dweller makes its final stand at this initiation.

But having reached the point where the intuition has been developed, and the mind can be held steadily in the Light of the soul; the disciple has earned the right for spiritual intervention on his part. The Angel of the Presence (the Solar Angel, representing this time the Spiritual Triad), intercedes. Here is the scene.

The Angel of the Presence stands on one side, the Dweller stands on the other. Between them, in the centre of the "burning ground," stands the disciple. The task is to hold this vertical alignment with the soul, with the Light, whenever negative thoughts or tendencies assail the mind. Whenever this can be done, the destroying light of the Angel can shine into the depths of the disciple's consciousness and destroy the Dweller's grip. This continues until the radiant Light of the Angel obliterates all trace of the Dweller and the entire nature is illumined.

2. Candidates for the 3rd Initiation.
   a. These disciples are fully self-conscious. They are mystics capable of pure vision and motivated by spiritual intent. They are trained occultists, mentally polarised and profoundly aware of the realities, forces and energies of existence and are therefore free from the ordinary glamours and illusions that colour the reactions and life of the average man. [2]
   b. They approach life from a level tableland of experience and not from the heights of aspiration or fanatical sacrifice. They have an adjusted sense of proportion and are forward-looking towards the soul and not backward looking towards the form nature.
   c. The disciple is trying to conform to a higher spiritual Law and is seeking to control the mind and manipulate thought matter to overcome illusion. [3]
   d. Self-forgetfulness and temperance in all things are now normal and natural.

3. Chakra Activity. The head centres are highly active and energy is being transferred from the base to the crown.

Solar Angel intervention 3--

The Solar Angel makes its third and final intervention at the Transfiguration initiation. As it gives the "Touch of Enlightenment," spiritual light breaks forth and the soul and the personality stand forth as one.

---

[1] Enlightenment is a relative term. The first enlightenment occurs when the personality is flooded with soul light. The second higher enlightenment is when the Monad floods the spiritual man with God-light.
[2] Gathered from Bailey, Alice. Esoteric Astrology, 307.
[3] Gathered from Bailey, Alice. Esoteric Astrology, 600.

▲ **Initiate consciousness.**

The initiate is a blend of scientific and religious training and has fused and blended the soul and personality. Consciousness has risen to the 2nd subplane of the mental plane.

The initiations so far equip disciples to receive impressions emanating from Shamballa (centre where the "Will of God is Known"), and this initiation brings the initiate into close proximity to it. The initiate has passed through a symbolic doorway, has left behind the close company of men and women below the rank he has attained and joins the spiritual impersonality of his ashramic group. Understanding the portion of the Plan of God [1] which the ashram he belongs to is responsible for, he takes on his share of the load and serves impersonally in the world.

> At the third Initiation of Transfiguration, the control of the personality in the three worlds is broken in order that the Son of Mind, the soul, may be substituted finally for the concrete and hitherto directing lower mind. Again, through the Law of Sacrifice, the personality is liberated and becomes simply an agent of the soul. [2]

4. Qualities demonstrated when the 3rd (Transfiguration) Initiation is taken.

   a. 3rd degree initiates have been born again, purified and transfigured. [3] They can now be trusted to ask nothing for the separated self and the personality is tempered and adjusted to group conditions. [4]

   b. The Monadic Ray controls the personality, [5] which means there is complete freedom from the claims and demands of the personality and its life. [6] All sense of separateness has been lost and the initiate is now identified with the Life Aspect.

   c. Consciousness is now planetary, [7] and is one with the "Father in Heaven." [8] Those at this level can therefore enter somewhat into the state of consciousness of our planetary Logos and sense His destiny and vision.

   d. Governed by the Law of Repulse, they reject all that is non-essential to their life of service in the world. They speak not of their achievements and make no reference to themselves or to their accomplishments save to deprecate the littleness of what has been done.

   e. Those working in the outer world will assume influential roles in groups or organisations working for the good of humanity. They may be misunderstood and criticised, but ignore this, realising his work will in due time help to fulfil the Plan.

Thus, the door and the past are left behind. Of this idea, St. Paul said: "Forgetting the things which are behind, press forward towards the prize of your high calling in Christ." [9] While world-service proceeds, the initiate likewise prepares himself to tread the Way of the Higher Evolution and of higher initiations.

---

1 The Plan of God for humanity (also just "the Plan"); the goal of the Plan is the fusion of spirit and matter, through the evolution of the soul of man. Bailey, Alice. Esoteric Psychology I, 353.
2 Bailey, Alice. Discipleship in the New Age II, 398.
3 Bailey, Alice. From Bethlehem to Calvary, 166.
4 Bailey, Alice. Discipleship in the New Age II, 406.
5 Gathered from Bailey, Alice. A Treatise on Cosmic Fire, 176.
6 Bailey, Alice. The Rays and the Initiations, 44.
7 Gathered from Bailey, Alice. Esoteric Astrology, 359.
8 Gathered from Bailey, Alice. Initiation Human and Solar, 19.
9 Bailey, Alice. Esoteric Psychology II, 72.

D. Arhats, Masters of the Wisdom and the Higher Initiations.

The 4th Arhat initiation is the final training period prior to taking the 5th Mastership initiation. It is most challenging, because all personal associations and relationships in the world are cut away. This also includes the ending of the long association with the Solar Angel.

▲ *Arhat consciousness.*

An arhat is an initiate of the 4th degree. Cutting away all the ties that bind, this includes the causal body, the soul lotus, which was required to bridge the divide in consciousness between the personality and the Spiritual Triad. It is no longer required because the Monad now has a direct link to the brain. The lotus shatters and the Solar Angel - having fulfilled its task, returns to the Sun.

After the 4th initiation and the disappearance of the causal body, consciousness has ascended to the Buddhic Plane. Now there is no form aspect to hold the Arhat prisoner. He stands in his intuitional (Buddhic) body and is one with the Monad.

> The disintegration that is a part of the arhat initiation leads to unity between the Ego [1] and the Monad, expressing itself in the Triad. It is the perfect at-one-ment.

▲ *Master of the Wisdom consciousness.*

These exalted personages who have taken the 5th initiation are called Masters because they have gained mastery over the forces of the five planes that souls in the human kingdom work through (the atmic, buddhic, mental, astral and physical). In consciousness, Masters are one "with the Monad", [2] are Masters of Compassion [3], Masters of the Wisdom. After Mastership, spiritual man moves beyond the Hall of Wisdom to higher initiations that finish solar system experience and lead to the cosmos.

> A true Master of the Wisdom has not only taken the lesser initiations referred to above, but has also taken the five steps involved in the conscious control of the five planes of human evolution. It remains for him then to take the two final initiations which make him a Chohan of the sixth degree, and a Buddha. [4], [5]

Emancipated and illumined Masters and Buddhas of the 7th initiation, have mastered all levels in the solar system and have control therein. They have broken free of the ring-pass-not of our solar system and have access to the open doorway to the cosmos.

1. Stages of the Master-Pupil Relationship. [6]

When we step onto the Path of Spiritual Development, we come under the guidance of one of the Masters - although this is not something that we are consciously aware of in the early stages. Our training is conducted by a disciple - or if we show promise, by an initiate.

---

1 Ego (Latin) The personal pronoun "I"; in philosophy and theosophy, the ego is the center of 'I-am-ship' or egoity in the human being. There are two such centres: the spiritual and impersonal, commonly called the individuality (as in this quote); and the personal, often called the soul or the personality. Theosophical Glossary.
2 Bailey, Alice. Initiation Human and Solar, 19.
3 Bailey, Alice. Initiation, Human and Solar, 10.
4 Bailey, Alice. Initiation, Human and Solar, 180.
5 Senior Masters Morya and Koot Hoomi have taken the 6th initiation, as have also the Buddha and Christ (Rays and Initiations, 17, 396).
6 Gathered from AAB. Letters on Occult Meditation, 278.

The ashram we become affiliated with is determined by our soul ray, past karma, any association we may have had with the Master in a previous life, and the need of the hour. Early entry into a Master's ashram can also come about if we have needed skills that will benefit the world work the Master has responsibility for.

No one is overlooked if they are ready to be admitted into an ashram for more intense training. The Master's attention is drawn by the brilliance of a student's indwelling light. When the bodies are sufficiently refined, when the aura is of a certain hue, when the vibration has been raised and the life sounds an occult note, it attracts the Master's attention.

Then, the Master makes a small image of the probationer [1] composed of emotional and mental matter that shows all the fluctuations of the nature. The Master works with this image to stimulate the pupil's bodies. For instance, applying a higher vibration to step up the student's vibration in readiness for initiation or to bring it into harmony with the Master's vibration. This takes place mostly at night when the student is out of the physical body, or during meditation. Other concerns of the Master are to expand the consciousness of the pupil, vivify the centres and their correct awakening, and develop the capacity to work in group formation.

Finally comes a time when on inspection of the image, the Master sees that the needed rate of vibration is held, the required eliminations have been made and a certain depth of colour has been attained. Then he takes the risk and admits the probationer into his aura. Consequently, the disciple becomes an "accepted disciple." At this stage, we may become consciously aware of this contact.

2. The Masters train students to be Esotericists. The Masters are esotericists and train their disciples to live a life that is in tune with the inner sacred realities and to use their energies to manifest the Divine Plan of Goodwill. They are light-bearers (carriers of wisdom, truth and love) and train their disciples to become light-bearers as well. To become an esotericist or light-bearer, students must step from the emotional, mystical world into the thinking world of the occultist and of energies.

Mystics walk the Path of Love, concentrate on the subjective and sometimes overlook the value of the outer life. A sense of duality distinguishes them - they love and adore their God, Master or Guru who they place above and beyond them. They pour their energies into the astral field, into yearning for the "beloved." Mystics must become occultists, must learn to value the form and bring the whole nature under rule. They must work on the mental body, study life intelligently and become knowledgeable and informed.

Esotericists or Occultists walk the Path of Mind. The words occultist and esotericist are used inter-changeably in the sense that they both refer to the intelligent use and manipulation of energies. Would-be esotericists need to learn to work from the mind and with the causal energies of life. Occultists analyse and study each body and level of nature. Exhausting each level, they go deeper - layer after layer, body after body until the form is lost sight of and the creator of the form is all that is seen. Occultists are mystics - lovers of God, functioning on the mental plane.

---

[1] Bailey, Alice. Letters on Occult Meditation, 278.

3. Students find their group.

Students should look for a group which studies the wisdom teachings and teaches spiritual practices that are sensible and safe. Above all else, avoid groups dominated by a glamorous or particularly powerful egocentric leader - it tends to encourage egoism and cult-like behaviours. Look for a teacher who seems wise, egoless, stable and grounded. When we have evolved to the stage where our view of the world is universal and we have found our soul vocation, then we will find our group of soul brothers and sisters who are likewise drawn to the same vocation. This provides the opportunity to participate in the mission of the group.

4. The ultimate goal is service.

True service is not a quality or a performance. It is not good intentions, mixed motives or the fanatical doing of good works. When the heart chakra is sufficiently open and love of humanity has grown, then we all turn to help manifest the greater good. True service is a spontaneous heart-felt response with no thought of personal gain. It is a soul instinct and is therefore innate. It is the outstanding characteristic of the soul - the urge to group good.

> Service is simply the first real effect that the soul is beginning to express itself in outer manifestation. [1]

Aspirants evolve into true servers by firstly doing the inner work. They use the physical body wisely to avoid ill health, cultivate emotional stability and serenity and a sense of secure dependence on Divine law. Training the mind to function scientifically, they equip it with information, knowledge and facts. Simultaneously they cultivate the qualities of selflessness, harmlessness and right speech. Then, skilled and prepared, discriminating, intelligent and accurate, they step forward to meet the need of the moment and to serve.

Service is a scientific process. It calls forth all the powers of the soul into full expression in physical plane life. If we are truly serving, it means we are drawing upon all the resources of our spiritual strength and light, all the wisdom we have accumulated over the aeons and pouring this out in the field of opportunity that most inspires us. True servers are found all over the world and may or may not have come in touch with the esoteric teachings and Masters in the current life.

> Some of the world's greatest servers are men and women who are very close to the spiritual Hierarchy and working under its direction, inspiration and impression, but who know naught of esotericism and (in their brain consciousness) remain unaware of Hierarchy or the Masters of the Wisdom.

True servers understand the need in the world and channel all resources to meet that need. Finding their niche in the general scheme, they use their capabilities to fill that niche. Adaptable, they step up into a higher position or step aside, if someone better equipped comes along. They are dispassionate and self-forgetful, do not waste time looking backwards in regret, but steadily press forward to the accomplishment of the next duty.

> The ultimate sacrifice and act of love is service to alleviate suffering. To this task all true servers are called.

> ***This concludes this section on the 3 Halls of Spiritual Training. In the next section, the Seven Rays are examined.***

---

[1] Bailey, Alice. Esoteric Psychology II, 125.

CHAPTER 2: THE 7 RAYS & PSYCHOLOGY

We are taught in the esoteric philosophy that seven great divine Emanations or Spirits came forth from God at the time of the Creation. The same teaching can also be traced in the Holy Bible. Upon one or other of these seven Rays, the souls of all forms of life are to be found as well as the forms themselves. These seven rays produce the seven major psychological types. [1]

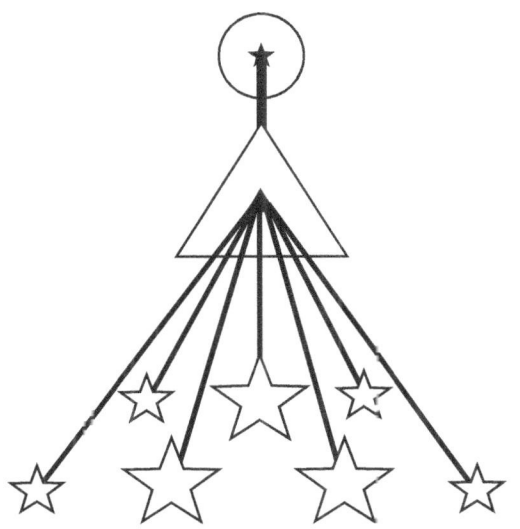

---

[1] Bailey, Alice. Discipleship in the New Age I, xiii.

I. THE 7 RAYS & PSYCHOLOGY.

The Seven Rays are the seven basic energies of the universe, of God, from which everything is made - Spirit, Soul and Body. Each ray has its own unique vibration and colour and in human psychology, gives a distinctly different character type. Esoteric Psychology is founded upon the Seven Rays.

The rays are the forces of God that keep the universe evolving. This chart shows the relation between the rays and the Divine Trinity.

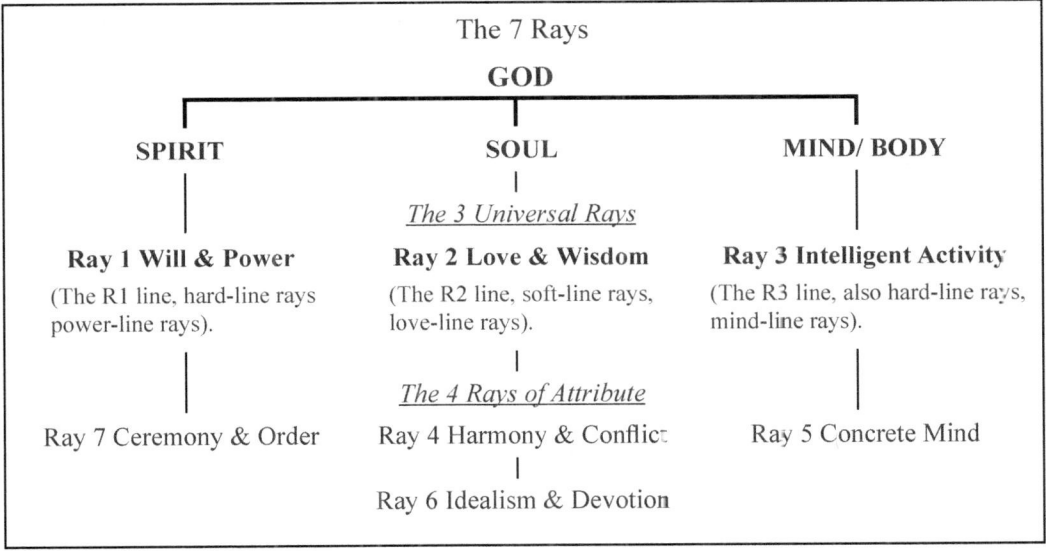

1. The Spirit, hard-line rays - 1 and 7. They are of the nature of "spirit", are "hard-line" rays. When these two rays colour human character, they produce leaders - people who have powerful and enduring wills and who see the bigger picture.

2. The Soul, soft-line rays - 2, 4 and 6. They are concerned with the development and expression of soul qualities, with the development of a wise and loving consciousness and therefore with self-understanding, human relations, health and education.

3. The Mind, hard-line rays - 3 and 5. They are of the nature of the "mind of God", and enhance the ability to think and reason.

In the following pages, each ray is analysed for the effect it has on human character and how it colours the nature of the soul. Then a guide is given on how to build a Ray Profile psychology chart and how to read it.

RAY 1 of WILL & POWER

This universal ray carries the energy of Spirit, the 1st Aspect, the 1st Logos, electric fire. It is considered a "hard-line" ray and is the power of LIFE and DEATH in the universe. It is the ray of the occultist and of born leaders.

Colour: red.

Ray 1 energy. The most powerful force in the universe, R1 builds and destroys, is destructive and hard, it takes life and is also the dynamic germinating force that seeds new life. R1 is there at the beginning - and such is its power to endure, it is there at the end.

Some Names of the Lord of Ray 1. *These names describe the nature of this energy and how it can affect human nature.* The Lord of Death, the Liberator from Form, the Fiery Element producing shattering, the Will that breaks into the Garden, the Ravisher of Souls, the Finger of God, the Breath that Blasts, the Lightning which Annihilates, the Most High, Lord of the Burning Ground.

Ray 1 Soul. Advanced men and women with R1 souls express this dynamic power always for the highest good. Their goal is to achieve spiritual liberation, freedom and right human relations for all. Courageous and absolutely fearless they are prepared to stand alone if necessary (and often do), to force through their goals. Steadfast, they can endure against all obstacles. Courageous and self-confident, they are very truthful and are ready to accept the consequences of what they say and do.

- Vocations: leaders and managers in any career or situation. Careers in politics and law that require great will power, strength, stamina, the ability to stand firm in the face of all obstruction, to destroy if necessary.
- Spiritual conscience: to preserve spiritual principles and values.
- Greatest contribution: strengthening and liberating others.
- Goals: to be powerful and benevolent leaders who serve the highest good, to free people from bondage and oppression.
- Most joyous activity: to discard all nonessentials and be in perfect freedom.
- Most sacred sense: the exhilaration at being in the presence of the power of Deity and identification with the One Self.
- Heart's desire: to be one with the "One and only".

Strengths
Courage, detachment, fearlessness, independence, large mindedness, masterfulness, perseverance, steadfastness, strength of will. Dynamic power to lead, govern, direct and initiate processes. To destroy and liberate old forms, to establish and enforce the law. Power to synthesise and centralise, to preserve values. R1 gives independence and detachment.

Weaknesses
Anger, arrogance, control issues, cruelty, hardness, impatience, inhibition, isolationism, power-hungry, separative, stubborn, unrelenting ambition and pride, violence, wilfulness.

Symbols
Crown, Diamond, Eagle, Flame, Hammer, Lightning bolt, Lion, Mountain, Point within the circle, Sickle, Spear, a straight line, Sword, Volcano.

Colour: Red.

Jewel: Diamond

Ray 1 colouring the Personality Fields.

Ray 1 unregenerated personality. There is natural power, great inner fortitude and a rocklike ability to endure in face of all obstacles. But this sort of power in an ego-centric, selfish and highly ambitious personality creates a dictator, an autocrat, a leader who believes in his "rightness" to rule, to dominate and control people. Being a law unto itself, this ego is proud, wilful, hard in nature, arrogant, obstinate, pitiless and very hungry for power. Then once it gets power does not want to let it go.

> In the early 21st Century, some examples are: President Xi of China, Supreme Leader Kim Jong-un of North Korea and President of Russia - Vladimir Putin. Certain actions of USA President Donald Trump indicate that he also belongs in this group.

Liking isolation, determined to do things entirely its way, the R1 personality tolerates no interference. It calls attention to itself as being the first and best in everything. It asserts its authority by intimidating opponents with its power and tries to annihilate opposition. It takes charge noticeably, strutting arrogantly, trampling over anyone foolish enough to get in its way. Gathering followers easily, it will use them as weapons to get its way.

For the soul, the purified R1 personality wielding this power is tremendously effective in getting things done, in bringing about the greater good, in uniting people and protecting them as they are led into higher ways of living and being.

Ray 1 Mind. An intense, fast and powerful mind that synthesises facts, focuses on principles and that sees the broad picture. Laser-like with diamond clear thought processes, it easily separates out the essential from nonessential and concentrates, organises and prioritises. It is independent, outspoken, decisive and firm in thought and speech. Its weaknesses are jumping to conclusions, making assumptions and aggression.

Ray 1 Astral Body: (only found in disciples). This is a coldfire type of emotional field. These disciples are not "touchy-feely" people. Standoffish, they can have difficulty relating emotionally with others. The intense power of this field could erupt periodically with volcanic outbursts.

Ray 1 Physical-Etheric Body: (only found in disciples). This body is lanky but steely strong - lean and mean is a good description. It is stiff, awkward and avoids human contact. The R1 brain expresses ideas sharply and assertively.

Famous figures
Hercules
Charlemagne
Adolf Hitler
Anwar Sadat
Bismarck
Josef Stalin
Franklin Roosevelt
General Kitchener
General Patton
Mikhail Gorbachev
Margaret Thatcher
Mohandas Gandhi
Mussolini
Napoleon
Nikita Khrushchev
Thomas Carlyle
Walt Whitman
Winston Churchill.

Signs & Planets
Aries, Leo, Capricorn;
Vulcan, Pluto.

Balancing Ray 1.

R1 Vices to eliminate: pride, isolationism, self-pity, use of power to destroy and control, arrogance and insensitivity to people's feelings.

R1 Virtues to cultivate: tenderness, humility, sympathy, tolerance, patience, inclusiveness.

The integration word *"Inclusiveness"* will help balance R1 and soften its hardness.

The words of power *"I Assert the Fact"* will maximises the positivity of R1 power.

RAY 2 of LOVE & WISDOM

This ray carries the energy of the 2nd Aspect, the 2nd Logos and solar-fire - the fire of mind. It is the power of the Love and Wisdom of God (of the Spiritual Soul) and its primary universal task is to develop the SOUL aspect in all living forms, to foster CONSCIOUSNESS and right-human RELATIONS. As gravity, it is the building force in the universe, holding all forms/ physical bodies together so they can be used by consciousness to grow and expand.

Colour. Indigo blue.

Ray 2 energy. It is an inclusive, enfolding, healing energy that embraces all. Its movement is spiral-cyclic. Pre-eminently the ray of applied consciousness it builds forms for the use of spirit, so that the indwelling consciousness can evolve. It is the ray of the true psychic, of teachers, healers, scholars and lovers.

Some Names of the Lord of Ray 2. *These names describe the nature of this energy and how it can affect human nature.* The Displayer of Glory, Lord of Eternal Love, the Cosmic Magnet, the Giver of Wisdom, the Master Builder, the Great Geometrician, Radiance in the Form, the Cosmic Christ, the Conferrer of Names, the One who hides the Life, the Cosmic Mystery, the Light Bringer, the Son of God Incarnate.

Ray 2 Soul. There are two psychological types:
　a. Love-types, who are heart-centred and express love.
　b. Wisdom-types who are wise intellectuals.

Both types express the love and wisdom this ray endows. They are intuitive, have a deep understanding of people and are patient, tactful and compassionate.

- Vocations: those requiring tact, foresight, personal magnetism, warmth and concern for others. Eg. Ambassadors, psychotherapists, teachers, healers and educators.
- Greatest contribution: wisely and lovingly helping people, in health, education and giving spiritual guidance.
- Goals: to develop a deep, intuitive, loving, understanding of people and help them in their troubles. Or, to become wise and knowledgeable in order to illumine people's minds.
- Most joyous activity: being in love and giving love. The pursuit and distribution of intuitive understanding.
- Most sacred sense: divine love, or divine wisdom.
- Heart's desire: to be in love with all, or knowing all.

Love Types

Strengths

Power to attract. Compassion, composure, empathy, sensitivity, faithfulness, inclusiveness. Being loving, magnetic, patient, serene, sympathetic, tactful, tolerant, wise. Power to salvage, redeem and heal through love.

Weaknesses.

Fearfulness, emotionally needy, indiscriminate, binding people through guilt, excessive love of comfort, hypersensitivity, fearfulness, impressionability, inferiority complex, non-assertive, over attached, overprotective, self-pitying.

Wisdom types

Strengths.

Clear perception and understanding, wise intelligence, power to teach, heal and illumine. Love of pure truth and simplicity.

Weaknesses.

Coldness, indifference, over absorbed in study, scornful of mental limitation in others.

Ray 2 colouring the Personality Fields.

Ray 2 unregenerated personality. This is a charming and magnetic personality. They draw people easily to their side with the radiance that they emit and the charm of their smiles and words.

The R2 ego uses this charm and magnetism to manipulate and control people, to get what it wants, to bring popularity, to ensure people love it so it gets the good things in life and can live in comfort and luxury.

> President Bill Clinton has a R2 personality. He was an alleged philanderer and got away with it - even when his indiscretions were exposed by political rivals. Charm and popularity saved his marriage and career.

Fearful of being alone, oversensitive, timid, the R2 personality controls people through evoking guilt and dependency.

- The "love" type needs to be popular, loved. It gets its way by binding people to it through need, by being a suffering martyr.
- The "mental" type can be cold, indifferent, an isolationist. It is contemptuous of mental limitations in others and lacks empathy.

For the soul, the purified R2 personality is a wonderfully wise and loving instrument through which many can be healed, educated and raised up - formally and in the higher mysteries.

Ray 2 Mind: (only found in disciples). These disciples are profoundly wise and knowledgeable. Natural academics, they are intuitive and capable of clear abstract thought.

Ray 2 Astral Body. This field is not that common. Most people have 6th ray astral natures. It belongs to people who have begun to develop spiritually and who have opened their heart-centre to a degree (R2 flows through the heart). Emotionally calm and affectionate, they want to include all and avoid causing harm. When prodded, this field is relatively non-reactive though it may dissolve for a while before it regroups. It is harmless, calm and does not have great emotional displays. Negatively, it is timid and fearful.

Ray 2 Physical-Etheric Body: (only found in disciples). This is a very sensitive and soft body, that tries to protect itself from pain and the "hard" knocks of life. Un-energetic, it prefers a life of ease and to be still. The R2 brain type would express ideas in a gentle and inclusive manner.

Famous Figures
Buddha, Christ, Abraham Maslow, Albert Schweitzer, Alice Bailey, Carl Jung, Mother Teresa, Plato, Pythagoras, Sigmund Freud.

Symbols
All-Seeing Eye, Book of Wisdom, Chalice Dove, Even Armed Cross, Giving Hands Mother and Child, Lotus, The Ocean, Owl, Radiant Heart, Rose, Sapphire, Shepherd's Crook, Spiral, the Sun.

Signs & Planets
Gemini, Virgo, Pisces. The Sun, Jupiter.

Colour: Indigo blue.

Jewel: Sapphire.

Balancing Ray 2.
Vices to eliminate: self-love, seeking approval from others, too attached to material things and relationships; or mentally cold.

Virtues to cultivate. Love types: independence and inner strength Wisdom types: love, compassion and unselfishness.

The integration word *"Centralisation"* will help balance and strengthen R2.

The words of power *"I See the Greatest Light"* maximises the positivity of R2 power.

RAY 3 of INTELLIGENT ACTIVITY

This universal ray carries the energy of the 3rd Aspect, the 3rd Logos and fire by friction (the fire of matter). It provides substance for all FORMS in nature. It is the power of the Mind of God at work in the world, and it promotes INTELLECTUAL ACTIVITY in living forms so they can adapt and survive in their environment.

Colour. Green.

Ray 3 energy. It is the highly energetic, adaptable, fertile and intelligent force found in all forms in nature. It gives to all souls in the subhuman kingdoms, an innate intelligence so they know instinctually what they have to do to survive and reproduce. In man, it gives mental brilliance when working through the mind.

Some Names of the Lord of Ray 3. The Keeper of the Records, the Lord of Memory, Unifier of the lower Four, Interpreter of That Which is seen, the Divine Separator, the Discriminating Essential Life, the Three-sided Triangle, Illuminator of the Lotus, the Forerunner of the Light, the One Who veils and yet reveals, the Dispenser of Time, the Lord of Space, the Universal Mind, the Great Architect of the Universe.

Ray 3 Soul. Men and women with ray 3 souls are endowed with a brilliant intelligence, power for abstract thought and creative reasoning. They speak with the voice of reason and intelligence. Adapting easily to cope with any situation, they are blessed with high levels of energy and resourcefulness.

- Vocations: those requiring excellent intellects, adaptability and resourcefulness. They make good tacticians, strategists, financial planners, business people, entrepreneurs and philosophers.
- Greatest contribution: stimulating the intellect and mental creativity of others. Creating plans that benefit humanity.
- Most joyous activity: mental activity to theorise, plan and then act on that plan. Physical freedom and activities.
- Most sacred sense: appreciating theories and proofs that explain the nature of things.
- Heart's desire: to plan along with God and manifest on earth the Divine Plan.

Strengths
Intellectual acuity, creativeness, mental fertility; capable of wide-ranging, philosophical abstract thought. The ability to plan, strategise, understand and explain complex patterns. Power to theorise, speculate and apply rigorous analysis. Communication skills, facility with languages. The power to manipulate for good. Natural executive and business skills. Skilled in money management. Philanthropic.

Weaknesses
Amoral and excessive materialism. Calculating, devious, dishonest, intellectual pride, manipulative and opportunistic. Excessive thought without practical action, scattered reasoning. Creating chaos, being disorderly, hyperactive. Restless wasted motion, being too busy.

Signs & Planets
Cancer, Libra, Capricorn; Saturn, Earth.

Colour: Green.

Jewel: Emerald.

Ray 3 colouring the Personality Fields.

Ray 3 unregenerated personality. This ray endows the personality nature with a very fertile, clever and resourceful nature that knows what it has to say and do to be successful in the material world, which is its main focus.

> 16th Century Niccolo Machiavelli, is a good R3 example. His famous and popular book "The Prince," revealed his nature. He told the ruler of Florence on how to manipulate events to stay in power.

This type is hyper-busy, restless, absent-minded, changeable and lacks continuity. The unprincipled man on this ray with no soul contact will try to assert his authority and control by being deceitful, devious, manipulative and untruthful. Sociopaths and psychopaths arise from the extreme negativities of this ray.

For the soul, the purified R3 personality is a brilliantly clever and resourceful instrument for its world-service work.

Ray 3 Mind: (only disciples). This combination gives a powerful and outstanding intellect, a wide-ranging mind that weaves, is incessantly active, fluid, versatile, highly verbal and communicative. It plans, strategises, reasons, is resourceful, analytical, deductive and non-empirical. It loves abstract thought. Its weakness is inaccuracy, generalising and absent-mindedness.

Ray 3 Astral Body: (only in disciples). Hypothetically, this astral field can be the servant of the mind.

Ray 3 Physical-Etheric Body. This endomorph body-type is found everywhere. It has a stockier body, thicker bones and a heavier body mass than the R7 type body. Very active it has a high pain threshold and is resistant to changes or impacts in the environment.

This is the body you see in careers that require a robust, stocky, strong, workhorse body, that can be pushed hard and keeps going for long periods and without food if necessary. For example, infantrymen, iron-man competitors and marathon runners.

Comfortable in its skin, the R3 body can be happy in an untidy environment or without an ordered routine. It likes spontaneity, to come and go as it pleases and resents having its activities curbed. If physical grace does not come from a higher ray, it plods firmly along, with graceless movements. The R3 brain expresses ideas in a fluid, energetic, sometimes inaccurate manner.

Famous Figures
Albert Einstein
Aristotle
Bertrand Russel
Jack Nicholson
John D. Rockefeller
Machiavelli
Lucrezia Borgia
Shylock
St. Thomas Aquinas

Symbols
Busy Hands, Busy Tongue, Emerald, Fleur de Lis, Gold, Golden Coins, Hour Glass, Kaleidoscope, Labyrinth, Loom, Money, Pen, Serpent, Spider and Web, Spinning Wheel, Tapestry, Triangle, Veil.

Balancing Ray 3.

Vices to eliminate: criticalness, coldness, disorganisation, lack of discipline, dogmatism, inaccuracy, intellectual pride, manipulation for personal gain, sectarianism, sexual excess, theological rigidity.

Virtues to cultivate: accuracy, common sense, concentration, focus, honesty, integrity, open-mindedness, stillness, sympathy, tolerance.

The integration word *"Stillness"* will help balance and quieten R3

The words of power *"Purpose itself am I"* maximises the positivity of R3 power.

RAY 4 of HARMONY through CONFLICT

Ray 4 is on the line of 2nd Ray of Love-Wisdom, so it is concerned with inner development and relationships. It is very powerful in humanity because it rules the (4th) Human Kingdom. This is why conflict is so deeply entrenched in human behaviour. Ray 4 is the energy that teaches us to RECONCILE differences - horizontally with other people, and vertically with the soul.

Colour. Yellow.

Ray 4 energy. It is related to the middle Buddhic plane. It oscillates and tries to bridge and reconcile opposites. Achieving a balanced central point results in harmony and beauty. Otherwise, instability, conflict and trouble continues.

Some Names of the Lord of Ray 4. The Link Between the Three and Three, the Divine Intermediary, the Hand of God, the Hidden One, the Seed that is the Flower, the Mountain whereon Form dies, the One Who marks the parting of the Way, Dweller in the Holy Place, the Corrector of the Form, the Master, Trumpet of the Lord, the Light within the Light, the Lower than the Three - the Highest of the Four.

Ray 4 Soul (very rare). *Bailey said in 1936 (Rays and Initiations, 605), there are (except in the ranks of disciples), no 4th ray souls in incarnation. More R4 souls will start coming in from 2025.* This is the artistic soul, who radiates beauty, colour and joy. Prodigious artistic talent may be present. Michelangelo and Leonardo da Vinci were on this ray. It creates unity, peace, beauty and someone to whom others come to be soothed, exposed to beauty, uplifted and inspired.

- Vocations: that create beauty, colour and harmony - actors, artists, musicians, writers. Also, those careers involved with conflict and its resolution - diplomats, counsellors and warriors.
- Contribution: help people resolve their conflicts.
- Soul-inspired aspiration: to bring divine harmony into every aspect of life, to express the exquisite and beautiful yet agonising and painful drama of life, in all its vibrancy.
- Most joyous activity: mixing, blending and harmonising to create balance, harmony and beauty.
- Most sacred sense: beauty and perfect equilibrium.
- Heart's desire: to live in beauty forever and become beauty itself.

Strengths
Power to create harmony from conflict, to grow spiritually and psychologically through crises and struggle. Warriorship, fighting to resolve injustices. Peacemaking, reconciling, negotiating, mediating. Intuitive, imaginative, loving beauty, creating colour and beauty. Dramatic, creative, spontaneous, musical, a natural ability to entertain and delight.

Weaknesses
Constant inner and outer conflict, extreme mood swings, self-absorption in suffering, agonising, worry, agitation, indecision, procrastination. The artistic temperament - emotional, exaggerating, dramatic, unpredictable and unstable. Moral cowardice, being too eager for compromise, fighting for the sake of fighting.

Signs & Planets
Taurus, Scorpio, Sagittarius. Mercury, Moon.

Colour: Yellow.

Jewel: Topaz.

Ray 4 colouring the Personality Fields.

Ray 4 unregenerated personality. It is endowed with a passionate, emotional, artistic and colourful nature that loves the dramatic pageantry of life in all its many shades and colours.

When unregulated, it lacks self-control, gets embroiled in personal dramas, has rapid mood changes, is inconsistent and unstable. Too ready to compromise, it fights with itself and others - it can be very aggressive. It tries to assert its authority and control through exaggeration, through humour (humiliating others), by being the drama queen, or attacking - verbally, sometimes even physically.

For the soul, the purified R4 personality is a colourful and joyful instrument through which to achieve its service mission. It has the ability and power to reconcile and harmonise differences.

Ray 4 Mind. This is one of the most common mind-types on earth - the right-brain, artistic type which is easy to distinguish from the R5 left-brain, scientific type. R4 oscillates and often when the ray 4 mind is at work, the head or features move from side to side.

This intuitive mind is passionate and very intense. On one hand it is conflicted, struggling, crisis-stressed, vacillating, ambivalent, indecisive, aggressive, antagonistic and contradicting. Changing the mind often is a distinguishing feature. Then it is the peacemaker, the "bridging" mind, linking, weighing, balancing, resolving, unifying, mediating and reconciling. Between the polarities it agonises - backwards and forwards, up and down, alternating between exhilaration and depression. When peaceful, it is serene.

Artistic, musical, literary and aesthetic, this mind is non-rational. It sees in pictures, an outstanding trait. Grasping concepts and translating thought images and colours into words can be a struggle. Often it communicates better through art. It is a pliable mind with a rapid grasp and recognition of mental truth. Quick and spontaneous, it likes to play.

Ray 4 Astral Body: (only in disciples). Hypothetically, a field that constantly agonises, or one that is harmonious and peaceful.

Ray 4 Physical-Etheric Body: (only in disciples). Hypothetically, a beautiful form with vibrant colouring and excellent proportions. The ray 4 brain type in a disciple would quickly find resolution in an argument.

Famous Figures
Beethoven, Claude Debussy, Fyodor Dostoyevsky, Isadora Duncan, Franz Schubert, Lawrence Olivier, Leonardo da Vinci, Lord Byron, Michelangelo, Mozart, Pablo Picasso, Richard Wagner, Robert Burns, Salvador Dali, Shakespeare, Vincent Van Gogh.

Symbols
Battlefields, Black + White, Bridge, Checker board, a Comic, Mandalas, Musical Chords, Seesaw, Square, Tetrahedron, Tragic Masks, Soldiers, Vortexes, Warriors, Yin and Yang

Balancing Ray 4.
Vices to eliminate: agonising, constant worry, dogmatism, emotional instability, fighting for the sake of fighting, indolence, lack of inner-discipline, selfishness.

Virtues to cultivate: accuracy, confidence, harmony, inner unity, mental-moral balance, purity, self-control, serenity, steadfastness.

The integration word *"Steadfastness"* will help balance and regulate R4.

The words of power *"Two merge with One"* maximises the positivity of R4 power.

Strengths

A fact based and scientific approach to life, facility with maths, technical expertise and mechanical ability. A mind that is analytical, lucid, keen, focused, intelligent, discriminating, accurate and precise in thought and then in action. Power to discover through research, investigation and experimentation. An approach to life that is impartial and that rejects nonsense.

Weaknesses

Separativeness. Excessive mental activity, rigid thought patterns. Being over-analytical, ultra-rational, over detailed, excessively objective. Narrow, prejudiced, and judgmental. Controlling through knowledge. Lacking sensitivity, emotional responsiveness and magnetism. Socially awkward.

Signs & Planets

Leo, Sagittarius, Aquarius. Venus.

Colour: Orange.

Jewel: Orange hued gems.

RAY 5 of CONCRETE MIND & KNOWLEDGE

Ray 5 is on the line of the 3rd Mental Ray, so is concerned with the development of the powers of the MIND. It is the ray of the logical mind and of science. It teaches its people how to use the mind factually in the physical world, and how to discover the mysteries of nature and life.

Colour. Orange.

Ray 5 energy. Related to the 5th Mental Plane this ray enhances the mind's ability to discriminate, analyse, measure, experiment in order to find the truth. Consequently, scientists, analysts and technicians are found on this ray.

Some Names of the Lord of Ray 5. Revealer of the Truth, the Divine Intermediary, the Crystalliser of Forms, the Threefold Thinker, the Cloud upon the Mountain-top, the Dividing Sword, Winnower of the Chaff, the Fifth Great Judge, the Rose of God, the Heavenly One, the Door into the Mind of God, the Initiating Energy, the Ruler of the Third Heaven, the Guardian of the Door, the Dispenser of Knowledge, the Keeper of the Secret, the Beloved of the Logos, Brother from Sirius, Angel of the Flaming Sword, Master of the Hierophants.

Ray 5 Soul. Souls who contribute greatly to the world of science are born on this ray. They take the lead in scientific discovery and exploration and their life service is to make contributions along this line. They are prodigious intellects and excel in focused concentrated thinking and scientific analysis. For example, Marie Curie, Louis Pasteur and Thomas Edison.

- Vocations: Mainly in science and technology. But any area for human good that requires scientific prowess, detailed analysis and observation.
- Greatest contribution: using the laser-like mental powers to discover new scientific truths, to advance the truth and reject error.
- Soul-inspired aspiration: to discover solutions to nature's mysteries through advanced scientific research and experimentation. To create inventions which uplift humanity.
- Joyous activity: discovering what was previously hidden.
- Most sacred sense: the contemplation of the wonderful and intelligent design of nature.
- Heart's desire: to "know" the mystery of life.

Ray 5 colouring the Personality Fields.

Ray 5 unregenerated personality. In stark contrast to the colourful R4 personality type, the R5 personality is relatively unexpressive. When it is in full flight trying to assert its power, it pours its force through the mind. So, when concentrating, the body and facial features can be held quite still. The voice can be monotone also. Consequently, this personality can appear to be colourless.

The selfish R5 personality focuses narrowly and exclusively on its own strictly mental, specialised and technical interests at the expense of seeing and taking part in the larger picture. It tries to assert its authority and control people by being excessively rationalistic, by having all the facts to prove that it is right and others are wrong, that it is the expert and more superior because of this. Separative, it can cut off its feelings and do things that a more compassionate type could not. For instance:

> Josef Mengele (1911-1979), the Nazi doctor at Auschwitz extermination camp who conducted medical experiments on inmates for racial profiling.

For the soul, the purified R5 personality is a lucid, clear and mentally precise explainer of scientific facts and data. It gains respect amongst the world's thinkers and can be very influential because of this, benefitting the soul's service-mission.

Ray 5 Mind. This is a very common mind-type that is found amongst the world's scientific, mechanical and practical thinkers. Taking time to think before speaking, it emphasises the facts. It is easily recognisable because it is analytical, precise and scientific when explaining something. Unbiased and unaffected by emotions, it is linear, rational, logical, highly detailed, lucid, very clear and accurate.

Negatively, it is irreverent and sceptical of the mystical, it is irreligious and dismissive of anything that cannot be proven scientifically. It is closed and fixed.

R5 minds are often found amongst the world's scientists, electricians, engineers, analysts, data technicians and operating surgeons.

Ray 5 Astral Body: (only found in disciples). Hypothetically, a flat, colourless feeling response.

Ray 5 Physical-Etheric Body: (only found in disciples). Hypothetically, a hard, compact, rigid and awkward body. The ray 5 brain type would express ideas in a methodical and linear fashion.

Famous Figures
Charles Darwin
Galileo
Gregor Mendel Isaac Newton
Louis Pasteur
Niels Bohr
Thomas Edison
Tim Berners-Lee
Dr. Anthony Fauci.

Symbols
Atom, Brain, Dictionary, Computer, Equation, Pencil and Ruler, 5-pointed Star, Laboratory, Laser, Magnifying Glass, Microscope, Pyramid, Scalpel, Telescope, Triangle.

Balancing Ray 5.

Vices to eliminate: a narrow mental focus, materialism, separativeness.

Virtues to cultivate: reverence, love, broadmindedness, sympathy.

The integration word *"Wisdom"* will help balance R5 and diffuse its too narrow and detailed focus.

These words of power *"Three minds unite"* maximises the positivity of R5 power.

They assert the fact that the Universal Mind, the higher mind and the lower concrete mind are blended through the projected antahkarana." [1]

---

[1] Rays and Initiations, 518.

RAY 6 of DEVOTION & IDEALISM

Ray 6 is on the line of the 2nd Ray, so is concerned with inner development and relationships. It is astral energy and it cooperates with the R2 mission to transform personal, selfish feelings, into universal and unconditional love.

Colour: Pale blue and rose.

Ray 6 energy. Related to the 6th Astral Plane, this fiery-emotional energy feeds human desire. It gives a passion for life and fosters the urge to adore all that is greater, more magnificent, more beautiful, more sacred and holy.

Some Names of the Lord of Ray 6. The Negator of Desire, the One Who sees the Right, the Visioner of Reality, the Sword Bearer of the Logos, Upholder of the Truth, the Breaker of Stones, the Imperishable Flaming One, the One Whom Naught can turn, Warrior on the March, the Crucifier and the Crucified, the Devotee of Life, the Implacable Ruler, the General on the Perfect Way.

Ray 6 Soul. There is an outstanding ability to dedicate oneself totally, completely, passionately and without reservation to a Teacher, Master or to a higher ideal. These are the servants of the Great Ones, who loyally and devotionally shoulder heavy responsibilities without complaint.

- Vocations: that require devotion and selfless service. Preachers, servers, orators, soldiers, nurses and carers.
- Greatest contribution: to inspire others to devote their lives to the highest ideal or Teacher they can conceive.
- Soul-inspired aspiration. Devotion and adoration to the highest source of guidance. Or, a passionate commitment to the highest ideal.
- Most joyous activity: Intimate sharing with the object of devotion. The fiery pursuit of an ideal.
- Most sacred sense: devotion to the Highest.
- Heart's desire: to love and be totally loved by the beloved. To perfectly express the highest ideals.

NB. Ray 6 has been the most powerful force in humanity for over 2,000 years. It has inspired many of humanity's greatest achievements and negatively, many of the atrocities committed in the name of "God" or for dogmatic reasons.

Strengths

Intense devotion, self-sacrificial ardour, transcendent idealism. Being one-pointed, single-minded, having unflagging persistence and unshakeable faith. Being receptive to spiritual guidance, to ecstasy and rapture. Earnestness, sincerity, loyalty and undimmed optimism. Profound humility, purity, goodness and sainthood.

Weaknesses

Being too emotionally rigid and idealistic. Too dependent on others, unreasoningly devotional, placing loyalty and blind faith in someone who is unworthy. Being superstitious, gullible and unrealistic. Unvarying one-pointedness in spite of evidence to contrary. Too extreme, intense, fanatical and militant. Selfish, jealous, taking things too personally, Being masochistic, assuming a martyr-complex, being self abasing.

Signs & Planets

Virgo, Sagittarius, Pisces. Neptune, Mars.

Colour: Pale blue.

Jewel: Ruby.

Ray 6 colouring the Personality Fields.

Ray 6 unregenerated personality. Driven by the egoism and power of the selfish personality, when pursuing its desires, the R6 personality is passionate, emotional, intense and fanatical. There are no half-measures. There is always a goal, object or person to which it is drawn and which it one-pointedly and avidly pursues.

The R6 personality tries to assert its authority and control by urging people to follow the banner it is waving. If they do not, it tries to force its beliefs on them - "If you're not with me, you're against me!" It sees those who hold contrary beliefs as "the enemy" or "betrayer." Militant and unforgiving, the R6 personality can be highly dangerous - "cruelty" is a R6 trait. This force has been behind the worst atrocities committed in the name of God. R6 governs fundamentalist religion.

For the soul, the purified R6 personality has the power to inspire people to rise up and follow their aspirations, their highest ideals. Advanced men and women of this type loyally carry out the service-commitments of the soul.

Ray 6 Mind: (only in disciples). Hypothetically, a mind that is fiery, which has an unremitting one-pointed mental focus and susceptibility to emotional bias.

Ray 6 Astral Body. Most people have a R6 astral field. It is very subject to glamour, distorts reality because of emotional bias. Unless the mind is strong, it can warp the truth, imposing its twisted version of the facts onto perception.

Emotionally, it is fiery, passionate, devotional and idealistic. It can be fanatical or one-eyed when pursuing its desires or ideals. When unstable, it is reactive, defensive, over-emotional and takes things personally. It is also very jealous and resentful when others have what it wants. Burning with desire to be with the one it adores; it suffers intensely when ignored. Rejection can cause it to go into depression, or become murderous and vindictive.

The refined R6 field reacts promptly to suffering with compassion and forgiveness. It provides ample fuel and inspiration to scale the heights of spirituality.

Ray 6 Physical-Etheric Body: (only found in disciples). A body very reflective of the emotions and may need extra attention because of this. The R6 brain can add an inspirational overlay to thoughts and words.

Famous Figures
Jesus of Nazareth
Sir Galahad
Joan of Arc
Florence Nightingale
Billy Graham
Rev Martin L. King
Jimmy Carter
Jesse Jackson
Pete Seeger
Pope Francis
Ronald Reagan .
Ayatollah Khomeini
Jane Fonda
Jerry Falwell

Symbols
Bleeding Heart, Beacon, Burning Candle, Dog, Flag or Banner, Halo, Horse, Praying Hands, Pulpit, Pyre, Rosy Cross, Torch.

Balancing Ray 6.

Vices to eliminate: beliefs that are separative and limiting, blind worship of gurus, creeds and causes. Cruelty, emotionalism, fanaticism, one-eyedness, sectarianism.

Virtues to cultivate: tolerance, serenity, balance, common sense

The integration word *"Moderation"* will help balance R6 and stop its thoughtless forward rush.

The words of power *"The Highest Light controls"* maximises the positivity of R6 power.

Strengths

Power to create order out of chaos; to plan, organise, manifest and work on the material plane. Power to perfect forms, to build a grand design, to renovate and transform. Power to understand and implement the law. Power to coordinate groups, to synthesise. A natural ritualist with a keen sense of rhythm and timing. Power as a magician, to work with devas and elementals.

Weaknesses

Rigid orderliness and formalism, subservience to habit, over concern with rules, laws and regulations. Bigotry and sectarianism. Crystallisation, materialism. Excessive perfectionism, snobbishness, superficial judgement based on appearances. Pompous ritual. Addiction to occult phenomena and black magic.

Signs & Planets

Aries, Cancer, Capricorn. Uranus.

Colour: Violet.

Jewel: Amethyst.

RAY 7 of CEREMONY, ORDER & MAGIC

Ray 7 is on the line of the 1st Ray, so it is a hard-line, power ray. It is the "MANIFESTING" ray and endows its people with the power to create on the physical plane. To synthesise, organise and build forms and civilisations that mirror the shape, colour and attributes of the Divine.

Colour. violet.

Ray 7 energy. At its most essential, R7 is the organising, ritualistic patterning in DNA that contains the instructions needed for an organism to develop, survive and reproduce. In human life, it gives the power to bring order out of chaos, to organise and reshape all forms so that they more perfectly reflect an ideal, an idea, a plan, or a divine archetype.

Some Names of the Lord of Ray 7. The Unveiled Magician, the Worker in the Magical Art, the Creator of the Form, the Manipulator of the Wand, the Watcher in the East, the Keeper of the Magical Word, the Temple Guardian, the Representative of God, the Lord of Death, Builder of the Square, the One Who feeds the Sacred Fire, the Whirling Fire, the Divine Alchemical Worker.

Ray 7 Soul. R7 souls are the magicians of the human family, those who seem to have an almost magical ability to bring order out of chaos or to manifest something from nothing. They are team-builders with power to bring together people who are necessary to the delivery of a project and can bind them together to achieve this. They are courteous, have exceptional people skills, and organisational, managerial and administrative prowess.

- Vocations: those requiring practical efficiency, finesse, organisational skill and the ability to manifest ideas on the physical plane. Leaders, organisers and ritualists.
- Greatest contribution: to help organise human life so it is in alignment with the living power of spirit.
- Soul-inspired aspiration: to invoke divine energies that relate spirit and matter according to the divine plan. To reshape human life in line with the Aquarian Age principles of universal brotherliness.
- Most joyous activity: manifesting perfection.
- Most sacred sense. Contemplating forms (divine or man-made) that reflect the Divine Plan.
- Heart's desire: to express the divine archetype in perfect form, and to see such forms manifest on earth.

Ray 7 colouring the Personality Fields.

Ray 7 unregenerated personality. The more common type lives its life locked into rigid rules of "must" and "must not", "should" and should not". It is rigid, resistant to change and locks itself into its preferred personal routines and customs.

Snobbish, haughty and judging by appearances, its chief attention-getter is efficiency, being good, doing things the right way and consequently, living a more superior life than its neighbours. It asserts its authority by insisting people follow the rules (its rules) and do the right thing (the way it thinks this should be done). Although not so extreme (perhaps), Emily Post is an example.

> Emily Post (1872-1960) was famous for writing about etiquette. Tall, pretty and spoiled, she grew up in a world of grand estates, her life governed by carefully delineated rituals like the cotillion with its complex forms and its dances. In her generation, she set the rules for "civilised" behaviour.

There is a R7 type that is unconventional and spurns the status quo. A free spirit who follows his or her own rules.

For the soul, the purified R7 personality is an excellent vehicle through which to manifest its service plans. It is courteous, has high standards, organising power and the power to manifest and build whatever is required. Ritualists, builders, architects, organisers and alchemists are often on this ray.

Ray 7 Mind: (only found in disciples). Hypothetically, a highly organised, coordinating and synthesising mind.

Ray 7 Astral Body: (only found in disciples). Hypothetically, a highly disciplined, non-feeling emotional body that desires a well-ordered physical plane life.

Physical-Etheric Body. This is a widespread body type. In contrast to the R3 stocky, strong and muscular body; the R7 body is refined, graceful. It is poised, dignified, walks gracefully and flutters the hands gracefully to emphasise what is being said.

The R7 body prefers to live in an ordered environment and functions better with routine - for example, rising in the morning and eating meals at the same time each day. Sensitive, it has a lower pain threshold than R3. However, it does have inherent strength and can be trained in sports requiring strength and grace, like gymnastics or ballet. The R7 brain expresses ideas in an ordered manner.

Famous Figures
Merlin
Aleister Crowley
Audrey Hepburn
Benjamin Franklin
Jackie Onassis
Kofi Annan
Sir Francis Bacon Sir Francis Drake Thomas Jefferson Tony Blair

Symbols
Altar, Coat of Arms, Cornerstone, Crystal, Hands (graceful), Lightning Rod, Official Seal, Peacock, Rainbow, Sceptre, Seven-pointed Star, Swastika, Talisman, Wand.

Balancing Ray 7.

Vices to eliminate. Being bigoted, judgmental, prideful, sectarian, snobbish and selfish. Slavishly adhering to meaningless routines, rules, rituals, schedules and forcing these onto others to standardize and control. Addicted to phenomena, the occult, black magic, to power.

Virtues to cultivate: wide-mindedness, tolerance, humility, gentleness and love.

The integration word *"Re-orientation"* will help balance R7 and.

The words of power *"The Highest and Lowest meet,* maximises the positivity of R7 power

The 7 Rays, Psychology and Disease.

This chart has been included for reader's interest. It links the rays to disease pathologies and resultant physical diseases and troubles.

Ray	Psychological negatives	Disease pathology	Disease examples
1	Aggression, egoism, hardness, inflexibility, inhibitions, megalomania, obsessions, wilfulness, repression.	Ages, atrophies, contracts, cripples, crystallises, hardens, scars, stiffens.	Arthritis, atherosclerosis, cancer, dementia, meningitis, multiple sclerosis, paralysis, scleroderma, stroke.
2	Amorality, excess, gluttony, greed, impressionable, emotionalism.	Excessive growth & vitality, over-develops, suffocates, too many atoms.	Blood disorders, cancer, heart disease, extra body parts, gluttony, tumours.
3	Avarice, dishonesty, hyperactivity, lying, manipulation, trickery, stealing, sociopathy.	Highly energetic, unstable diseases, quick moving, subtly invasive, they trick the body.	Breathing troubles, certain brain disorders; gastric, stomach, intestinal disorders; sexually transmitted diseases.
4	Constant agonising, inner conflict, mental-emotional instability, mood swings.	Devitalisation & debilitation opens the body to disease & epidemics.	Chronic fatigue, debilitation, influenza, susceptibility to indigenous diseases - cancer, tuberculosis, syphilis.
5	Aloofness, antisocial, disassociating, divisive, separative.	Builds barriers, separates, hardens, cleaves, splits apart.	Many modern psychological disorders. Brain lesions, consciousness thread trouble, imbecilities, migraine.
6	Anger, delusion, fear, frustration, hurt, jealousy, fanaticism, warped ideals, unstable emotions.	Destabilises homeostasis, upsets body rhythms and energy flow.	Emotional disorders. Carcinogenicity, digestion problems, causes susceptibility to viruses. Trouble in any part of the body.
7	Perfectionism, regimentation, perversions, sexual promiscuity.	Promiscuity at a cellular level.	Genetic mutations, germs - bacterial infections. Blood circulation problems, epidemics, sexually transmitted diseases, reproductive problems.

II. THE 7-RAY PERSONALITY PROFILE METHOD.

1. The 7-Ray Personality Profiling method is unique amongst personality profiling methods because it differentiates between the energies of the soul, of the personality, of the mind, of the emotions and of the physical body.
2. The goal in this work is to identify the rays that condition these fields, to balance and integrate these energies, then to bring the integrated personality into alignment with the Soul (Ray). This accelerates spiritual growth.
3. Note that the personal rays are not found via the astrology chart, but only by observation. To find the ray that conditions a body, the body is observed as it goes about its daily affairs, its actions are analysed and noted - then compared to ray qualities until the closest match is found. This is done for each of the bodies/ or fields.
4. The Ray Chart is a compilation of a person's energy makeup, their energy strengths and weaknesses. Two rays in particular are important. First, the body-ray which is out of balance and which needs balancing. Second, the body-ray which requires strengthening, because it is the higher body-faculty, which a person is growing into. In the masses, the higher body is the personality. For those on the Path, it is the soul.

A. Formulate the Ray Profile Chart.

In this section, readers are taught how to assemble a Ray Chart - how to find the ray that governs each of the soul, personality, mind, emotions and physical bodies.

In all people, the rays for the mind, emotions and body can be found. But many have not yet developed their personality natures, nor are they in touch with their souls. In these cases, the personality ray has not yet formed and the soul ray is not yet expressing through the nature. So, the ray chart for some people will consist of just three rays (no personality or soul), or four rays (no soul ray).

Important points.
1. The soul ray and the personality ray are always different. They are never the same ray.
2. Of the five rays in a chart, sometimes there is a doubling-up of rays. For example, the soul and emotional rays may both be R6, or the personality and physical both R7.
3. While disciples can have any ray for any body, the rest of us do not. The average person and aspirant will have their bodies on the following rays:
   - The soul ray: it can be any of the seven rays.
   - The personality ray: it can be any of the seven rays.
   - The mind ray: is 4, 5 or 1.
   - The emotional-astral ray: is mostly 6, occasionally 2.
   - The physical ray: is 3 or 7.

1. The Physical-Etheric Ray - 3 or 7.

The physical-etheric ray (and karma), determines the shape and size of the body, its energy levels, powers of endurance, the way it moves, what it likes to do and the mode of living that best suits it. It also determines how the brain works. The brain receives information from both the soul and from the outer world via the senses.

a. How it looks. The R3 physical is robust, stocky, strong, muscular, thick in girth and in the ankles and wrists. R7 is more refined, slender, dignified-looking, slimmer, smaller ankles and wrists. However, it can also be strong and do sports requiring strength and grace, like gymnastics or ballet.

b. How it moves. R3 plods firmly along, is graceless. It likes physical movement and becomes restless and fidgety if constrained. R7 is graceful, walks and dances with grace, emphasises points with graceful hand movements. It is more serene and highly strung.

c. How it spends its day. R3 has very high energy levels and reserves. R7 has to conserve energy, keeps it topped up with regular snacks. The R3 physical is a workhorse body, highly energised and active, it likes to keep doing and moving and can do so all day if necessary. It is happy in an untidy environment or without an ordered routine. R7 likes to live in a well-ordered environment and prefers a routine - for example, rising in the morning and eating meals at the same time each day. R3 has a high pain threshold. R7 is sensitive, it has a lower pain threshold.

d. How the brain works. The R3 brain expresses ideas in an energetic and sometimes rambling manner. It likes to talk. The R7 brain is more orderly and reticent.

Find the Physical-Etheric Ray.

Search for this ray first because it is usually the easiest to find. Observe the body and its daily habits.

Is the body muscular, strong, stocky, active and busy (3), or more delicate (7)? Is it graceful when moving and dancing (7), or more vigorous and athletic, perhaps with poor timing (3)? Can the body be pushed to work long hours without nourishment, fall asleep anytime, anywhere (3)? Or, does it need regular meals, operates better with order and ritual and a comfortable bed to fall into at the end of the day (7)?

Once you feel more confident, then also check to see if your ray choice for the physical also coincides with the way the brain works - how the brain interprets the thought productions of the mind ray and communicates them through speech. A R7 brain is very good for grounding and expressing ideas so they are coherent and workable (if perhaps dogmatic). If the R3 body is undisciplined, so may the thoughts and communications be.

2. The Emotional Ray - 2 or 6.

The 6th ray emotional force rules most people's astral natures.

a. Positive emotional expression. The R6 field is highly reactive, fiery, intense and passionate. It tends to place people on a pedestal where they can be adored. It is intensely loyal and will passionately support those it loves. When its power is rightly directed by a balanced mind, this emotional force provides the fuel to achieve great things.

R2 is highly sensitive and is quick to sense need in others and to give support. It is non-reactive, harmless emotional field and people like being around it. They feel included.

Owners of this field, because it is quieter, are less likely to allow their feelings to influence judgment. It tends to remain relatively calm and does not have great emotional displays

b. Negative emotional expression. The unbalanced R6 field is highly reactive, fiery and it takes things very personally. It is jealous and resentful when it cannot get what it wants - burns with righteous indignation when people contradict or oppose what it stands for. Easily glamoured by its prejudices and bias, it becomes blind to the truth and sees only what it wants to see. If it gets to the stage that it is fanatical and lacks humour, it can incite cruel, vicious, even murderous behaviour.

R2, because of its hyper-sensitivity can be easily overwhelmed in stressful circumstances. Then it frets, can be very fearful and over-anxious that it has hurt someone. If there is not a strong personality or mind, this emotional field can cause its owner to become a door-mat, be easily beaten down. When prodded, it does not react with fire like the ray 6 field, but rather can dissolve for a while (in tears or by withdrawing) before it regroups.

Both types try to attach themselves to others in unhealthy ways. R2 because it fears being alone, R6 because its passion compels this. Both types will put up with abuse rather than face rejection. But R6 will fight back, while R2 will take what is dished out.

c. How love is expressed. R6 is fiery and urgently passionate in love. It burns with desire to possess the one it adores and places that person on a pedestal. But all idols fall in time when seen to be less than perfect. If this happens R6 can quickly discard the old love prior to a hot, new pursuit. If rejected, love can quickly to hate.

R2 is warm and affectionate, is more inclusive and forgiving that R6 types. Its people are patient and supportive to those they love. But they can attach themselves to others as payment in return for a life of comfort and luxury, or just to have someone around.

Find the Emotional Ray.

Observe the emotional displays.

Do you take things very personally (6); or do you find it easy to be relatively impersonal (2)? If betrayed by someone you love and trust, are you disappointed and deeply hurt, but otherwise quietly non-reactive (2)? Or, are you intensely passionate, reactive, fiery, angry and jealous (6)? Have you been trying to transform your behaviour because fiery anger has got you into trouble in the past; but now you are more serene and can channel your fire serenely (6)? Do you react immediately if attacked and fight back (6)? Or do you timidly back off in fear (2)?

3. The Mind Ray - 4 or 5 (sometimes 1).

Most people have either a R4 feeling-type mind, or the R5 scientific mind. A smaller number have a R1 mind.

a. How the mind thinks. The R4 mind is intuitive, artistic and more easily influenced by the emotions. It sees in pictures and trusts or relies on impressions and the intuition. It's thought-forms (though colourful), can be vague and imprecise.

The R5 mind is analytical, scientific, precise and unemotional. Unbiased, it concentrates on the facts. Irreverent and sceptical of the mystical, it is dismissive of anything that cannot be proven scientifically. R5 builds precise, highly detailed, lucid and clear thought-forms. In extreme cases this mind can be coldly judgmental and heartless.

R1 mind is laser-like and fast. It rapidly synthesises facts, focuses on principles and sees the broad picture. Trusting in its own judgment it can jump to conclusions and make assumptions. It builds diamond-clear thoughts.

b. How it communicates. R4 minds often prefer to communicate non-verbally, through an art form or entertainment. They use pictures, colour, diagrams, props, laughter and playfulness to support what they say. The R4 mind is either making trouble or is peacemaking and reconciling. Its people are skilled counsellors and diplomats.

R5 minds communicate in a monotone voice and use facts when presenting their point of view. Their discussions are usually orderly. R1 minds push their points of view loudly, assertively or aggressively. They are compelled to win any argument and have the last word. They often raise their voices to drown out opposition.

c. If attacked or upset. The R4 mind will react aggressively, throw tantrums or dissolve in tears. R5 will try to win with words and with irrefutable facts. R1 may blow up with rage and use words as weapons to try to destroy opposition.

d. Body movement when communicating. The R4 head tends to move from side to side, and the whole body may move to better express what the mind wants to say. R5 people tend to hold the head and body very still. R1 people tend to thrust their head forward and may punch the forefinger forwards to emphasise a point.

Find the Mind Ray.

Observe the mind, how it thinks and communicates its thoughts.

How do you think and speak? Are you logical, detailed, perhaps colourless and monotone focusing only on facts (5)? Or entertaining, humorous, colourful, dramatic, intuitive, poetic but short on details (4)? It is easy for you to get into arguments (4)? Or do you jump to conclusions, go straight to the point and then defend your point of view arrogantly, beating your opponent down with will-power and assertion (1)?

Do you agonise over decisions, get torn about what to do it is exhausting (4)? Or are you disciplined in problem-solving and take a pragmatic and logical approach (5)? Do you summarise matters quickly and come swiftly to a synthetic conclusion (1)? If someone attacks you verbally, can you get so emotional you cannot think clearly or coherently, it seems the mind gets "drowned" in the upset (4)?

If you were asked to organise a workshop.

Would you do research first to gather all the facts and information you can about the subject before you start (5)? Or would you jump straight in by choosing the location and whether the atmosphere, location and colour-scheme of the venue suits your topic (4)? Or, would you immediately see in a comprehensive flash all that needed to be done, and organise the endeavour from the larger picture working inwards (1)?

If the workshop was science or technology based, would you feel at ease with your topic as long as you had time to research it (5)? Or feel out of your depth (4)? Or how would you feel if a workshop was humanities or art based? Uncomfortable (5), or right at home (4)? Or, whatever the topic, you would just do what needed to be done because you are a great organiser and you would recruit others to help if necessary (1)?

4. The Personality Ray - any of the 7 rays.

The personality ray cannot be found before it forms. Then it is easy to see because it is how the personality tries to control people and the environment.

1. Personality rays 1 and 7 carry the power of God.

Ray 1 is a major ray and those who have it exude natural power. R7 is its lower counterpart and though also strong, its power is expressed in a more civilised and polite manner.

a. Positive personality expression. R1 is a natural ruler and leader. It exudes power which it uses to drive through all obstacles and has the will to endure until it achieves victory. People are drawn to its power and confidence. R7 is also a leader, but is group-conscious and understands that developing and working harmoniously with a team is important to its personal success. It is also a great organiser - and politically correct, which R1 is not.

b. Outstanding negative traits. R1 is a law unto itself, is proud, ambitious powerful, wilful, hard, obstinate, angry and dominating. It demands to be first and best, the alpha ego, the top dog. It is aloof and separative. R7 is snobbish and judgemental. It exudes a superior attitude because it knows what is right and wrong and how things should be done.

c. How they try to dominate others. R1 is an arrogant bully and will try to destroy resistance with brute force and violence. It demands blind allegiance. R7 sets the rules, the standards, then polices the performance of people to ensure they follow them. It tries to standardize people's behaviour to better control them.

2. Personality rays 2, 4 and 6 carry the love of God.

a. Positive personality expression. These are the feeling, emotional rays that focus on relationships. Ray 2 is a major ray and these personalities sparkle with light and radiance. They are warm, serene, kind and charming. They make others feel good by shining their light and warmth on them. R4 types are the artists and entertainers, who make people feel good through play, laughter and by transporting them to another world in their imagination. R6 types are pure devotees and idealists who make others feel good by inspiring them to lift themselves up to God or to follow their highest ideal.

b. Outstanding negative traits. All these rays are fearful of being alone and of rejection, but none more so than R2. Its people are the most fearful, oversensitive and timid. R4 lacks self-control, has rapid mood changes, is inconsistent and unstable. It is aggressive and fights with itself and others. R6 is the fiery, intense fanatic, the crusader, who tries to force its beliefs onto others - "if you're not with me, you're against me." R2 is warm, R6 is fiery, R4 gets hot and conflicted.

c. How they try to dominate others. R2 uses charm, warmth and magnetism. It binds people through selfish love, guilt, dependency, or by playing the suffering martyr. R4 exaggerates what is going on, plays the drama queen, will throw a huge temper-tantrum to try to force people to do what it wants. It will "go to war" if thwarted. R6 tries to inspire people to follow its belief or ideal. If they do not, it can attack them as if they were devils.

3. Personality rays 3 and 5 carry the mind of God.

a. Positive personality expression. R3 is a major ray and is the super-thinker. It is knowledgeable about the material world and how it works. It uses intellectual creativity, mental astuteness, resourcefulness and adaptability to solve life's problems, to benefit financially and materially. R5 is the scientific-thinking type, who uses concentrated thought and analysis to find the answer it is searching for. They are the technical experts that others come to when they want specific and specialised knowledge. They use these skills to benefit society.

b. Outstanding negative traits. Hypercritical and intellectually proud, R3 needs to be cleverest, the wittiest. Over-busy and over-thinking, it gets caught up in a multitude of plans so that life becomes a tangled mess. It is restless, absent-minded, changeable and can be deceitful. R5 is more disciplined - but where R3 casts its net too wide, it is too restricted. It focuses narrowly and exclusively on its own strictly mental, specialised, scientific and technical interests, at the expense of seeing and taking part in the larger picture. It tends to suppress empathy. Consequently, it can be separative, cold and "heartless" when dealing with those who violate what it considers to be "the law".

c. How they try to dominate others. The R3 personality uses its intellectual superiority, its wits, to manipulate and inveigle people - it gets what it wants through lies and deceit. It is "the early bird that gets the worm" type. Bending the rules to suit itself, it will do whatever is required to win the day. R5 becomes excessively rationalistic, lists all "the facts" to prove that it is the expert, that it is right and others are wrong. It is the "hanging judge" type.

Find the Personality Ray - any of the Seven Rays.

Analyse the Personality Ray Checklist chart in the Appendix. If the personality ray is fully formed and the soul ray is not yet controlling it, this ray will be a dominant force and the ray negatives will be easy to see. If a certain level of soul-alignment has been achieved, the personality ray positives will be easy to see.

Identify outstanding negative traits. Observe how the personality seeks to assert its authority. How it tries to get attention and "big-note" itself. How does it go about fighting for its rights or control people? Do you see hard line, pushy, mental (1, 3, 5, 7) or soft, cooperative, emotional (2, 4, 6)? Go through all the rays, dismiss those that do not fit, then focus on the remaining.

- Does the person use power, might and bullying coercion to control (1)?
- Does she just have to smile and exude charm and an incredible magnetism to get people to give her what she wants (2)?
- Does he easily manipulate people through his rapid-fire quick wit, deceitfulness and lies (3)? Is he successful because he is clever, adaptable and highly energetic (3)?
- Does she get her way by exhausting people because of the huge dramas she creates, the screaming tantrums, the unstable emotions (4)?
- Is she cold and clinical and tries to convince others she knows best because she has all the facts and information (5)?
- Does he draw people in with his amazing enthusiasm and conviction in the rightness of his beliefs. Or reject people, feeling betrayed if they disagree (6)?
- Does she control situations by proving she is the best person to get things done? The one with the best credentials, the most efficient and best organised (7)?
- Does he radiate such impressive power and inner strength, he intimidates all those around him (1)?
- Is he cruel (6)? Can get into a hot rage when pushed?

- Does she get away with things by claiming she is an artistic soul, and that being outrageous is what she does best (4)?
- Is he needy and so desperate not to be left alone, he would make a doormat of himself, try to shrink in size to avoid being seen and becoming a target (2)?
- Does she look elfin-like, other-worldly, and is interested in nature, fairies and magic (7)?

5. The Soul Ray - any of the Seven Rays.

Analyse the Soul Ray Checklist in the Appendix. Once the personality ray is alive and is assertive, the soul ray becomes more active and begins to clash with it for control.

1. Hard-line souls on the Power Rays.

Ray 1 Will & Power Soul. This soul expresses its power dynamically and with directed purpose. Leading from the front, it is strong, hard, courageous, fearless and truthful. The R1 soul goal is to be a powerful and benevolent leader who serves the highest good, and who frees people from bondage and oppression.

Ray 7 Ceremony, Order & Magic Soul. This soul expresses its power courteously. Leading the team from the front, it has organisational, managerial and administrative prowess. The goal is to bring order out of chaos, to organise affairs and the workings of the group so things run efficiently and forms and constructions are manifested that are not only functional but are beautiful (the better to achieve the greater good for all).

Some R7 types are drawn to ceremonial or ritual work such as Masonry.

2. Soft-line souls on the Love Rays.

Ray 2 Love & Wisdom Soul. The "love" type soul expresses the power of inclusive love, kindness and compassion. The "Wisdom" type soul expresses its power wisely, with kind concern, by being understanding and tactful. The goal is to facilitate the inner spiritual growth of people and alleviate their suffering. Love-types focus on healing, wisdom-types on education.

Ray 4 Harmony through Conflict Soul. This soul expresses its power with feeling, with a deep and empathetic understanding of the pain and suffering of others. To alleviate suffering, it surrounds people with beauty, tries to lift spirits with laughter, or will go into battle with the one causing the suffering. Its goal is to be a reconciling and harmonising agent so that individuals find inner peace. R4 works through diplomacy, counselling or the arts.

Ray 6 Devotion & Idealism Soul. This soul expresses its power with fiery and dynamic passion. It dedicates itself totally, completely, with one-pointed devotion and without reservation to the service of its teacher, leader or to its highest ideal. Its life-duty is to inspire people so they also find the same teacher, the same truth or the same pathway to God.

3. Hard-line souls on the Mind Rays.

Ray 3 Active-Intelligence Soul. This soul expresses its power as intellectual brilliance - a weaving, dancing play of mind that speaks with the voice of reason and that can clarify the complexities of life so that people better understand. The goal of this soul is to stimulate the intellectual and mental creativity of others, to solve complexities and create plans that benefit humanity.

Ray 5 Concrete Mind & Science Soul. This soul expresses its power through scientific brilliance, concentrated thinking and factual accuracy - to bring about justice and fairness for all. The goal is to use the laser-like mental powers to discover new scientific truths that benefit the greater good, to advance truth and reject error, to find the soul.

The Vocation of the Soul.

The mission of the soul is to serve humanity. So, if the heart-vocation is identified, often it will reveal the soul ray.

R1: Vocations requiring exceptional leadership, will, power, strength and stamina, to overcome all opposition and see projects and plans succeed - such as in law, order and politics.

R2: Vocations that require tact, foresight, personal magnetism, warmth and concern for others. Particularly in health, education and spiritual growth.

R3: Vocations requiring exceptional intellectual adaptability and resourcefulness to solve ethical, moral and philosophical problems in business, finance and in life generally.

R4: Vocations that require the creation of some form of beauty, colour and harmony. The arts, music, writing, counselling and the diplomatic service.

R5: Vocations that require a keen intellect and analytical accuracy - scientists, engineers, technology workers, analysts, data and medical technicians and surgeons.

R6: Vocations requiring devotion, dedication and selfless service - preachers, orators, generals, matrons, nurses and carers.

R7: Vocations requiring practical efficiency, finesse, organisational skill and the ability to manifest ideas on the physical plane. Business leaders, legal heads and advisors, political advisors, architects, ritualists and white magicians.

Find the Soul Ray - any of the seven.

Meditate upon the following questions, searching in the heart for answers. What is my heart-vocational goal? What vocation would most fulfil the urge in my heart to help people?

R1: My goal is to use my power, management and leadership ability - in government, politics or law, to strengthen and liberate others.

R2: My goal is to help and heal people so I can alleviate suffering. Or, to develop a deep intuitive loving-understanding of people, to become inclusive and wise so that I can teach, illumine and help people find their own wisdom.

R3: My goal is to speak with the voice of reason and intelligence, to cultivate the intelligence of students and help them develop the powers of the mind so they can help solve the complexities of life.

R4: My goal is to help harmonise and resolve conflict, to beautify life through art, music or drama.

R5: My goal is to use my scientific expertise and laser-like mental powers to discover new scientific truths, to advance truth and reject error, so I can alleviate the suffering and hardship that many experience on earth.

R6: My goal is to use my faith, devotion and idealism to inspire people to search for the same high God, truth or faith.

R7: My goal is to use my organising expertise wherever it is needed, so that people's lives run more efficiently, and life can conform more closely with the beauty of the divine plan

Ask yourself, "what are my most joyous or sacred moments?"

R1: My most joyous activity is to discard all nonessentials and be in perfect freedom. To identify with the One Self and to stand in the presence and the might and power of Deity.

R2: My most joyous activity is "being in love" with all (love-type), or pursuing wisdom and distributing understanding (wisdom-type).

R3: My most joyous activity is to use the mind to theorise, plan and then act on that plan to solve problems. I love theories and proofs, which explain the nature of things.

R4: My most joyous activity is to create beauty, and to perfectly harmonise and equilibrise that which was previously imbalanced.

R5: My most joyous activity is to discover the previously hidden, to contemplate the wonderful and intelligent design of nature.

R6: My most joyous activity is to be in pursuit of the one I adore and to love and be totally loved by the beloved. To have the freedom to pursue my highest ideal with fiery ardour and to express that ideal. To be in devotional communion with Deity.

R7: My most joyous activity is to bring order out of chaos. I love contemplating forms (divinely created or man-made) which perfectly embody some aspect of the Universal Design.

6. The Monadic Ray

Only very spiritually advanced initiates are consciously in contact with the Monadic Ray. This is the energy stream that relates us to the Spirit or Father aspect of God. When consciously employed, it gives the initiate the "freedom of the solar system." Ultimately, our Monads are on one of the three rays of aspect - rays 1, 2 or 3.

- R1 Monads of Power. There are few in incarnation at this time. They destroy when necessary to promote the Plan of God - usually at the beginnings and endings of cycles. Form does not count to them. When they destroy it accelerates evolution in a manner that is beneficial for the souls working in the system.

- Our solar system is of the 2nd Ray and there are more R2 Monads on earth than on other rays. These Monads guide and rule through love and wisdom.

- 3rd ray Monads dominated in the previous solar system. They are masters of knowledge and are expert manipulators of energy in the material world. They are in this system to learn to love,[1] and to use their ingenuity wisely.

Definitions for Monad.

> The Monad, or pure Spirit, the Father in Heaven.[2]

> Monad. The One. The threefold spirit on its own plane. In occultism it often means the unified triad—Atma, Buddhi, Manas; Spiritual Will, Intuition and Higher mind,—or the immortal part of man which reincarnates in the lower kingdoms and gradually progresses through them to man and thence to the final goal.[3]

---

[1] Bailey, Alice. Esoteric Psychology II, 295. Only initiates are in a position to sense, determine, or discover the nature of their Monadic ray. It is the "unknown quantity" in a man's nature and remains relatively quiescent until after the 3rd initiation, though it basically conditions the etheric body itself.

[2] Bailey, Alice. Initiation, Human and Solar, xii.

[3] Ibid, 221-222.

Example. assembling a Ray Chart for Carl Jung (1875-1961).

Carl Jung was a theoretical psychologist and practicing clinician and became well known for his pioneering work in dream analysis. He also explored Eastern and Western philosophy, alchemy, astrology, sociology, as well as literature and the arts. Jung's wisdom and global influence indicated he was at least a disciple. Here is his hypothetical chart.

It can be written like this:

II - IV: 3. 6. 3, or as follows:

R2 soul.
    R4 personality.
        R3 mind.
        R6 emotional.
        R3 physical.

Ordinarily you would start a ray search by working from the physical ray inwards. But when you are dealing with giants of men and people in history who have become famous because of their vocational work (like Jung), the soul ray is like a blazing beacon. In Jung's case, he was a teacher and healer - R2 vocations.

- *Soul R2, wisdom line*. Jung's passion was healing and teaching, R2 vocations that point to a second ray soul. Souls on the wisdom line take ideas emanating from the Divine and make them attractive to the public and easy to understand. They train others to carry these ideas forth, to maximise the good that people can do with them. This was Jung's life. He lived to think, write and teach his ideas.
- *Physical R3:* his bulkiness points to a third ray physical nature - the "work horse" physical vehicle. He was extremely active.
- *Emotional R6:* Jung was fiery and passionate in expression. He had a rich personal life and it is reported that he had a long-term mistress who was good friends with his wife (who knew of the affair). He also had many fiery battles with his opponents. These point to a R6 astral field.
- *Mind R3:* Jung's wide ranging and philosophical approach on many subjects is typical of the R3 mind. He wrote prodigiously, produced many books on mental-health and various esoteric topics, confirming R3.
- *Personality R4:* Jung had a colourful personality, laughing and joking; his humour came across during his lectures and talks. He was also a talented artist - R4 gives a desire to produce art and beauty and the talent to do so. When trying to assert his authority, he would go into battle. The conflict side of this ray was evident in the public animosities he had with Sigmund Freud, his former mentor and friend. He also struggled in the earlier part of his life to rise above depression, which is often associated with this ray.

Validate the Ray Selections.

Once a ray chart has been formulated, it must be tested for its validity. Very often, after observation over months, even years, you may change a ray because you notice that a different ray is more influential.

B. Reading the Ray Profile Chart.

Once a ray chart has been assembled, then read it. The goal in a Ray Profile Reading is to harmonise and integrate the personality rays then bring the Personality Ray into a harmonious alignment with the soul. In the counselling session, help people understand themselves energetically, how to harmonise any energy imbalances, and how to integrate their fields so they become more spiritually aligned and effective in their service work.

1. Identify the problem ray.

There is always one body and its ray that is strongest, which dominates the nature in a negative way and stands in the way of spiritual progress. In most it is the emotional ray. A smaller number will have the mind ray as the major problem. In dominant people it will be the personality ray. If the latter has formed it will be fighting the soul ray for control of the life.

Once identified, explain to the person how this force is hindering spiritual progress and the requirement for balancing. Then give advice on how this can be done. We all have a wealth of information to draw upon and will give advice based on our particular expertise and knowledge.

Example. The person is Atlantean (emotional) in consciousness and the emotional ray (6) is the problem. Explain the positives and negatives of R6, what you have observed in the person's emotional expression that needs to be changed. Then the benefits of doing so. Finding happiness is the goal at this level. So, mentioning for instance that greater happiness and a more stable and long-lasting love will be found if the inner work is done. This will be highly motivating for the R6 person. Include in the consultation the integration word "Moderation," and the need to moderate and balance the life. Give a meditation or exercise to balance the emotions when they are upset.

2. Identify and strengthen the higher ray.

a. Identify the highest ray the person is consciously active in and encourage the development of this ray/ body.

Suppose in the previous example, the mind ray was the highest ray. Identify the mental ray (either 4, 5 or 1) and explain its positives. How it can be used to help overcome emotional suffering. Give advice on how to strengthen the mind. Although at this level, the soul ray is not yet apparent, ask mystics how they would like to help humanity. Then based on the answer, suggest a ray-type service vocation that would be suitable.

b. There will be times when the Personality Ray is the higher level to be attained. In such a case, the mind will be awake but it struggles to bring the emotional nature under control. (A study of the life will reveal a lack of ambition or dedicated purpose in any direction).

Encourage the person to choose one (very achievable) goal, then to make it a high priority to reach that goal. Then to be self-congratulatory when successful. Then set another achievable goal and repeat the process. When successful, this will integrate the personality.

c. If the Personality Ray is evident and is in control of the life, then the soul will also be active. Identify the Soul Ray and bring it to the attention of the person concerned. Highlight the fact that the Soul Ray needs to be strengthened (and how to do this), to bring the personality under control and the benefits of doing so.

1. Ray Readings.

1. A reading for Carl Jung.

Imagine that Jung had come for a consultation and was asking for advice. From preliminary consultations, a ray chart had been drawn up. Here is how such a reading could be presented.

> You have a ray 3 physical body, which is a work-horse physical vehicle. This is fortunate, because it enables you to work long periods - without nourishment if necessary.
>
> Your emotional ray is 6, which explains why you are fiery and passionate in expression and why you can become fanatical sometimes in the battles you have with those who offend you. This needs to be balanced.
>
> Your mind is on ray 3. You have wide-ranging mind that searches far for information. Your mind is also very fertile hence the many books and writings you have produced. It is an asset.
>
> Your personality ray is 4: hence your colourful, artistic nature and the way you use humour during your lectures. It is also an asset. But this is also your problem ray, which is clashing with your soul ray for dominance. Aided and abetted by your 6th ray fiery fanaticism, you can fly into battle and create huge and unnecessary conflicts. It also explains why you have been prone to depression. You can swing from the heights to the depths. Your task is to stabilise and balance this force and be more diplomatic - over the years you have managed to do this, but more needs to be done. For instance, [offer advice].
>
> Your soul ray is 2, on the wisdom line, which means your heart-vocation is to heal and educate through your writings. Souls on the wisdom line take ideas emanating from the Divine and make them attractive to the public. They train others to carry these ideas forth, to maximise the good that people can do with them. This is your life. You live to think, write and teach the wisdom you have acquired. Keep moving in this direction.

2. Example reading 1, from Master Djwhal Khul (paraphrased).

The next two cases were analyses given by Djwhal Khul, to explain how psychological problems can arise. The bracket insertions are by the author.

R1 soul. R4 personality. R3 mind. R6 emotional. R1 physical.

> This man will be ambitious for power (R1), but with right motive, because he is truly idealistic (R6). He will fight intelligently (R3) to achieve power (R1), and will fight fanatically (R6) to bring about these ends because his R4 personality and R6 astral body will force him to do so, and his R1 body and brain will enable him to put up a strong fight.
>
> At the same time, his R1 soul energy is seeking to dominate, and will eventually do so through the medium of R3 mental energy, influencing the first ray brain.[1] The first result of soul influence will be an intensification of everything in the personality (the R1 soul). The trouble [DK used this as an example of mental trouble], will be localised in the mental body or in the brain and can range all the way down from idee fixe and mental crystallisation to insanity [a

---

[1] Rays/ bodies on the same line will team up together in the personality expression. Rays 1 and 3 are both hard line rays.

negative result when rays 1, 3, 6 combine] (if the stimulation becomes unduly powerful or the heredity is not good). He can express arrogant success in his chosen field of work, which will make him a dominant and unpleasant person (R1), or he can express the fluidity of the third ray mind which will make him a scheming manipulator or a fighter for immense schemes which can never really materialise.

In this analysis I simply sought to show one thing: that the conflict of energies within a man can produce serious situations. But most of them can be corrected through right understanding. [1]

3. Example reading 2, from Master Djwhal Khul (paraphrased).

In this example, Djwhal Khul allocated a R2 physical body, which is highly unusual. Three bodies were on the love/ soft-line - 2 and 6. DK said this was a problem.

R1 soul.
  R2 personality.
    R5 mind.
    R6 emotional.
    R2 physical.

The personality, astral and physical bodies are on the ray 2 line creating a psychological problem. The soul (1) and mental body (5) are along another line. This combination presents both opportunity and difficulty. The second ray quality of his physical body relates him to the personality (both R2).

In the lower expression: It gives a person who is intensely sensitive, inclusive (R2) and self-willed (R1). Emphasis will be upon material inclusiveness and tangible acquisition (prominence of R2). Because the R2 personality and physical body are related by similarity of ray, there will also be a clearly pronounced tendency to lay the emphasis upon material inclusiveness and tangible acquisition, and there will, therefore, be found (in this person), an exceedingly selfish and self-centred man. He will not be particularly intelligent, as only the R5 mental body relates the person directly to the mind aspect of Deity. His R1 egoic (soul) force enables him to use all means to plan for himself, and to use the will aspect to acquire and to attract the material good he desires or thinks he needs. His predominant R2 equipment, however, will eventually bring the higher values into play.

Higher expression: when the evolutionary cycle has done its work - a sensitive, intuitive, inclusive disciple whose wisdom will flower and whose vehicles will be a channel for divine love. [2]

Djwhal Khul was a master psychologist and we can learn much by studying how he analysed these ray charts. In the next section, is advice he gave to his disciples based on their behaviours and associated rays.

---

1 Bailey, Alice. Esoteric Psychology II, 443-444.
2 Bailey, Alice. Esoteric Psychology II, 297-298..

2. Rays of the Tibetan's Disciples

The ray allocations shown in the chart are of great interest. They were made by Djwhal Khul in the Alice Bailey books Discipleship in the New Age (DINA), volumes I and II. Each disciple was identified by initials, which referred to qualities the disciple needed to build into his or her psychology. The most famous person was Robert Assagioli, author of the Psychosynthesis Psychology technique, identified as FCD. The letters may have referred to fidelity, compassion and detachment. Because they were disciples, they could have their bodies on any rays. As students, we can learn much by studying the advice which DK gave. Some quotes are paraphrased and bracket insertions are by the author.

1. The Physical Ray.

R1 there were 6.
R2 there was 1.
R3 there were 12.
R6 there were 2.
R7 there were 15.

(To JWKP) Your physical body is on R7. Hence your Masonic opportunity and your ability to organise and to rule. I would remind you all that when the statement is made that the physical body is upon the seventh ray, it means that the atoms of the brain, in particular, are coloured and motivated by seventh ray energy. So it is with all the rays upon which a physical vehicle may be found. (DINA I, 168)

(To RVB) Your physical body is on R3; it is here that your major problem lies. It is closely connected with your mental problem which is that of an increased dynamism. The dynamic power of your soul [R2] must pour through your fourth ray mind [both soft-line rays], galvanising it into a renewed, inclusive, loving, harmonising activity. Be more outgoing (as a part of your self-initiated training) to those, for instance, with whom your daily lot is cast. They need help. Give them of that help freely and fully. R3 which governs your physical body is unduly quiescent and should be awakened to increased coordinated purpose. (DINA I, 275).

2. The Emotional Ray.

R1 there were 6.
R2 there were 7.
R6 there were 22.

(To BSD) Your astral body is on R6, so you have a line of force direct from the soul [it was also on R6]. In your case, this R6 energy shows itself predominantly as devotion to duty as realised, and to responsibility as recognised, and not so much in devotion to persons or even ideals. This has constituted a paramount balancing factor in your life. (DINA I, 120).

3. The Mind Ray.

R1 there were 6.
R2 there were 3.
R3 there were 2.
R4 there were 18.
R5 there were 7.

(RAJ) Your mental ray is R4, the Ray of Harmony through Conflict, of beauty through order and of unity through understanding. This, being on the line of your soul ray [R2], will tend to bring about rapid contact with the soul, via the mind, if you apply yourself with diligence to the task involved. Your whole life problem is, therefore, that of relationships, both within yourself and in your chosen field of service. This is naturally true of all, but your particular battlefield in this connection lies in the reconciling of the forces warring within your own nature and in your particular environment. It is not the Kurukshetra of the "pairs of opposites," wherein Arjuna sits in the middle and seeks to balance the warring forces. It is the battlefield of higher relations—those between the soul and the personality, and between what you are in this life and the environment in which you find your chosen field of service. Your personal release lies in the production of harmony through conflict, and your best technique is to produce this harmonising influence within your environment as the result of your inner conflict, silently waged in the shrine of the mind. (DINA I, 178-9)

Rays of 39 of the Tibetan's Disciples

Disciple	Soul	Personality	Mind	Astral	Physical	DINA 1
AAB	2	1				
BSD	3	6	5	6	3	105
BSW	1	7	4	6	7	621
CAC	1	2	4	6	1	203
CDP	2	6	5	6	6	504
DAO	7	1				278
DEI	2	1	2	1	3	497
DHB	2	6	1	1	7	416
DIJ	2	6	4	1	7	454
DLR	1	5	5	6	7	301
DPR	1	5	4	2	3	382
EES	7	6	4	6	1	645
FCD	2	4	1	2	7	138
GSS	7	6	1	6	3	406
HSD	6	1	1	6	7	571
IBS	1	6	4	6	3	235
ISGL	6	1	1	6	1	210
JSP	2	6	4	2	7	662
JWKP	1	2	4	2	7	157
KES	2		4	6	7	544
LDO	2	4	4	2	7	127
LFU	1	3	3	6	6	225
LTSK	1	6	5	1	3	2-724
LUT	2	1	4	6	3	471
OLRD	1	5	3	6	1	551
PDW	2	6	5	6	7	433
PGC	2	7	5	6	7	342
RAJ	2	7	4	6	2	173
RLU	2	4	5	6	3	531
RRR	2	1	4	6	1	649
RSU	2	3	1	1	7	355
RSW	2	7	4	2	7	637
RVB	2	4	4	2	3	253
SCP	1	6	2	6	1	321
SRD	2	6	4	1	3	560
SSP	2	5	4	6	3	189
WDS	2	1	2	1	3	375
WOI	2	5	4	6	7	441
WDB	2	4				291

4. The Personality Ray.

R1 there were 7.	R2 there were 2.
R3 there were 2.	R4 there were 5.
R5 there were 5.	R6 there were 12.
R7 there were 4.	

(SSP). Your personality ray is the fifth and your physical body is the third. It will be apparent to you then, why your physical vehicle is such a good response apparatus to mental impression [because they both were hard-line, mental rays]. (DINA I, 200-201).

(BSD) Your gift to this group is that fiery, dynamic, zealous aspiration which is the spiritual quality of the sixth ray, which governs your personality. (DINA I, 107).

Your personality ray is focussed in your astral body [also R6]. The rays 3, 5 an 6 are your controlling factors. [He only had rays 3, 5 and 6 in his chart]. This gives you devotion and mental control and it should give you balance but, unfortunately it does not, because the mind aspect is unduly emphasised and you fear devotion. Yet it is your devotion which has brought you to us and not your mental ability. It is your devotion which has led you steadily all these years and produced your service in the world. (DINA I, 126).

(ISGL). Your personality, mind and physical rays are all on R1 and this predisposes you to loneliness which is based on a sense of isolation. Fortunately, and also owing to the quality of your R6 soul and to an achieved measure of control, your effect upon those you seek to serve is good. You are aware of the powerful influence you can call into play and thus affect other people's lives - and the powerful reaction you can evoke from them. The effect of R1 when focussed on the physical plane. It is both an asset and a problem. You came into incarnation to learn to wield this force rightly. (DINA I, 221-2).

5. The Soul Ray.

R1 there were 10.	R2 there were 23.
R3 there was 1.	R6 there were 2.
R7 there were 3.	

(CAC) Your soul ray is the first Ray of Will or Power. Your personality ray is the second Ray of Love-Wisdom and this enables you safely to evoke and use your first ray Will, for it will then be inevitably modified by your personality focus. this tends to make you fairly well-balanced, when you act as a personality or as a soul. (DINA I, 204-5)

(FCD). You have the *vices* of your second ray [soul] *virtues*. You suffer from attachment and from a too rapid identification with other people. This can be handled if you stand steadfast as a soul and do not focus as a personality in dealing with people. (DINA I, 130).

Your soul, personality and astral rays [2, 4, 2], are on the same line of force (of R2). I would ask you—as far as you possibly can—to insulate yourself from fear [1] and from the effect of the world situation and its allied problems. The future for you is planned and you can take the right steps through the power of your illumined mind. (DINA I, 156).

This concludes this section on the Seven Rays. In the next section, in the Esoteric Psychology chapter, mental troubles are examined.

---

[1] This was within the period of WWII..

CHAPTER 3. ESOTERIC PSYCHOLOGY.

The foundation of the new psychology must be built upon the premise that this one life is not man's sole opportunity in which to achieve integration and eventual perfection. The great Law of Rebirth must be accepted and it will then be found to be, in itself, a major releasing agent in any moment of crisis or any psychological problem case. The recognition of further opportunity and a lengthened sense of time are both quieting and helpful to many types of minds; its interpretative value will be found illuminating as the patient grasps the fact that behind him lie points of crisis wherein it can be demonstrated by his present equipment that he achieved integration, thus guaranteeing to him victory in his present point of crisis and of difficult conflict. The light which this throws on relationships and environment will serve to stabilise his purpose and make him comprehend the inevitability of responsibility. When this great law is understood in its true implications and not interpreted in terms of its present childish presentation, then man will shoulder the responsibility of living with a daily recognition of the past, an understanding of the purpose of the present, and with an eye to the future. This will also greatly lessen the growing tendency towards suicide which humanity is showing. Alice Bailey. Esoteric Psychology II, page 431.

Psychology problems fall into two major groups.

I. Psychology Problems which affect the wider community.

'**II. Problems of Mystics and Disciples.**

INTRODUCTION.

Psychology is what scientists and philosophers of various persuasions have created to try to fill the need to understand the minds and behaviour of man. The requirement for this arose as humanity developed the powers of the mind under the influence of the 5th Ray. But with this growth, as people began to think more about themselves and their lives, came the realisation by some that they were unhappy. This began a search to understand why, and this in turn gave rise to the science of psychology. In the 20th Century there were impressive breakthroughs with Freud and Jung among the forerunners.

1. Overview of Mental Health.

1. What is a psychological disorder?

Defining exactly what constitutes a psychological disorder is fluid and definitions change. In 20th Century psychology, the term "neurosis" was generally used to refer to any mental imbalance that caused distress but did not interfere with rational thought or the ability to function in daily life. Examples were depression and anxiety disorders. More serious conditions were called "psychotic". The term "neurosis" is no longer used but some still do use psychotic to denote a clinical condition that consists of delusions, hallucinations, and thought disorders. Here is a recent (2021) definition for mental illness.

> Mental illness, also called mental health disorders, refers to a wide range of mental health conditions — disorders that affect your mood, thinking and behaviour. Examples of mental illness include depression, anxiety disorders, schizophrenia, eating disorders and addictive behaviours. [1]

Tremendous advances have been made in understanding mental problems and its treatment. But still, such people are often considered to be deficient in some way or defective, even lazy or irresponsible. Mental illness is often seen as being less real or less legitimate than physical illness, leading to reluctance on the part of policy-makers and insurance companies to pay for treatment. "Why don't you just snap out of it," is a common attitude. However, a growing realization of the extent that mental illness affects health care costs and the number of lost work days is changing this.

> Nearly 50% of adults experience a mental illness at some point in their lives. More than half of these people experience moderate to severe symptoms. In fact, 4 of the 10 leading causes of disability among people aged five and older are mental health disorders, with depression being the number one cause of all illnesses that cause disability. Despite this high prevalence of mental illness, only about 20% of people who have a mental illness receive professional help. [2]

---

[1] https://www.mayoclinic.org/diseases-conditions/mental-illness.
[2] https://www.msdmanuals.com/en-au/home/mental-health-disorders/overview-of-mental-health.

2. An esoteric explanation for ill health.

From an esoteric point of view, the single cause of all disease and psychological distress is the result of an inhibited soul life. [1] The soul is continually trying to express its energies through the personality and when it cannot because of negative thoughts and emotions, the result is a clashing of energies and general upset to the flow and distribution of energy throughout the body.

This means that prior to enlightenment, which is that advanced state when soul-personality illumination occurs and the flow of soul energy through the form is full and free; physical disease or a psychological disturbance is inevitable. Ill-health is the soul's way of letting us know that its flow is blocked and that an adjustment or easing of that blockage is required.

> Troubled emotions or rampant desire lie at the root of most of our problems. The mind thinks, it plans, it idealises and has ambitions. The thoughts it creates descend to the astral plane where they blend with astral force. When disappointments and frustrations set in because things don't go the way we would like them to or because we cannot get what we want, bitterness sets in.

Our mental health suffers first. Then disease follows according to the weaknesses we have inherited in the physical body. Stoics who repress their worries so they can continue to function in life and at work are more likely to collapse with a serious physical disease or mental problem than those who express their discontent. Repressed emotional energy is virulently toxic and is the major psychological cause of ill-health.

3. General steps for good Mental Health.

Good mental health is the basis for a creative and joyful life. That so many suffer mentally, is due to the stresses and demands that modern competitive society places upon the individual and the lack of support and understanding in providing adequate assistance when the need arises.

The essential requirement for good mental health is considered to be a flexible and adaptable mind and balanced emotional expression. If our thoughts and emotions are positive and filled with joy, then energy flow will be smoother and the result will be more wholesome and health benefiting. A person who is mentally and spiritually healthy:

a. Is in touch with his or her emotions and has learned to expresses them healthily.
b. Takes responsibility for his or her life and actions.
c. Is flexible and adaptable, is able to change the mind, is spontaneous, laughs easily and feels free.
d. Has integrity and honesty and feels comfortable being transparent about his or her life.
e. Is content with life.
f. Is authentic, is connected to the soul and speaks and lives from the depths of the self and not from the surface.
g. Has courage to face insecurity and go forward into the unknown.
h. Is socially cooperative and feels integrated with the community.
i. Has a purpose for living, a holistic outlook and affirms truth and goodness.

---

1 Bailey, Alice. Esoteric Healing, 5.

2. Three forms of "insanity" that will not respond to counselling.

According to Eastern wisdom, there are three groups of very serious insanities that are incurable [1] and which cannot be helped with psychological intervention. The term "insanity" is not used clinically today although it is used in legal cases.

1. Serious organic damage to the brain.

The first group occurs when there is serious damage to brain tissue and cells - such as caused by structural head defects or injuries, tumours and other growths, abscesses and the various dementia disorders. Because of this damage, it is impossible for the soul to communicate through the brain.

2. Impaired mental cognition due to the soul not being present.

In this group, there are 2 types. Both are caused by trouble with the consciousness thread.

a. The consciousness thread is not connected to the brain. This is the most serious type of this problem. Because the consciousness thread is not connected to the brain, the soul remains unaware of the body and so is not controlling it. The body lives on but it is being run by the "animal-brain" or body intelligence. In such a case, the "human" is simply an animal responding to basic need. "In these cases, you have idiocy, or simply a very low-grade human animal." [2]

b. The consciousness thread is connected to a foreign entity. This is the reverse of the first case and it results in serious and rare cases of obsession. The brain-end of the thread is intact, but there is trouble at the soul-end. For one reason or another, it is not connected. That end, having been abandoned, has been snatched up by an opportunistic bypasser, a disembodied person or entity. There is nothing to be done in this situation.

3. An uncontrollable Astral Body - "Astral Maniacs."

This is a desire-body problem. The mind functions adequately but it cannot be used to stop the expression of an uncontrollable and rampant desire. This because the person keeps brooding and salivating over some desire and this builds a thoughtform encapsulating that desire that becomes so powerful, dominating and compelling; it controls the person. The person becomes a prisoner of his own creation. This is the cause of the problem and how the trouble arises. The desire is not always dangerous, but often is.

> The mind remains useless and inert whilst the man expresses (with violence or subtlety as the case may be) some basic desire. It may be the desire to kill, or desire to have abnormal sexual experience, or even the desire to be ever on the move and thus constantly active. There is no remedy but the protection of the man from himself and his own actions. [3]

Two serious criminal behaviours that fit this criterion are paedophilia and serial killings. A common remark serious offenders of this crime make on being caught is, "I could not stop myself." When true, this confirms the uncontrollable nature of the desire and that such people fit the astral-maniac description. Science is recognising that the worst of these offenders cannot be rehabilitated with methods currently being used.

---

1 Bailey, Alice. Esoteric Psychology II, 459-460.
2 Bailey, Alice. Esoteric Psychology II, 458.
3 Ibid, 459.

The Pedophilic Disorder.

Those affected. Those in whom rays 3, 6 and 7 are strong. R3 gives active thoughtform making, R7 rules the sexual sacral chakra, and R6 is the energy of desire.

How the problem arises. Many perpetrators were themselves sexually abused as children and some psychologists say this is a cause. But the true cause is the improper use of the imagination. The condition begins or is perpetuated by reading, watching or imagining child sexual abuse and pornography. A desire-thought that enjoys these scenes becomes firmly lodged in the emotional brain and is fuelled by recurring fantasies that induce intense sexual-arousal in the body. Doctors diagnose paedophilia when people feel greatly distressed or become less able to function well because of their attraction to children or when they have acted on their urges.

How it affects the life. It causes great evil. It warps the life of the perpetrator who has physically acted on the impulse. Such a person often cannot have normal sexual relations with an adult, which means they cannot form a healthy relationship. If caught, they are vilified and permanently ostracized by society. But the greatest harm is on their victims. Many cannot overcome the trauma, are unable to have a normal life and self-medicate with alcohol and drugs. Some also commit suicide.

Sexual abuse proliferated in many government and religious institutions where small children could be targeted. Amongst these, the Catholic Church stands out as the worst. Abuse had been reported as far back as the 11th century by Peter Damian. Instead of addressing the evil and rooting it out, there has been a heinous cover-up by church hierarchy and officials. Those who complained were threatened, harassed, paid off, ignored or made to think it was their fault. Once a complaint was made which could not be ignored, the perpetrator was simply moved to another diocese. Theodore McCarrick is a grim example.

> McCarrick (b-1930), was a Cardinal [1] in the USA Catholic Church - a serial child-abuser and coverer up of abuse. He had been accused of engaging in sexual misconduct with adult male seminarians for decades, but allegations of sexual abuse against minors did not come to light until this was revealed by the New York Times newspaper (in 2018). After a Church investigation and trial, he was found guilty of sexual crimes against adults and minors and abuse of power and dismissed from the clergy in February 2019.

McCarrick is the first known case of a Cardinal being laicized (defrocked), for sexual abuse in the church. It means the church still recognises him as a priest, he just cannot practice. The carefully calculated pious facade he presented to hide his activities; indicates he could fit the psychopathic criterion.

Therapy. Mainstream treatment involves long-term psychotherapy and drugs that alter the sex drive and reduce testosterone levels.

> *But generally, all that can be done for astral-maniacs in these three groups is to keep them in custodial care if protection is necessary for them or for society. Only death "shall bring to an end this interlude in the life of the soul."* [2]

---

[1] Cardinals are leading dignitaries of the Roman Catholic Church. Nominated by the Pope, they form the Sacred College which elects succeeding popes.
[2] Bailey, Alice. Esoteric Psychology II, 459-460.

3. Points that distinguish Esoteric Psychology.

1. Emphasis is laid upon the Soul and relating the Personality to the Soul.

This is a vital point. The major shortcoming in modern exoteric psychology is ignorance of the soul and its role in the psychology of a person who is mentally distressed. This results in blame being placed solely on the personality aspect for any trouble. The relation between the soul and the personality is not explored and this results in an incorrect and incomplete diagnosis as to the cause of the trouble.

Psychology eventually will have to recognise the fact of the human soul and that the personality is its "apparatus" or means of expression in the world. Psychology troubles experienced are indirectly related to the soul's effort to express its energies through the personality.

Psychology also has to recognise that the soul has a plan of development in the current incarnation. The character we are born with is a continuation of the one we had in the previous life with all its negatives and positives, but given new opportunities for growth and correction. The soul chooses the rays and astrology signs it wants for the new incarnation and the type of challenges required so the personality can become more rounded-out in its development and more responsive to the soul.

The psychologist must recognise that the "pushing" effort made by the soul is the true cause of our many physical and mental ills. The psychologist must understand all of this and in order to do so, must become proficient in several esoteric sciences.

- Gain an esoteric understanding of the constitution of man and of the initiation process, which forces development. This forcing process causes the imbalances in the force centres, in the mind and body. This process needs to be understood if a correct diagnosis is to be made.
- Knowledge of the Seven Rays is required so that the true nature of a man's temperament and the real subjective cause of his varied reactions and complexes can be seen.
- An understanding of Esoteric Astrology is required. It gives a blueprint of the psychology of a person, the underlying energy disturbances found in the nature, the purpose of the soul and a time-map as to when major develops will occur.

When to modern exoteric psychology, esoteric knowledge is added, the diagnosis of mental disorders and physical disease will be more factually scientific and accurate.

2. Esoteric Psychology includes Eastern Wisdom.

Gautama Buddha laid the groundwork for the science of psychology. He said the cause of pain and suffering was desire for material objects. This simple statement encapsulates the psychological problem.

> When the mind is ignorant of its true spiritual nature, the false "I" of the lower ego arises. This "I" desires happiness and looks for it in the external world. It reaches out and grasps after things and attaches itself to people or objects it thinks will bring it happiness. If it gets what it wants there is temporary happiness. But after a while, the value placed on an object diminishes and then it grasps after something else. If it does not get what it wants, it is unhappy and thinks life is unfair or cruel. Then anger and bitterness rises. As Buddha said, desire for material objects is the true cause of unhappiness and it leads to our many psychological problems and disease.

There comes a point in time when we all must break the cycle of material-grasping and engage with the world of spiritual realities. The techniques involved are covered in the Raja Yoga section of the book. When modern western psychology includes this eastern knowledge as foundational in its work, then true and lasting progress will be made.

3. Psychology problems are viewed as those of clashing energies.

Essentially, we are all energy beings working through fields of energy (mind, emotions, etheric), living in a world of swirling repulsive and attractive forces, interacting with other people's energy fields. The task is to balance and harmonise any clashing energies in our nature or in our relationships.

> As long as we regard our problem as consisting of the inter-relation of many energies, their fusion and their balancing, we shall arrive at some measure of understanding and subsequent solution. [1]

4. Goals of Esoteric Psychology.

Goal 1. Relate the Soul and Personality.

When working with a client, the counsellor should give suggestions that will lift the eyes of the client to the soul. For instance, introduce the Wisdom Teachings if it is appropriate. Hearing about the Plan for Humanity, the journey of the soul, reincarnation, karma, etc., can have a powerful impact and bring far-reaching changes. The Law of Rebirth when accepted is a major releasing agent - the realisation that further opportunities lie ahead and that more time is given to achieve unsatisfied goals can bring a sense of peace. The teachings are practical and if adopted lead to sane, joyful and healthy living.

Some people have an aversion to "New Age nonsense". In this case, modify terms. Introduce the Law of Karma under the name of "what goes around comes around". Meditation is widely accepted as a way of improving health and life quality and people who may choose not to meditate for spiritual reasons, may do so for health reasons. Many who have had difficulties with fundamentalist or rigid religions may find the words spirit, God, etc, repellent. Find alternative words that describe the same truth. Talk about the purity, beauty and power of one's inner nature. Most Buddhists do not accept that there is a reincarnating soul but do embrace the notion that the mind is capable of being illumined and becoming wise. Substitute the word "soul" with "mind wisdom".

Goal 2: Enhance the ability to stand in spiritual being.

Psychoanalysis will come into its real usefulness when it emphasises achievements rather than the unearthing of mistakes and disasters. Dwelling on past failures anchors consciousness in the past and the unhappy state of affairs that led to the trouble in the first place. This is depressing. Emphasising achievements inspires, it lifts the spirits and encourages people to rise up and move forwards.

a. Reframe the person's life. Talk about the beauty and sacredness of (the client's) soul and the wonderful spiritual destiny that lies ahead. Mention that future lives offer new opportunities to start over.

---

[1] Bailey, Alice. Esoteric Psychology II, 424-425.

b. Eliminate guilt and any sense of sin. Reframe any mistakes or failures as marks of success because greater wisdom has been gained. Explain that we are here to learn and so-called failures are a normal and natural part of the process of growing in spirit.

c. Give an esoteric explanation for the cause of inner conflict and pain. Explain how identification with the "flawed" lower nature results in feelings of unworthiness, powerlessness and low self-esteem. When identification is made with the soul, with its beauty, love and compassion, suffering goes. Add that the soul has initiated the process because it is seeking integration. Give a suitable meditation or affirmation to use to aid the process. Add that the evidence that similar crises in past lives have been met successfully, is because he or she is here now. That this period will also pass and be survived.

d. Help the person anchor in the present and orient to the future. Recommend meditations to anchor attention in the present, such as "observing the breath". Encourage the cultivation of a wider life view and to join a group that shares the same (higher) ideals.

e. Emphasise the fact that the power to heal is found within. Karma aside, one is a soul, a child of God, with all the spiritual power and creativity that this implies. That invoking the "power of the soul", God or Jesus etc., really works.

f. If the mind is deeply troubled, recommend physical activities that will fill the present moment with constructive creative effort. Also recommend finishing one task before starting another. These steps will help to restore balance.

g. Help clients see crises as opportunities for growth and progress, especially around the ages 28-30, 35, 42-45 and 57-59. In these periods, we go through karmic experiences, are required to face the consequences of our decisions. If we have been shirking important life responsibilities or have been living life in a delusory or dishonest way, we will be held accountable. This information is very helpful when it is included in a counselling session. In astrology, these years coincide with Saturn transits. Saturn is the Lord of Karma and the soul uses these periods as an opportunity to get the life back on track. Often, people will find their way to counselling during a Saturn transit.

Goal 3: Help people find and serve in their chosen field.

Another important aspect of this work is to help clients discover what it is they would really like to do in terms of a vocation or useful project. Once identified, then work out a plan, with a series of steps that will help the person reach that goal. For clients who are more spiritually advanced, identify the soul ray and an associated vocation the client is strongly drawn to.

This brief introduction lays the groundwork for the examination of mental troubles and problems.

I. PSYCHOLOGY PROBLEMS AFFECTING THE MASSES

In this section, the psychological problems that afflict the masses of humanity are categorised into their specific energy-conflict groups. When energies in the nature swing out of balance, when they are repressed, expressed violently, or when they clash and do so for a prolonged period; then psychological and physical disorders appear. Resolution is achieved by balancing these forces.

Master Djwhal Khul said:

> As long as we regard our problem as consisting of the inter-relation of many energies, their fusion and their balancing, plus the final synthesis of two major energies, their fusion and their balancing we shall arrive at some measure of understanding and subsequent solution. [1]

Three Problem Groups affect the Masses.

Remember to think of the root cause of all our psychological troubles as being due to misaligned or unstable energies.

Three Major Groups of Psychology Problems affecting all Humanity				
1. Cleavage	2. Integration	3. Mental Problems due to (over) Stimulation		
Divisions in the nature that are at war with each other. The root cause of most modern psychological complexes.	When a cleavage heals, the over-inflated ego feels powerful, able to achieve anything & this brings in new problems.	*Overstimulation due to intense mental activity.*	*Overstimulation due to higher energies pouring in.*	*Overstimulation due to psychic unfoldment.*
		Leading to fixed-mindedness and narrow-minded thinking.	Causes delusion if the nature is unstable & there is no discrimination.	People who lack discrimination, mistake psychic phenomena for the real thing.

1. Problem group 1 is "**CLEAVAGE**," the energies are divided and fight.

2. Problem group 2 is "**INTEGRATION**," arising when a cleavage heals and the energies are unstable, swinging back and forth.

3. Problem group 3 is "**STIMULATION**" (or overstimulation). It occurs when soul energy impacts an unstable mind or emotional body.

---

[1] Bailey, Alice, A; Esoteric Psychology II 424.

A. THE PROBLEM OF CLEAVAGE.

> The Problems of Cleavage, leading frequently to the many ways of escape, which constitute the bulk of the modern complexes. [1]

The basic cleavage problem appears when two different fields of energy are antagonistic to each other. All the cleavages we experience are tiny reflections of the dual Spirit-Matter dichotomy of the universe. These opposing forces are gradually reconciling as fragmented spiritual sparks and souls finding their way back to their Source. Evolution proceeds as cleavages are bridged, then integrated and balanced.

Cleavages are found everywhere. Within our nature (between the physical, emotional, mind, personality and soul fields of energy), between individuals, groups, different schools of thought, between races and religions, etc.

Today, people are at all different stages in the cleavage-integrative process and are in crisis as a result.

The cleavages covered are:
1. A weakness between the dense physical body and the etheric web.
2. A cleavage within the astral body and with the environment.
3. A cleavage between the mind and brain.
4. A cleavage between the mind and emotions.
5. A cleavage between the personality and soul.

General therapy guide to heal cleavages.

The goal of cleavage therapy is to overcome any existing conflicts and establish harmonious rhythm in the life. This will eventually lead to integration.
1. The therapist recognises the existence of a cleavage
2. Between which two bodies - or in which body, the cleavage lies.
3. How the conflict is affecting the life (Eg. Wild unrest, frustration, a sense of futility, a nervous breakdown, a trail of broken relationships).
4. Then applies a bridging process that is appropriate for the cleavage and for the status of the person who is in conflict.

1. Weakness between the dense Physical Body and Etheric Web.

There is no longer a full cleavage between the physical and etheric bodies - only a weak integration between them which can lead to problems.

Those affected. Over-sensitive souls who are reluctant to incarnate, who do not want to be in the world or involved in its affairs. And/ or, those in whom the emotional body is dominant and who have the sensitive, soft-line rays 2, 4 or 6 prominent.

How the problem arises. It occurs during gestation or around birth. A definite and decisive integration between the web and the body is not established. This can occur if the soul is reluctant to incarnate, because of an accident or for a karmic reason.

---
[1] Bailey, Alice. Esoteric Psychology II, 404.

How it affects the life. Due to this loose connection, there is under-vitalisation of the body and slowness to mature. It causes immaturity, introspection, a lack of interest in the world, difficulty handling the practicalities of life, possession and physical debilitation.

General therapy. Stimulating the etheric body through sunshine, nutrition, exercise and by balancing the endocrine system, increases vitality and helps to strengthen the connection.

1. Split or Multiple Personalities, Possession.

How the problem arises. Because the rightful owner only has a weak grip on the body, control of the consciousness thread can be lost, only to be snatched up by an opportunist disembodied person or persons. The lay term for this condition is "possession". Medically, terms used today for the split and multiple personality problem, are "dissociation," "alternate personalities" and "identity fragmentation"

How it affects the life. Because the soul is struggling to reclaim the body, it can do so for as long as the connection is held. When the connection is lost, other beings gain control. This causes havoc, confusion, fear and despair.

> Chris Sizemore (1927-2016), was an American woman who was diagnosed with multiple personality disorder. Her condition was made famous in the 1957 film "The Three Faces of Eve." There is evidence from Sizemore's bio and astrology that she was Atlantean (emotionally ruled) in consciousness with a R6 emotional body. She is a classic case of a soul that only has a weak grip on the physical. Consequently, at times, discarnate entities took control of the consciousness thread.

Therapy. Because the soul is trying to fighting off the interlopers for control, the condition can be helped. The goal is to strengthen the etheric body and the will, and to ground the personality into the physical body and into physical life interests. All mystical practices should be stopped, which includes religious practices if they are weakening personality integration. Strengthen the will through counselling and the physical body through sunshine and exercise. Take steps to eject the intruders.

2. Physical ailments associated with a weak physical-etheric link.

a. Epilepsy and fainting fits.
Because of this loose connection, the consciousness thread can temporarily withdraw from the brain, which abstracts all self-consciousness and intelligence. Only physical-life and cell-consciousness remains. This is the root cause of epilepsy and fainting fits.

b. Debilitation.
This loose connection can also lead to a devitalised and debilitated condition, and many ongoing illnesses and complaints.

c. Sudden Infant Death Syndrome (SIDS).
SIDS is unexplained death occurring during sleep of a seemingly healthy baby. In normal sleep the consciousness thread temporarily withdraws, then reconnects when the baby wakes. During this process, the life-thread remains intact. In SIDS however, the life-thread withdraws as well as the consciousness thread, and the baby dies.

> Early withdrawal from incarnation can be part of the soul's plan for the incarnation. If there is a specific karmic or growth experience that requires only a few short weeks or

months to complete, hypothetically, the SIDS situation can occur. As previously stated, this may be part of the soul's plan for the incarnation.

> [In] cases of sudden death, on occasion the "soul may leave the door of protection open so that the forces of death itself may enter anew in order more rapidly to obliterate past penalties." [1]

d. Euthanasia.

Euthanasia is the legal ending of someone's life if that person is suffering from an incurable and painful disease or is in an irreversible coma. Although it is not a psychological problem, it is an ethical dilemma that is hotly debated whenever governments attempt to bring it into law. It is bitterly opposed by some religious people who believe that only God can give life or take it, a teaching called "the sanctity of life". Harmlessness to all, which includes *not* committing murder, is a spiritual commandment. But just as human beings make exceptions such as in times of war or where food is involved (eg. killing animals, harvesting vegetables), so are exceptions made by the Guides of the Race (very spiritually advanced souls who guide human evolution). Here is what the Master Djwhal Khul said.

> Frequently, today, lives are preserved that could be well permitted liberation. They serve no useful purpose and cause much pain and suffering to forms which nature (left to herself) would not long use and would extinguish. Through our overemphasis on the value of form life, through the universal fear of death, through our uncertainty as to the fact of immortality and also through our deep attachment to form, we arrest the natural processes and hold the life, which is struggling to be free, confined to bodies quite unfitted to the purposes of the soul. This preservation is, in the majority of cases, enforced by the subject's group and not by the subject himself—frequently an unconscious invalid, or an old person whose response apparatus of contact and response is imperfect, or a baby who is not normal. [2]

According to these teachings, "forced living" is out of step with nature. Love and compassion lie always at the root of the teachings of Buddha and Christ and holding fast to fixed ideas and laws that inflict unnecessary pain are in conflict with what they taught.

2. A Cleavage within the Astral Body and the Environment.

Those affected. People who are primarily Atlantean or emotional in consciousness. Ray 6 that governs the astral plane is the problem ray.

How the problem arises. It is generally due to the level of evolutionary development that has currently been reached. Such people are trying to stabilise consciousness on the mental plane, but there is emotional instability and over-sensitivity. If the faculty of discrimination has not yet been developed, this cleavage may form.

How it affects the life. This cleavage results in emotions that swing back and forth or up and down from exhilaration to despair. There is fear, anxiety and deep distress. It leads frequently to the many ways that people try to escape unhappy situations they find themselves in - such as through suicide, alcohol and drugs. It creates major difficulties in relationships and with the environment generally.

---

1 Bailey, Alice. *Esoteric Healing*, 472.
2 Ibid, 350-351.

Mental Disorders that are caused by an Emotional Cleavage.

In mainstream medicine, mental disorders are grouped various ways. Most popular is a 5-group category, in which an emotional cleavage is responsible for the first 4 groups. The exception is the 5th group of disorders comprised of dementia, organic and structural brain problems. These of course do not involve the emotional body.

1. Anxiety disorders.

This is the most common category - excessive, ongoing anxiety and worry that is difficult to control and interferes with day-to-day activities.

a. Panic attacks. Even though there is no real danger, intense and sudden fear triggers severe physical reactions.

b. Phobias. An overwhelming and unreasonable fear of an object or situation that poses little real danger. Common phobias involve fear of snakes, spiders or heights.

c. Post-traumatic stress disorder (PTSD). If there is exposure to a terrifying event or ordeal in which grave physical harm occurred or was threatened, the trauma of this can be re-experienced through flashbacks and nightmares.

d. Self-harm/ self-injury. Cutting or burning are the most common forms of this problem. It is an unhealthy way to cope with emotional pain, anger and frustration.

e. Social anxiety disorder. There is an inability to form healthy, social connections and this leads to becoming anti-social, unpopular, developing a fear of life, etc.

f. Obsessive-compulsive disorder (OCD). Unreasonable thoughts and fears compel sufferers to do repetitive behaviours.

> Rafael Nadal (b-1986), is a Spanish professional tennis player famous for his match rituals of squaring the court, lining up his water bottles, etc. He has the classic signs of OCD. His actions indicate an unstable R6 emotional body that he tries to control through these rituals. They help alleviate stress and anxiety.

2. Mood disorders.

A mood is a dominant emotion. In a mood disorder, emotions are so distorted and inconsistent with reality, they interfere with the ability to function at an everyday level.

a. Major depressive disorder. A persistent feeling of sadness and loss of interest.

b. Borderline personality disorder. Feelings of emptiness, intense emotions and poor self-image lead to a pattern of instability in personal relationships, displays of inappropriate behaviour, intense anger and attempted suicide.

c. Bipolar disorder (formerly manic depression). It is characterized by alternating mood-swings that cause alternating states of euphoria and depression.

> Amy Winehouse (1983-2011), was an English singer and songwriter, known for having an amazing voice, a deep, rich, expressive contralto. She told an interviewer she was bipolar. She would have had an artistic R4 mind or personality and a R6 emotional. Insecure, emotionally unstable and torn within, she self-medicated to cope and died from alcohol poisoning in 2011, at age 29.

3. Psychotic disorders.

a. Schizophrenia. A serious mental disorder where people interpret reality abnormally. It may include hallucinations, delusions and extremely disordered thinking and behaviours. Paranoid schizophrenia is the most common form.

b. Delusional disorder (paranoid disorder or psychosis). A person cannot tell what is real from what is imagined. There are delusions, an unshakable belief in things untrue

4. Eating disorders.

Obsessing with food and weight are unhealthy ways of coping with emotional problems and trying to regain control of the life. Imagined imperfections are blamed for not being universally loved and accepted - personal worth is measured by one's looks. A negative voice within tells the person he or she is fat, and therefore is ugly and has no value.

a. Anorexia nervosa. Sufferers starve themselves and may exercise excessively.

b. Bulimia nervosa. Episodes of binge-eating are followed by feelings of guilt and self-loathing, then vomiting.

> Princess Diana (1961-1997) was sensitive, emotional, reactive and defensive Cancer Sun person with a R6 emotional. She admitted to her auto-biographer Andrew Morton, that she had a long battle with bulimia. It began when she got engaged - then her insecurities surged. After the wedding, in 1981, it is alleged Charles remarked she was "chubby", which exacerbated the problem.

Therapy for emotional cleavages.

Regard the problem as requiring emotional healing, balancing and integration - achieved primarily by helping the person develop a healthier outlook on life. Encourage healing or self-help groups with supportive people.

a. Have the physical checked first, especially the endocrine system. Often the thyroid gland requires balancing and the diet needs to be free of fatty or sugar-rich foods.

b. Observe physical coordination and movement. Look for any jerkiness, which can reflect inner disharmony. Then, a rhythmic exercise such as Tai Chi would be beneficial.

c. Re-interpret the person's life and environment in terms of appreciation.

d. Resorting to unhealthy lines of thought and feelings must be stopped. Cultivating an urge to help others will bring a sense of satisfaction, accomplishment and appreciation.

e. Eliminate any sense of sin by emphasising the person's divine nature and that so-called mistakes are normal and natural in the soul's journey.

f. Encourage the person to strive towards a higher goal, which may include educational or vocational training suitable for the point in evolution. Formulate a step-by-step plan to help the person achieve this, avoiding any steps which are impossible to reach. Later, encourage the development of any creative faculty or talent, thus meeting the desire to be noticed and to contribute.

3. A Cleavage between the Mind and the Brain.

In the activity of the 5th ray will be found eventually the source of many psychological disorders and mental troubles. Cleavage is the outstanding characteristic - *gaps* in the relation of the *physical body [including the brain]* to the subtle bodies [the mind in this case], which show as imbecilities and psychological troubles. [1]

Autism Spectrum Disorders (ASD).

Different types of ASD - autistic disorder, Asperger's syndrome, pervasive developmental disorder and childhood disintegrative disorder; used to be diagnosed individually. But now they are grouped under the umbrella term, Autism Spectrum Disorders. "Spectrum" refers to the wide range of symptoms and severity. The condition is related to brain development that limits how a person perceives life and socializes. Scientist's report the ASD brain can have fewer alpha and beta waves and under-connectivity to strategic areas that have to do with the emotions and relating.

Those affected. Those who's mental or personality ray is the 5th Ray.

How the problem arises. The 5th ray is the mental energy that discriminates. If this faculty is used to judge the world as being very scary, a place the owner does not want to be - and this attitude is carried across a life or lives; it can result in an incarnation where there is a cleavage in consciousness such as autism. Consequently, the problem is karmic.

How it affects the life. Symptoms of ASD are: a lack of social or emotional exchanges, lack of non-verbal communication and difficulty developing and maintaining relationships appropriate to the age. Some have only mild impairment and can live independently. Others have severe disabilities and require life-long care and support.

Childhood disintegrative disorder is the rarest and most severe part of the spectrum - because it involves seizures. In this case, not only is there a cleavage, but the consciousness thread is abstracting.

The great danger of prolonged withdrawal to an inner world is that the sense and normal nervous system activities ("vrittis" in eastern science), can become severely impaired. This is mentioned in Raja Yoga, where the great Teacher Patanjali wrote:

> Book I:10 The vrittis are those activities of the mind that relate the sense employed and that which is sensed. By withdrawing one from active sense perception, by no longer utilising the "outward-going" consciousness and by abstracting that consciousness from the periphery to the centre, can bring on a condition of passivity - a lack of awareness, or a form of trance. [2]

Although this is a different condition to autism, the avoidance of life tendency is similar and can have similar negative repercussions on the nervous system.

Therapy. Early intervention is vital to turn autism around in a child. It can make dramatic improvements. Greater success seems to come with programs using love, play and encouragement that invite the child to engage. Love seems to be the key. Children require a home structure that is loving and orderly. This will help them feel comfortable and encourage them to engage with life.

---

[1] Bailey, Alice. Esoteric Healing, 302. Inserts in brackets are by the author.
[2] Bailey, Alice version. Light of the Soul, 21-22.

4. Cleavage between the Mind and Emotions.

Those affected. Any of the mind or emotional rays could be involved. The mind is being developed and attempts are being made to use it to control the emotional life.

How the problem arises. It is a natural stage in evolution, when consciousness is moving from a 6th astral-plane focus, to the 5th mental plane. The intellect is being developed and is being trained to discern essentials from nonessentials, between right direction and wrong goals, between satisfactions of the lower nature and higher.

How it affects the life. In such a case, because emotional satisfaction is the path of least resistance, the astral ray fights any attempt by the mind to rein it in. The two rays vie for control and this creates a war between the goals of the mind and those of the desire nature which would go in another direction.

Unhealed, this cleavage has two outcomes. Either the man or woman - refusing to be moulded by environing circumstance, uses the conflict as energy to drive towards a higher goal and achieves success. Or, is broken on the wheel of life physically or mentally and ends up mired in feelings of futility and in depression.

This cleavage can cause a second one - between one's life task or vocation.

> The cleavage found between a man and his life task, or the life activity to which fate ordains him and predisposition inclines him. The difficulty here lies in a definite break or failure of continuity between the mind nature, determining purpose, and the astral nature, governing impulse.

Many find themselves in this situation. They want a job that is heart-fulfilling, but find themselves stuck in mundane work "because life-circumstances demand it". In the western world where opportunities are available, the cause of this lies in the inability to discipline the life and hold firm to one course of planned action. The astral nature resists such discipline. It wants to be gratified moment by moment. Any rewards are too far away in the future. The will that calls on sacrifices to be made in the immediate so that long term goals can be achieved, has not yet been sufficiently developed. Hence the problem.

The person with this cleavage is aware that this inner problem exists but lacks the will or wisdom to fix it. Consequently, there is intense frustration and suffering. The understanding help of a trained psychologist or the intervention of the soul is required if fusion is to be made and the individual is to be "made whole".

Therapy. Help people distinguish between achievable goals and those that are not (eg., wanting to be a rock-star when you cannot sing in tune), to be realistic about any talents, recognised assets, capacities and potential. Many conflicts would be solved by such recognitions because this would eliminate impossible goals and consequent frustration. When this part of the conflict has been overcome, then will come a clearer recognition of one's true potential and what can be achieved if due effort is made. This is empowering.

> Thousands (perhaps millions) of people in the world have already bridged the cleavage between the emotional nature and the mind and they are now becoming aware of the major task - to bridge the gap between the personality and the soul. Due to this, it is fair to say that the integration of the One Soul of Humanity is progressing very well.

5. A Cleavage between the Personality and Soul.

Those affected. All ray types.

How the problem arises. Disciples who have integrated the personality vehicles and have exhausted desire; now they are consciously striving to bring the personality ray under the control of the soul. This is a natural cleavage due to status on the Path of Spiritual Development, and one we will all face at some time.

How it affects the life. This cleavage produces first a dominant selfish personality and then later, a practical mystic conscious of the need for fusion and unity. When steps are taken in this direction, a war occurs between the personality and the soul for control over the entire life. There is a contest between personality goals and satisfactions, and the desire for unity with the soul and to serve the higher good.

Therapy.

a. Once we have reached this level of advancement, an innate impulse rising from our mystical side, urges us to heal the breach between the personality and soul. This is in response to the essential oneness which exists on the inner side of life, a oneness that negates all separativeness. The sensing of this inner union causes us to continually try to reproduce this harmony in ourselves. This sense should be encouraged.

b. The mind must be used to gain a clear understanding of the cleavage that is preventing union between the soul and personality; and what needs to be done to bridge it.

c. An intelligent study of the soul must be made and of the laws which govern soul unfoldment. (See the side-panel). These must be observed. This is not so difficult at this stage. The call of the soul is so strong, directing our energies into spiritual observances and group service comes naturally.

d. There needs to be an acceptance of group purpose. Soul consciousness is group consciousness. So, working within one's chosen service group and learning to adapt and bend the forces of the personality so that the mission of the group becomes more important that any personal ambition is required.

There are greater cleavages, such as between humanity as a whole and the Spiritual Hierarchy. The work we do individually helps to bridge these.

The 7 Laws of Soul Unfoldment and Group Work.

1. The Law of Sacrifice. We must let go of material concerns and focus on the inner life and service. This brings blessings in return: "Having nothing and yet possessing all things."

2. The Law of Magnetic Impulse. It urges us to align with the soul, to find other like-minded souls and our soul-group.

3. The Law of Service. Service to the race through a cultivated self-forgetfulness, is the spontaneous effect of soul contact. Serving comes naturally as soul-alignment increases.

4. The Law of Repulse. It causes us to naturally repulse all that would impede us from realising our spiritual destiny and service goals.

5. The Law of Group Progress. Urges us to find our true soul group and work cooperatively within it to progress the group and its world-service work.

The final two laws concern group activity at a spiritually advanced stage.

B. The PROBLEM OF INTEGRATION.

> The Problems of Integration, produces many of the difficulties of the more advanced people. [1]

How the problem arises. It is caused when a cleavage heals and there is an energy integration. But because the nature is unstable, there is a huge over-reaction.

How the integration problem affects the life. Integration brings in an influx of unaccustomed energies which expresses as high voltage ambition, a sense of power and as a desire for personality influence. The person is, temporarily at least, selfish, dominant, over-confident and arrogant. Over-excitement is triggered by the increased opportunities that are now suddenly available, in a world that seems larger and with wider horizons.

There is another side to this problem - an inferiority complex. This can happen if a person feels unable to measure up to the wide vista of opportunities suddenly presented. The vision is too big and the person feels unable to make the grade. This results in a sense of futility, failure and impotence.

1. Integration, leading to a tendency to over-emphasise.

Those affected. Ray 6 will be strong in the nature.

How it affects the life. While in the "integration" period, self-absorption and the tendency to over-emphasise can turn people into fanatics for a time. But note, this is a gentler group than the die-hard fanatics who are driven by narrow ideologies and who would destroy all to achieve their goals. With the highest motives, this fanatic seeks to drive everyone the way that he has come, "because it worked for me and will for you!" Such a person becomes a source of distress to himself and to others.

Therapy. If the problem is not excessive, then it is best to leave such a person alone to the directing purpose and guidance of the soul - once the fact of the soul is admitted, and provided that the person understands what is happening. This understanding will bring a sense of peace. In time, the energy swings will even out.

2. Integration, leading to an over-developed sense of direction or vocation.

Those affected. All ray types.

How it affects the life. When the gap between the emotional body and the mind is bridged, people can be so greatly affected by the vast field of mental activity that has opened they become selfishly preoccupied with their own plans and goals, and their important role in saving the world.

Therapy as for Problem 1.

3. Integration, leading to an over-inflated sense of power.

Those affected. Ray 1 strong in the nature. People who are intellectually advanced, but still relatively selfish and separative.

How it affects the life. Sensing new power available and greater opportunities, the person is temporarily filled with arrogance and wants to dominate the world. If this ambition is not checked, it can lead eventually to a serious state of egomania, the outstanding problem of

---
[1] Bailey, Alice. Esoteric Psychology II, 405.

integration. What sets this egomania-type apart from narcissists and megalomaniacs, is the person has good intentions, thinks he or she can improve the world. Megalomaniacs and narcissists put themselves first, they want to control the world or have its adulation. But all types create chaos and disharmony in their environment

> This type of person, under the influence of this extension of consciousness, is often beautifully motivated and actuated by the highest intentions, but only succeeds in producing inharmony in his surroundings. [1]

Therapy. Offset these difficulties by helping sufferers realise that they are an integral part of a much greater whole. When successful, personal values will adjust and the exaggerated sense of power will balance out.

4. Integration, resulting in major internal conflicts.

Those affected. All ray types who have integrated the entire lower nature and have fused the personality.

How it affects the life. For a long while after integration - and strictly within the realm of personality, there are major conflicts as first one energy and then another will assert itself and battle for supremacy. Djwhal Khul gave an example using the following rays.

> R1 soul, R4 personality, R3 mind, R6 emotions, R1 physical.
>
> This hypothetical man is highly intelligent (R3) and ambitious for power (R1), but with right motive because he is truly idealistic (R6). He will fight intelligently but also fanatically to achieve what he wants because his R4 personality and R6 astral force him to do so. And his first ray body and brain will enable him to put up a strong fight. At the same time, his first ray soul energy is seeking to dominate, and there is an intensification of everything in the personality.
>
> The trouble will be localised in the mental body or in the brain [because rays 3 and 1 are hard line, as is the R1 soul], and the problem can range all the way down from *idee fixe* (fixed mindedness) and mental crystallisation to insanity (if the stimulation becomes unduly powerful or the heredity is not good.) He can express arrogant success in his chosen field of work, which will make him a dominant and unpleasant person, or he can express the fluidity of the third ray mind which will make him a scheming manipulator or a fighter for immense schemes which can never really materialise. [2]

Therapy. Such a conflict of energies can produce serious situations, but most can be corrected through right understanding if the issue is dealt with early enough. Help the person understand the cause and nature of the conflict, the rays involved and the need for their harmonising.

---

1 Bailey, Alice. Esoteric Psychology II, 433.
2 Bailey, Alice. Esoteric Psychology II, 443-4.

A Basic Counselling Method
for the problems of Cleavages and Integration.

The following method of analysis was provided by Djwhal Khul (paraphrased).

1. Ask, "What are your reasons for wanting to be "straightened out?"

2. "What brought this need to your attention and evoked in you the desire for a specific process of interior adjustment?"

3. Determine the five ray energies conditioning the subject.

4. Determine in which vehicle there is a need for the bridging process. Where the point of cleavage is, and, therefore the nature of the present crisis? Is this difficulty a major or a minor crisis?

5. How far does the man's life pattern, his life vocation and his innate coherent desires, coincide with the trend set by his Soul Ray and the Personality Ray? With disciples much difficulty will be found to lie in the personality expression.

6. Is this problem of *cleavage* - requiring a bridging process and fusion of energies; or one of *integration*, requiring right understanding of what has happened, and right adjustment of the fused powers to environing conditions?

7. To approach the counselling session in the wisest way, establish at which level a client may be working. Is the person at the point where he should be?
   - Integrating the personality and therefore becoming more strictly human.
   - A mystic who recognises that the soul and personality aspects need to be unified.
   - A trained occultist whose soul and personality aspects are beginning to function as one.

8. Determine what in the last analysis must be done to make the consciousness enlightened enough so that the ray of the mind can be turned at will to light up the subconscious and the mind can become a search light, penetrating into the super-consciousness and thus revealing the nature of the soul?" [1]

When a cleavage is healed and the initial duality had been resolved into a unity, then there comes a growing recognition of a fresh realm of choice, based upon the emergence of the higher values. This will be followed by a new period of conflict as the individual tries to resolve this higher duality. [2]

---

[1] Bailey, Alice. Esoteric Psychology II, 446.
[2] Bailey, Alice. Glamour: a World Problem, 110.

C. THE PROBLEM OF STIMULATION

This section deals with problems which arise in the mental nature due to the power to create in mental substance. There are three subgroups in this section.

1. The problem of a too-intense and narrow mental focus.
2. The problem of Illusion, Glamour and Maya.
3. Problems caused by psychic development.

Stimulation problem 1.
A too-intense and narrow Mental Focus.

Those affected. Leader types who are pronounced intellectuals, independent in thought and are capable of clear thinking. But psychologically unsound, they lack balance, humour and right-proportion, are narrow, crystallised and rigid thinkers. This causes the trouble. They include violent partisans in any group, church, order or government. People who give blind adherence to ideas and personality devotions.

How the problem arises. It is a misuse of the thought-form making process. A vision is held about what is believed to be right and true. The person broods about this vision and what should be done for this ideal to manifest. The thought grows, takes on colour and beauty. This evokes a response from the desire body, swinging the entire lower nature into unison with the recognised mental urge and the dominant mental demand. When this happens the thought is now capable of holding the man mentally and emotionally and it is at this point that danger ensues.

> If, there is no sense of balance, proportion or humour and the entire mental equipment is focused in just this one direction, the thoughtform can imprison the man. He becomes a devotee to this entity which he created in his own mind. It holds him captive - mentally and emotionally. He can see nothing and believe nothing and work for nothing except that embodied idea which imprisons him. It possesses him. He is its victim and he acts in accordance with what this embodied thought tells him to do.

How it affects the life. Compelled to act to manifest the beloved vision, if there are people or groups perceived as preventing its accomplishment, this type of man (or woman) could act to remove them by any means. Frequently sadistic, such types are willing to sacrifice or to damage anyone who prevents them achieving their avowed goal.

> The men who engineered the Spanish Inquisition and those who were responsible for the outrages in the times of the Covenanters are samples of the worst forms of this line of thought and development. [1]

These people fall into 3 groups - by ray-type.
1. The mentally introverted: 2nd, 4th and 6th ray personalities.
2. Those who are amazingly aware of themselves as centres of thought - 1st and 5th ray.
3. The strongly extroverted: 3rd and 6th ray personalities.

---
[1] Bailey, Alice. Esoteric Psychology II, 456.

Intense thinkers type-1. The mentally introverted (rays 2, 4, 6).

Those affected. Introverted types with ray 2, 4 and 6 personalities. This is the soft-line group of rays where people are naturally more introspective.

How the problem arises. Such people are completely preoccupied with and absorbed in a world that revolves around one dynamic thoughtform which they have built, and to which they are deeply attached. Such introverted brooding about a central thought is not destructive on its own - scientific or creative geniuses are in this group.

How it affects the life. If soul contact has not been made, the mental equipment is unstable, there is low self-esteem, resentment and anger, then the compelling central thought which arises will be negative. In such a case, this is how it could play out:

> There is emotional sensitivity and vulnerability (R2), overlaid with a R4 tendency to agonise and brood over perceived injustices. Imaginative movies created in the mind replay painful incidents. Anger rises (R4) and thoughts of revenge (R6). Feeling victimised (R2, 6), an urge to retaliate arises (R4 and R6).

This highly combustible mix festers away in the mind of the introvert until something triggers a explosive and violent reaction against those perceived as being the cause of trouble. Today this problem is a phenomenon amongst introverted young people in the USA who commit school shootings.

Charles Joseph Whitman (1941-1966), is an example of a mental introvert with issues.

> Whitman was an engineering student and former marine. On the 1st of August 1966, he killed seventeen people and wounded thirty-two in a mass shooting in and around the Tower of the University of Texas. Whitman was never diagnosed. But he was polite, courteous and well-mannered and (as far as we know) never spoke publicly about the dark thoughts and menacing urges that eventually led to his rampage. He kept these hidden away. He fits the profile.

Another example is the "Unabomber," Theodore Kaczynski (b-1942).

> Kaczynski was an American domestic terrorist. A mathematics prodigy and former mathematics professor, he abandoned his academic career in 1969 to live in isolation in a remote wilderness. He became obsessed by the thought that people advancing modern technology were destroying the environment. So he decided to do something about it and started a nationwide bombing campaign. Between 1978 and 1995, he killed three people and injured 23 others. [This photo is his mugshot on his arrest. His family turned him in to the FBI]. Kaczynski would have a R5 mind, a R6 emotional and could also have a R6 personality.

Therapy. If intervention is made early enough, the situation may be retrieved. Some form of healthy, creative, imaginative, emotional release is required. Explain why undue emphasis upon one line of thought is undesirable and what it could lead to. Give examples of people in the world who succumbed to this problem. Encourage a more rounded-out unfoldment, and for those who are ready a meditation to bring about fusion with the soul. Otherwise, if the person has become irretrievably dangerous, incarceration for public safety will be necessary. Only death (which allows the soul to reset the life), will help.

Intense thinkers type-2. Megalomaniacs (rays 1 and 5).

Those affected. Rays 1 and 5 are involved, giving a powerful and intense (R1) personality and mind (R1 and R5).Today, science considers megalomania to be a subset of the narcissism group of disorders. Although narcissistic traits do exist in the megalomaniac, esoterically, megalomania is a stand-alone problem.

How the problem arises. Intensely preoccupied and obsessed with oneself, there is an inflated sense and admiration for one's wisdom, power and relevance. Delusional thoughts are harboured and fantasies about relevance and omnipotence All thought life is directed towards the planned aggrandisement of the self and how to control others. Unchecked, the intensity of these thoughts can completely wall a person off, leading to complete isolation (R1), separateness (R5), and the establishment of acute megalomania.

How it affects the life. With a psychological makeup that is unstable and a distorted perception of the self, such people force their way into positions of exalted leadership and authority. They achieve this through the power of their personality and forceful rhetoric, which convinces people to follow them and do what they say.

Jim Jones, Charles Manson and Adolf Hitler have all been described as megalomaniacs. With an evil genius for destructiveness, all controlled people through their rhetoric (1 and R5) and were responsible for murderous acts (R1). They fit the megalomania profile.

Jim Jones (1931-1978), was an American cult leader, preacher and faith healer who led the Peoples Temple religious organization. He loved absolute power and was obsessed about getting it. But his criminal activities attracted the attention of the USA authorities and unable to face up to the consequences of his actions, he killed himself and ordered 908 of his followers in Guyana to also be killed.

Charles Manson (1934-2017), was an American criminal megalomaniac who led the Manson Family, a cult based in California in the late 1960s. They were behind a series of nine murders in 1969. Manson had a magnetic control over his followers. He predicted a coming apocalypse and told his family that "Helter Skelter" was coming, the uprising of a racial war between "blackies" and "whiteys".

Adolf Hitler (1889-1945), had a ravenous hunger for power, which he chose to pursue through politics. Psychiatrists agree he was a pathological narcissist and megalomaniac who knew what he was doing and chose to do it with pride and enthusiasm. In 1939, Carl Jung met Hitler and wrote, "Hitler never laughed, was sexless and inhuman, with a singleness of purpose: to establish the Third Reich and use it to overcome all of the previous insults in Germany's history."

Therapy. This condition is found in varying degrees. If the behaviour is persisted in, the sufferer becomes imprisoned by a barrier of thoughtforms concerning himself and his activities and gradually becomes untouchable. If the problem is caught early enough, an effort should be made to decentralise the central focus through the evocation of another higher interest, development of a social consciousness and contact with the soul. Otherwise, only death and a new incarnation will provide a new opportunity to reset the life.

Intense thinkers type-3. Mental extroverts (rays 3 and 6).

Those affected. Rays 3 and 6, extrovert thinkers and intellectuals who are unstable.

How the problem arises. The 3rd ray of Intelligence gives an active and versatile mind that weaves thoughts. It also gives a natural shrewdness, a cunning nature and a natural extroversion. When it teams up with the devotional 6th ray - and the nature is unstable, a compelling desire to impose conclusions upon others arises.

How it affects the life. The urge to impose conclusions on others may be expressed relatively harmlessly - such as by well-meaning theologians and dogmatic indoctrinators found in practically all schools of thought. But when the nature is selfish, unspiritual and unstable, then very unpleasant and often dangerous types emerge - such as fanatics who try to impose their views on others, and maniacs who become so obsessed with their visions that for the protection of society, they must be locked away.

Restless with a short attention span, they are always looking for distractions, ways, means and opportunities to get what they want. Scheming manipulators, they find it easy to con people. Lying, deceitfulness, manipulation and disregard for the rights of others are typical, negative, R3 traits. These types are naturally drawn to white-collar type crimes such as embezzlement, fraud and identity theft. They enjoy the thrill of the game and of the chase.

Therapy. Two methods can help. The first takes a long time - the wise and understanding counsellor holds a steady, loving presentation of a wider vision before the person's eyes. Second, the counsellor evokes the power of the soul to either bring about an instantaneous transformation (such as a conversion), or the problematic walls of thought are gradually broken down over time.

1. Antisocial Personality Disorder (APD): Sociopaths and Psychopaths.

This is the most extreme condition in this category. Sociopaths and psychopaths are types of APD. Both conditions have many common traits. This criterion comes from Britannica Encyclopaedia. Note that most are 3rd ray traits.

Both psychopathy and sociopathy are characterized by
- An excessively high self-appraisal (arrogance, conceitedness, or cockiness).
- A pronounced lack of empathy (R3).
- Contempt for the rights, interests, or feelings of others (R3).

There is an abiding pattern of disregard for and violation of the rights of others, as manifested through three or more of the following habitual or continual behaviours:
- Serious violations of criminal laws.
- Deceitfulness for personal gain or pleasure - lying, swindling, or trickery (R3).
- Impulsiveness or failure to plan ahead (R3).
- Irritability and aggressiveness often resulting in physical assaults (R6).
- Reckless disregard for the safety of oneself or others (R3).
- Failure to meet important adult responsibilities, including job and family-related duties and financial obligations (R3).
- Lack of meaningful remorse or guilt - to the point of complete indifference regarding the serious harm or distress one's actions cause other people (R3). [1]

---
[1] Britannica Encyclopaedia online.

Distinguishing traits of Psychopaths (note these are R3 traits).
- A nearly complete inability to form genuine emotional attachments to others. A compensating tendency to form artificial and shallow relationships, which the psychopath cynically exploits or manipulates to benefit himself (R3).
- A corresponding ability to appear glib and even charming to others (R3).
- An ability to maintain the appearance of a normal work and family life (R3).
- A tendency to carefully plan criminal activities to avoid detection (R3).

Distinguishing traits of Sociopaths (note these are mostly R6).
- Usually incapable of anything even remotely resembling a normal work or family life.
- Exceptionally impulsive and erratic and more prone to rage or violent outbursts (R6).
- Criminal activities are spur-of-the-moment rather than carefully premeditated (R6).

When either case is extreme and appears beyond rehabilitation, they would fit into the "Astral Maniac" category. Psychopath, sexual sadist and killer, Dennis Rader would fit there.

Dennis Rader (b-1945), is an American serial killer known as the BTK Killer (Bind, Torture, Kill). Between 1974 and 1991 he killed ten people in Kansas, and sent taunting letters to police and newspapers describing the details of his crimes. Cunning, he avoided apprehension for years. He was completely detached from the awful suffering he inflicted on his victims and when he recounted details to authorities, did so coldly and clinically. Rader remains unrepentant (in 2021) with no remorse or regrets except for having been caught.

Rader was a psychopath, sexual deviant and astral maniac. It is possible he was but a shell used by evil entities. Here is what Djwhal Khul said about this type of obsessed person.

> [They] are "shells," obsessed by evil entities, hence their extreme skill and cunning, based on very ancient evil experience, devoid of all true feeling, lacking the light of love and understanding. [1]

Many other serial killers would fit this profile. Overshadowed by evil, a long period of salvaging must occur, else they could end up as lost souls. [2]

2. Sectarian and Obsessive Fanatics.

Sectarians have a narrow-minded adherence to a sect, party or denomination. When coupled with humourless fanaticism, serious trouble can arise. They gather believers to support their crusades (a R6 phenomenon). Through pen or word (R3), or violent action, they attack those who oppose their point of view. Relentless, they never let up (R6).

Ian Paisley (1926-2014), was a Northern Irish loyalist politician and Protestant religious leader. A fiery and driven crusader for his sectarian cause, mentally brilliant and with powerful oratory, Paisley is an example of a mental-extrovert fanatic. Hypothetically, he had a 6th ray personality; working through a R3 physical body-brain. Paisley mellowed with age, became more conciliatory with his old political foes, the mark of someone approaching the Path.

---
1 Bailey, Alice A. *Esoteric Astrology*. 544.
2 Lost souls. Those who are irretrievably evil because they deepen the trend from life to life. In such a case, the Monad cuts the soul away, abandons it.

3. Stalking and cyber-bullying.

Modern psychiatry does not consider stalking and cyber-bullying to be a mental problem until it becomes extreme and serious harm is inflicted on others. Such people are placed into the Antisocial Personality Disorder category.

a. Stalking.

"Stalking" is defined as an unwanted or obsessive attention by an individual or group toward another person. Stalking behaviours are related to harassment and intimidation and may include following the victim in person or monitoring them. Obsessive devotion is a 6th ray trait. The obsession could be the idolising of a person and wanting to possess his or her love; or if rejection is the motivating impulse, hating that "fallen idol" and wanting to harm or kill. Victims are bombarded with unwanted attention. They manipulate (R3) from behind the scenes, behind their computers and from the shadows.

> Maria Marchese was the perpetrator in the worst case of stalking in the United Kingdom (up to 2007). Developing a fatal attraction for psychiatrist Dr Jan Falkowski, she stalked, harassed him and tried to ruin his reputation. She threatened to kill his fiancee, bombarding the couple, their families and colleagues with chilling text messages, phone calls and emails for four years. She burgled and wrecked the psychiatrist's riverboat home. Then, having destroyed his marriage plans and relationship, she accused the doctor of drugging and raping her in his hospital office. In 2007, Marchese was jailed for nine years.

Marchese's 6th ray obsessive fanaticism is evident. So is her ingenious 3rd ray trickery and deceit. Her actions, forcing herself onto her victim, fits the mental-extrovert problem criteria. When her photo is examined, she appears to have a 3rd ray physical body (stocky, strong). She could also have had a R3 personality. The real problem would be a R6 emotional body, giving her a fanatical desire, which when attached to a target, she could not resist. Obsessive types will stop at nothing to try to satisfy their 6th ray thirst. In this case, it was aided and abetted by a R3 brain.

b. Cyberbullying.

To cyberbully is to use electronic communications to bully a person, typically by sending messages of an intimidating or threatening nature. Here is an example from Missouri, USA.

> In 2006, about five weeks before her death, on the social networking website MySpace, a supposed 16-year-old boy named Josh, asked Megan Meier to be friends. The two began communicating online regularly. After a few weeks, Josh said he did not want to be friends anymore. He started sending cruel messages which accelerated in their viciousness and concluded with Josh telling Megan, "The world would be a better place without you." Within 20 minutes, Megan was dead. She hung herself.

The aftermath. Josh was not real, but was created by a neighbour, Lori Drew, Drew's teenage daughter and an employee. Drew was convicted for Computer Fraud and abuse Act, but this was overturned on appeal. Megan's mother attempted to bring in a law to curb cyberbullying but it was not enacted. 59% of U.S. teens have been bullied or harassed online.

Stimulation problem 2: Illusion, Glamour, Maya.

On the journey of the soul, we are all exposed to the tests of Illusion, Glamour and Maya, three ways the indwelling soul is beguiled by what it sees and hears in the world. We fall prey to "glamour", which is a blanket term that includes different ways we distort reality and delude ourselves mentally and emotionally. Here is a chart which describes how the three aspects of glamour can play out.

The 3 Aspects of Glamour

Illusion	Glamour	Maya
Affects mental types. The mind is full of its own conclusions and ideas are misinterpreted.	*Affects emotional types.* Perception is distorted by the breeders of glamour: pride, criticism and separativeness.	*Affects most people.* It is the unthinking, emotional mess in which most people seem always to live.
For example: An aspirant realises he has to purify the life to progress spiritually.		
Misinterprets the message: "This means I will have to be 100% pure. I will go into a monastery to do this & so I will not be contaminated by others."	*Distorts the message:* "I am doing what needs to be done because I am a vegetarian. This makes me more spiritual than others who still need to purify themselves."	*The effect on the life.* Has good intentions & talks a lot about doing something. But it all gets put aside as more "important" issues arise.

1. Illusion - The Misinterpretation of Ideas.

Those affected. Primarily R3 and R5 people, but all intellectual types.

How the problem arises. The mind is full of its own conclusions and ideas are misinterpreted

How it affects the life. The truth is misinterpreted because of preconceived narrow conclusions, which occurs often because vast illusory thoughtforms surround varying schools of thought (philosophy, science, religion, sociology, etc).

Therapy. Encourage the development of the intuition or soul apprehension, which destroys illusion. It develops as we become more inclusive and wise, through occult meditation and the study of symbols (such as through the study of astrology). Understanding is broadened, and the soul is trained to look for the truth behind the form.

2. Glamour - Distortion of Reality because of Emotional Bias

Those affected. Primarily ray 4 and 6 people succumb, but all emotional people who have not yet developed discrimination are susceptible. All rays produce their own glamours.

How the problem arises. Unable to accept that others may not see it as being superior, the ego imagines itself to be so anyway and feels self-satisfied and smug as a result. It puts people down, so it can go "up", to maintain this pretence. Lacking discrimination, it sees what it wants to see, easily accepts untruths if they confirm or align with its prejudices. Such people wander through life as if in a mist.

Therapy. All spiritual practises to develop lower psychic powers must be stopped. Evoke pride of status by explaining the difference between the Atlantean and Aryan consciousness, that lower clairvoyant powers are shared with animals and should be left behind. The breeders of glamour - "criticism, pride and separativeness" should be avoided. Encourage the development of the intellect and discernment. If appropriate, recommend the use of the Formula for the Dissipation of Glamour, given later.

3. Maya - Glamorous Activity on the Physical Plane

Those affected. All people who are not yet enlightened.

How the problem arises. This is the activity produced when glamour and illusion play out on the physical level, in daily life.

How it affects the life. It is that vital, unthinking, emotional mess in which most people seem to live.

Therapy for Maya. The only remedy is to bring all the centres under soul control, achieved at an advanced level. In the meantime, discrimination must be cultivated.

<u>Glamours associated with the Rays.</u>
(From Glamour a World Problem, 120-125)

If a ray has been identified, the glamours listed here will give insight into a person's potential glamours. Conversely, if glamours are being displayed, this list will help to identify the ray that is responsible.

Ray 1: smugly sees itself as having a divine right to rule.
The glamour of ...
- physical strength.
- personal magnetism, personal potency.
- self-centredness, of "the one at the centre."
- selfish, personal ambition.
- rulership, of dictatorship, of wide control.
- superimposed will - on others and groups.
- Messiah complex, the divine right of kings.
- glamour of destruction.
- isolation, of aloneness, of aloofness.

Ray 2: smug for being self-sacrificing, unconditionally loving.
The glamour of ...
- the love of being loved, of popularity.
- being wise.
- being selfishly responsible.
- self-pity, a basic glamour of this ray.
- a Messiah complex.
- fear, based on undue sensitivity.
- self-sacrifice; selfish service.
- selfish unselfishness, self-satisfaction.

Ray 3: smugly sees itself as being mentally superior.

The glamour of ...
- busyness.
- active scheming.
- creative work without a plan.
- good intentions, which are basically selfish.
- being "the spider at the centre."
- devious and continuous manipulation.
- smug about knowing it all.

Ray 4: smugly sees itself as being the peacemaker, the colourful one.

The glamour of ...
- harmony, for personal comfort/ satisfaction.
- fighting/ war for war's sake.
- creating conflict to impose righteousness/ peace.
- vague artistic perception.

Ray 5: smugly sees itself as the expert with all the facts.

The glamour of ...
- materiality, or over-emphasis of form.
- having a superior intellect.
- possessing superior knowledge and facts.
- being right, based on a narrow point of view.
- emphasising the form (to the detriment of reality).

Ray 6: smugly sees itself as the righteous one, the special and chosen one.

The glamour of ...
- devotion and idealism to loyalties and creeds.
- (misused) emotional response.
- (inappropriate) sentimentality.
- attachment to World Saviours and Teachers.
- the narrow vision. Fanaticism.

Ray 7: smugly sees itself as superior in efficiency, in following the rules.

The glamour of ...
- magical work, of subterranean powers.
- emphasising the physical body.
- (unhealthy) sex magic, the mysterious, the secret.
- being efficient and organised.
- (over-emphasising) the appearance.

Glamour Dissipation Formula
(From 'Glamour a World Problem', 215-221)

Part 1. Preparation

1. Preparatory stages

   a. Recognise the glamour to be dissipated, how it affects the life and relationships.
   b. Focus mentally. Align the brain-light with the light of mind. Lift the lower light up into the mind-light, forming a pin-point of light like a small torch light.
   c. Briefly meditate on the soul, recognising the power of this greater light.
   d. Build the searchlight: blend the soul light with the torch-light, fuse them together forming a searchlight that is ready to be turned in the needed direction.

2. Align the personality with the soul. See the soul accept the personality, forming one unit. Say "I dedicate my personality to the soul."

3. Brace yourself for the work to be done. Turn your mind <u>to the astral plane</u> and focus on the glamour to be eradicated. (Do not focus on yourself or your astral body).

Part 2. The Formula

1. Endeavour to see and hear the soul - the source of light and power, breathing out the **OM** into the mind. Retain and hold this soul light. Feel strong, positive.

2. Build an intense brilliant powerful searchlight from the three blended lights; a vivid brilliant disc light not yet radiating.

3. Focus all your will behind this light.

4. Relate the searchlight being held, and the glamour out there on the astral plane. Briefly affirm that the searchlight will destroy the glamour.

5. **Turn on the light**. See a broad, brilliant, beam pour forth from your mind and impact the glamour on the astral plane.

6. Silently say

   The power of the light prevents the appearance of the glamour (Name it).
   The power of the light negates the quality of the glamour from affecting me.
   The power of the light destroys the life behind the glamour.

7. Sound the OM: see the light penetrate the glamour and being absorbed by it. See the light slowly dissipate the glamour.

8. Withdraw to the Mental Plane, turn off the light and identify with the soul, with God, with the Real. Feel free and clear.

Glamour is never immediately dissipated because it is of too ancient an origin. But persistent use of this formula will weaken the glamour and slowly it will vanish. Observe the results and continue if the glamour is being weakened. Otherwise discontinue the formulas use.

Stimulation Problem 3: Guidance and Dreams

1. Problems of Guidance

Those affected. 6th ray emotional and devotional people.

How the problem arises. Mystics who lack discrimination. They yearn so intensely for union with God (Jesus, Mother Mary, the Master, etc), they convince themselves that the images they see of God in their imagination, and the words they imagine God would speak to them; are really coming from God.

How it affects the life. People believe they are hearing voices or urges from God, the Christ, Baba, etc., comforting them or telling them what to do. But usually only the person's own internal dialogue is heard. This type of guidance may sweep people into quite harmless activities, but not always. Susceptible people who open themselves to blind, unreasoning guidance may become negative, impressionable automatons, helpless victims of circumstance, self-hypnotised tools that are used by others. [1]

Wise teachers such as Gautama Buddha told us that blind acquiescence and acceptance is not asked of students. The goal of all true teaching is to develop the mind and intellect, so that students can think for themselves and reason their way to enlightenment.

The desire to contact revered Saints and Masters is natural. But emotional mystics of this type want this so powerfully, they imagine communications that in fact are only the product of their wish-life. It is naive to think that these advanced beings would make direct contact with people who have not built the inner mechanism through purification and right living that makes such contact possible

It does not happen according to the Master Djwhal Khul. To think otherwise is to be deluded. Khul said for instance, that there was an astral effigy of him "living" on the astral plane, which had been constructed by the devotion of some of his followers. Because the race is increasingly becoming mystical, the guidance problem is widespread.

Sources from which guidance can come:

a. Supposedly from God. Those susceptible to this problem are introverts who are mystically inclined and naive about religion. Sometimes there is the recovery of old spiritual tendencies from a previous life that appear new. Imagined divine injunctions are perceived as coming from God. People wanting to escape life's difficulties may join a church and blindly follow the "will of God", believing they hear God speak to them.

b. Words previously heard and remembered, either good or bad. These replay through the mind and susceptible people believe a person or entity is talking to them.

c. From contacts made by the person on the astral or mental planes. These planes are full of thoughtforms that may be used by undesirable entities demanding blind and unquestioning acceptance.

d. From trained minds giving instruction to disciples. But true guides and teachers do not try to control students. They make suggestions. It is then up to the student to either follow that advice or ignore it.

e. From a man's own soul when through meditation, discipline and service, he has established contact and there is a direct channel of communication from soul to mind to brain.

---
[1] See the example of Teresa Musco in the Mystical Vision section.

Therapy. All spiritual practises should be stopped. Any voice that demands control of the life or that has personality or separative implications should be rejected. Sometimes, being a cynic is a healthy thing. Those affected should focus on creative, mental and physical interests. Any occupation which takes the person out of the problematic emotional body and into the mind or the physical body is desirable.

A technique which can be used for all types of psychological problems is for the sufferer to consciously invoke the power of the soul using affirmations. However, it is only effective when mental focus can be held.

A simple technique is to affirm "I invoke light and love of the soul," while visualising white light pouring through the personality vehicles and life, cleansing and purifying all aspects of the lower nature.

"I wash myself through with love and light of the soul," is another.

2. Problem of a distressing Dream Life.

Those affected. 6th ray emotional and devotional people.

How the problem arises. Through frustrated desire.

a. Sexual frustration: it leads to an overemphasis of sex, an uncontrolled sexual thought-life, sexual jealousies and sexual dreams.
b. Frustrated ambition: it dams up the life force, producing constant inner fret, envy, hatred, bitterness and intense dislike of people who are successful. It causes abnormalities of many kinds, including dreams that reflect this unhappiness.
c. Frustrated love: disappointment spill over into the dream life.

How it affects the life. When these three types of frustration exist, you will frequently have a vivid, unwholesome dream life, physical liabilities of many kinds and a steadily deepening unhappiness.

Therapy. Some therapists believe dream interpretation will help current problems. But there is danger with such work. For instance, it could bring to the surface things that are undesirable in the unrecognised wish-life or penetrate the past and tap into ancient racial evil. On a more mundane level, it could cause sleep disorders. Although dreams can come from the soul and sometimes from higher sources, students should avoid analysing dreams. Deal with the underlying frustration by filling the life with constructive and creative projects and invoke the power of the soul through meditation and positive affirmations.

3. The Problem of Depression

Those affected. Wholesale depression is seriously affecting all of humanity. The 4th Ray of Conflict is the problem, aided by the 6th ray that rules the emotional plane.

How the problem arises. A primary cause of depression is the lowered physical vitality of the race.[1] There is conflict in the world (R4) and when there is also conflict in the personal life, it taps into this global problem. This is why it is often very hard to break out of deep depression - it is being fed by the global phenomenon. When this goes on for an extended period it is very debilitating. When conflict lowers global vitality, health epidemics can break out with devastating consequences. Nature is at war with man.

---

1 Bailey, Alice. Esoteric Psychology II, 512.

A second cause of depression occurs when people feel inadequate and unable to measure up to presented opportunities and are troubled by a sense of failure. This affects everyone including aspirants and disciples.

> Depression is frequently the result of a sensed incapacity to measure up to the realised opportunity. The man sees and knows too much and can no longer be satisfied with the old ways of living, with the old satisfactions, and old idealisms. He now longs for something larger, for new and vibrant ideas, and for the broader vision. The way of life of the soul has gripped and attracts him. But his nature, his environment, his equipment and his opportunities appear somehow to frustrate him consistently, and he feels he cannot march forward into this new and wonderful world. He feels the need to temporise and to live in the same state of mind as heretofore, or so he thinks, and so he decides. [1]

Disciples are told to ignore depression and continue their service work. But this advice should not be given to non-disciples. Djwhal Khul also said there is a "glamour of depression." This is what he said to one of his disciples.

> The glamour of depression, based on a sense of spiritual inferiority which is not warranted, being not based on facts. Read the list of failings which you give. Even if there is some basis of truth in your enumeration, still your replies remain untruthful, for you omit all recollection or reference to the other side of the picture. A clear vision of yourself is needed. [2]

How it affects the life. Under the influence of the 4th ray, uncontrolled emotional bodies can swing rapidly back and forth from exhilaration to depression. This is very tiring for the stressed person. This swinging back and forth in an unstable emotional body is the root cause of the bipolar disorder. It is not surprising that many artists suffer from depression, since the artistic 4th ray will be in their makeup somewhere.

> Lady Gaga (Stefani Germanotta, b-1986), the pop star, said that she has dealt with both depression and anxiety for her whole life. In an interview with Billboard magazine, she admitted she takes medication for depression and said she thinks it's important for people to talk about their mental health. "If we share our stories and stick together, we're stronger." Artists often have a R4 mind (as does Stefani), and many also have a R4 personality.

Therapy. Advise sufferers to cultivate and express goodwill. A meditation/ visualisation exercise which is helpful is to create an imaginary garden.

> Garden Meditation. Spend a few minutes every day, tending and creating this garden, filling it with fragrant and beautiful flowers, bushes and trees. Then imaginatively spend time in the garden to heal and relax. Tending to a physical garden will also help. It is very therapeutic to be outside in the sun and working with the magical plant kingdom. (See also a guide in the Meditation section).

This concludes this section on the psychology troubles that affect the masses. Next we examine those that affect mystics and disciples.

---

[1] Bailey, Alice. Esoteric Psychology II, 466.
[2] Bailey, Alice. Discipleship in the New Age I, 425.

II. PROBLEMS OF MYSTICS & DISCIPLES

MYSTICS are spiritually orientated, but they sense the divine realities from the heights of emotional aspiration. This emotional orientation poses a problem, because this is the body of delusion and such people often have delusory experiences or are susceptible to being deluded by false teachers and prophets.

Further, though mystics can sometimes experience a spiritual vision or ecstatic union with God through prayer, adoration and worship; they are often unable to repeat this experience. This is because the mental bridge of light - the antahkarana, which connects the brain to the spiritual realms, has not yet been built. The mystic must eventually become an occultist, and build this bridge.

Occultist Helena Blavatsky equated the term "occultist" with "the true mystic."

> [There are few] students of occult sciences, for rarely is the *true mystic* born. Few, alas, have so yearned after the discovery of Nature's secrets as to be willing to pursue that hard and unselfish course of study. [1]

That "hard and unselfish course of study" is what distinguishes the emotional mystic from the occultist or true mental mystic. The Master DK concurred with this definition.

> *The occultist, is only the mystic functioning on a higher plane - that of the mind.* These are the brilliant people [who] rise to the top of their profession, who have outstanding creative ability and are phenomenally magnetic and influential; they unify and blend and gather around them groups of people. [2]

DISCIPLES are Occultists. They earnestly follow in the footsteps of advanced human beings who have trodden the Path ahead of them - the Path that leads from "darkness to light and from the unreal to the real". Having tasted all pleasures in the material world, these no longer have the power to satisfy and hold them. They are transitioning into a new state of being, are vibrating between the condition of form awareness and soul awareness, are seeking to enter a new and higher field of experience. Spiritual perception is growing and the intuition is developing. Pledged to a Master and to co-operate with the plan of the Great Ones, they are striving to take initiation and become enlightened

<u>There are three groups of Mystic - Disciple Problems.</u>

1. Problems due to Chakra Development.

2. The Problem of Psychic Powers.

3. The problem of Directed Group Thought.

---

[1] Blavatsky, Helena; Collected Writings 2. 442-3.
[2] Bailey, Alice. Esoteric Psychology II, 710.

A. PROBLEMS DUE TO CHAKRA DEVELOPMENT

Those affected. Mystics and disciples.

How the problem arises. When there is the first faint stirring of spiritual orientation in the mystic, then begins a transference of energy from the lower chakras (sacral, solar plexus and base), to the higher chakras (throat, ajna, heart and head). These transferences simply reflect the change in orientation being made, and the new and higher perspectives of life which are developing.

The process of energies lifting from a lower chakra to a higher one has three main steps - from sacral to throat, from solar-plexus to the heart, and from the base to the crown. This triple transference represents the eventual transference of energy from the personality (symbolised by the solar plexus) to the soul (symbolised by the heart centre) and from the soul to the Monad (symbolised by the head centre).

There are other smaller incremental steps. For instance, the masses of average intelligent people (the educated who recognise world news and discuss world events and trends), are in the process of transferring energy from the sacral centre to the solar plexus. This is responsible for much turmoil in the world. The awakening and vitalisation of the ajna chakra - which is not in one of these pair groupings, comes alive after the throat is vital and stimulated.

How the problem affects the life. While these transfers are going on from lower to higher chakras, the energies swing back and forth between the two centres - mirroring the uneven life of the aspirant. This creates disruption in both chakras, in their functioning and it creates imbalances in energy. This lasts until the focal point of attention stabilises in the higher centre.

These disruptions and imbalances cause mental health problems and physical diseases in the organs vitalised by the chakras. Over-activity of a centre overstimulates the organs in that area, with congestion, cell overbuilding and inflammation. Under-activity denies vitalisation and the organ atrophies, which inhibits its activities.

> If he has succeeded (as a result of a long evolutionary history) in awakening in some fashion, however slight, the centres above the diaphragm. The moment that occurs he becomes subject, for a long cycle of lives, to difficulties connected with the heart or the nervous system. An aspirant or a disciple, may have freed himself from inherited taints, but will succumb to heart trouble, to nervous disorders, mental imbalance and overstimulation - they are classified occasionally as the "diseases of the Mystics." [1]

The transferences involving the solar plexus chakra are happening in so many people at once, it is releasing astral forces into humanity that are causing widespread fear, desire of a wrong kind and many other emotional upsets. This is temporary and will be resolved given time.

This phenomenon is positive in a spiritual sense. Collectively, those doing this work constitute the "world aspirant," and the fact that their efforts are having a global effect testifies to the number of people who are either approaching the Spiritual Path or who are actually upon it.

---

[1] Bailey, Alice. Esoteric Healing, 55-56.

The Transferences.

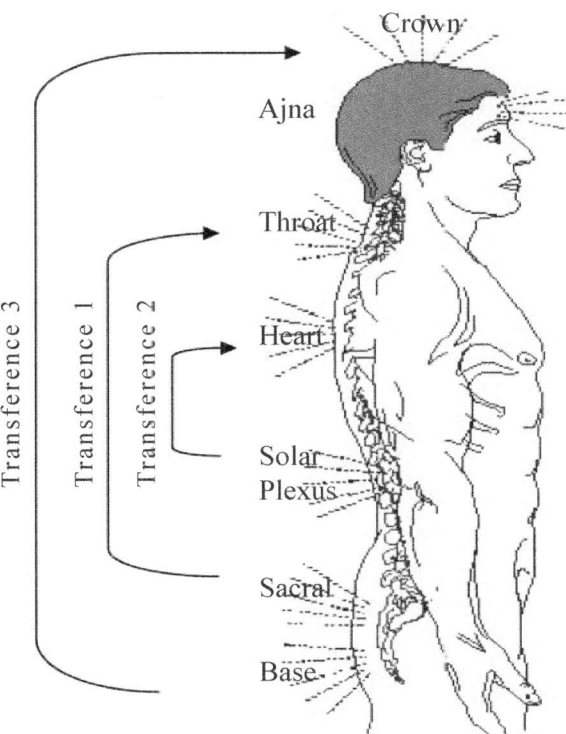

- *First Transference – Sacral to Throat. Coincides with the 1st Initiation.*

This is the highly intelligent citizen and aspirant stage. It can last several lives. The centres below the diaphragm are fully awakened and active, with the solar plexus dominating. It receives energy streams from the base and sacral centres, and when it begins to deflect them to the higher centres (sacral force to the throat [1] chakra), it means the personality has developed or is in the process of doing so. When the throat centre is functioning, it means a fairly high state of evolution has been reached and the man is beginning to take his place in the work of the world.

The developmental task associated with this process (of transferring the fire from the generative organs to the throat centre), is to moderate and balance the sex impulse and throw the mind into creative projects. This period is a long and very difficult one, lasting several lives. Please also note, the fire in the lower centre is minimised - it is not extinguished.

With the throat centre becoming active, and while energies are still imbalanced, physical problems can develop in the throat and thyroid gland, and also in the reproductive organs and glands. Later, solar plexus force (in a very small measure), will begin to rise to the heart chakra, which is stirring. While reactions are still selfish, group consciousness will gradually develop. The person at this stage is conscious of dualism in the nature and is ready to tread the Probationary Path. [2]

---
1 The throat centre is situated in the lower part of the throat, and properly belongs to the torso and not to the head. Bailey, Alice. A Treatise on Cosmic Fire, 864.
2 Bailey, Alice. Esoteric Psychology II, 525.

- *Second Transference – Solar Plexus to Heart. Coincides with the 2nd Initiation.*

In the first stage of this transference, the ajna centre becomes active and dominant and the zenith of the personality life is reached. This is the dominant personality stage. The man or woman is selfish, powerful, ambitious - but also very creative. The mental and selfish personality stage is a temporary development designed to round out the nature.

> § Sometimes, even if mystical attributes have been awakened in a previous life, the soul may put these into abeyance in the new incarnation so that the mind and personality qualities awaken fully. When the needed developments have been achieved, the mystical qualities will resurface again. This may be in the same incarnation or a later one. For example: a business person is ruthless and appears uncaring about how he deals with others. Then a crisis happens and the person changes completely, becomes selfless, giving and caring. The mystical side has been re-awakened.

Next comes the mystic-discipleship stage. As the fires of the solar plexus continue to rise to the heart centre, the desire for worldly satisfaction becomes less magnetic. Aspiration for a life based on spiritual values grows and the mystic definitely emerges again. By this stage, the ajna centre is vivid and potent, the throat centre is intensely active and the heart centre is rapidly awakening. The aspirant is being drawn to both the world of man and to the world of souls. As the work continues, devotion is transmuted into love and idealism into wisdom. The disciple (for this level has now been reached), develops group-consciousness and is now inclusive in attitude to people and to life. No longer antagonistic and exclusive in attitude, he knows and understands, he pities, loves and serves.

- *Third Transference – Base to Crown. Coincides with the 3rd Initiation.*

The initiate stage. The soul pours its energy into all the chakras, via the head centre. The point at the heart of each centre (the jewel in the lotus), comes alive and is radiant and magnetic. This awakens the base centre fully and all the psychic energies are drawn up to the head centre, up to the soul. This is the final transference. Then the great polar opposites symbolised by the head centre (organ of spiritual energy) and the base centre (the organ of the material forces) are fused and blended and from this time on the man is controlled only from above, by the soul.[1]

Therapy. Try not to brood over any physical condition that has arisen in the chakra-region of transference. This could over-energise the centre or feed the condition. The practise of spiritual disciplines such as right-detachment and meditation will help stabilise the fluctuating energies, as will endeavouring to live a stable and practical life of service. Aligning oneself daily with the love and light emanating from the soul, from God, will have a very beneficial effect. Esoteric healing and chakra balancing will also help.

This quote highlights the benefits of occult meditation on health.

> The goal of meditation is to bring about the free play of all the incoming forces so that there is no impediment offered at any point to the incoming energy of the soul; so that no obstruction and congestion is permitted and no lack of power—physical, psychic, mental and spiritual—is to be found in any part of the body. This will mean not only good health and the full and free use of all the faculties (higher and lower) but direct contact with the soul.[2]

---

1 Bailey, Alice. Esoteric Psychology II, 527.
2 Bailey, Alice. Esoteric Psychology II, 593.

This chart provides further information about the transference process and subsequent problems that can arise.

Chakras and Levels of Consciousness	*Problems*
1. CROWN. 1000 Petals. This centre is dominant after the 3rd Initiation and is active in initiates. Occultists work from the crown. It is the seat of the soul. With the onset of the **3rd transference**, all centres are synthesised from the crown. At the 4th Initiation, kundalini rises from the base to the head, and all chakras are controlled from the crown by the Monad.	Pineal gland problems, brain inflammation and trouble such as tumours and stroke.
2. AJNA. 96 Petals. This centre links us to the mental plane. It is the organ of imagination and higher creativity. This centre comes alive prior to passing onto the Probationary Path (Esoteric Psychology, 304) and is active in integrated personalities, mystics, aspirants and disciples. 1st initiation: ajna energies are active and sweep down into the lower centres. The person at this level is intelligent but also materialistic and selfish. 2nd initiation: soul energy flows up from the sacral to the heart centre. The ajna becomes dominant after the 2nd Initiation.	Problems with the pituitary gland, the eyes, ears and nasal passage; in the lower brain and nervous system.
3. THROAT. 16 Petals. This centre links us to the mental plane and is active in advanced humanity - the intelligentsia and creative artists. At the **1st Initiation** and **1st Transference,** physical appetites are being purified and sacral energies rise to the throat.	With the thyroid, the bronchial tree, lungs, larynx, lymphatics. Also with communication.
4. HEART. 12 Petals. This centre relates us to the Buddhic plane and to the Love-Wisdom aspect. It is active in all types of spiritual people and starts to dominate after the 1st initiation. At the **2nd Initiation** and **2nd Transference**, the solar-plexus gathers up the energies of the lower centres and transfers them to the heart. This centre opens fully at the 4th Initiation	Problems with the thymus gland, with the heart, cardiovascular, circulation and immune systems.
5. SOLAR PLEXUS. 10 Petals. This is the portal for the astral plane and the expression of emotions and desires from the crudest to the most high. It is dominant in average humanity. Working closely with the sacral and base centres, it gathers up these lower forces and transfers them to the heart at the **2nd Transference**.	Problems with the pancreas gland, with digestive and elimination functions.
6. SACRAL. 6 Petals. This is the centre of lower desire (for food, comfort and sex), and is still very powerful in average man. At the 1st Initiation sacral energies begin to be raised to the throat centre (**1st Transference**). Eventually the creative output of the aspirant will work primarily through the higher centre.	Problems with reproductive glands and organs, with childbearing and sex.
7. BASE. 4 Petals. This centre is related to the physical plane and vitalises the dense physical body. People with powerful, selfish wills focus in this centre as well as in the ajna. The base chakra is awakened in its true and final sense at the 3rd and 4th Initiations.	Problems with the adrenal glands, the urinary tract, and body structure including the spine, bones and joints.

B. THE PROBLEM OF PSYCHIC POWERS.

Psychic is derived from *Psyche* (Greek), soul, and refers to the powers of the soul. There are two types of psychic powers available in the human kingdom - the powers of the spiritual soul and the powers of the animal soul.

The soul on its own plane is constituted of the energies of light and love and its powers are the higher psychic powers. But when it incarnates, it takes on bodies formed from the air, fire, water and earth elementals, primitive lives whose collective "intelligence" we call the animal soul. The latter works through the lower nature and the lower psychic forces that are problematic for man, rise from the solar plexus chakra.

Higher psychics: are the spiritually advanced people who use the powers of the spiritual soul through the third eye, which is located near the ajna chakra.

Lower psychics: are the ordinary clairvoyants, clairaudients and mediums who use the lower animal powers through the medium of the solar plexus chakra.

The higher spiritual worlds are largely formless. So, when the lower psychic sees beings and other phenomena that mirror happenings on the physical plane, he is working on the astral plane, the plane of delusion. On this plane we learn to distinguish truth from error, so lower psychics who work here are mistaking the unreal for the real. They have not yet developed discrimination.

The average thinking person does not use either powers. He is occupied with developing the mind - which drives the animal powers below the threshold of awareness. As we become soul-aligned, we develop the higher powers.

Lower and Higher Psychic Powers.

Atmic plane	*Higher .. Psychic .. Powers*	Beatitude	Active service	Realisation	Perfection	All knowledge
Buddhic plane		Comprehension Understanding completely, all-knowingness.	Healing Power to heal by touch.	Mystical vision Power to sense the emerging reality or unknown.	Intuition	Idealism
Mental plane		Higher clairaudience Telepathy.	Planetary psychometry En rapport with all living things.	Higher clairvoyance Seeing geometric symbols.	Discrimination	Spiritual discernment
Astral plane	*Lower Psychic*	**Clairaudience** Hearing words, messages, sounds not discernible by ordinary hearing.	**Psychometry** Be en rapport with an absent person by touching an object belonging to him.	**Clairvoyance** Sees images on the astral plane.	Imagination *Not a lower psychic power.*	Emotional idealism *Not a lower psychic power.*
Physical plane sense		Hearing	Touch, feeling	Sight	Taste	Smell

The chart shows 5 physical senses and their application and development on each of the higher planes of consciousness, up to the Atmic spiritual plane. (Information from Esoteric Psychology II, 561).

Those affected. Mainly mystics whose consciousness are still dominated by the emotions. But intelligent people can also be affected. In both, R6 is strong and is most likely the emotional or personality ray, or it rules both bodies.

How the problem arises.
a. These powers can emerge naturally in people whose evolutionary stage is still Atlantean (ruled by the emotions).
b. Over-emotional and susceptible people who choose to dwell in the emotional world can overstimulate the solar plexus centre and open the door to the astral plane. This removes the veil that usually hides the astral world from ordinary sight and the powers emerge.
c. "Sitting for development", as the practice is called in some spiritual groups. They deliberately cultivate the lower powers, forcing them to emerge again.

How it affects the life. Use of lower psychism that was normal and right in old Atlantis is undesirable today - it is an animal faculty and is shared by the animals. Their development and practice retards evolutionary development and wastes time as far as higher progress is concerned. Consciousness is going backwards and downwards instead of forwards and upwards.

Such people interpret the astral, delusory images as spiritual phenomena that is wonderful, true and desirable. The practice is delusory, the unreal is being interpreted as being real. The practice can also be dangerous. Dark things reside on the lower levels of the astral plane and if the door to that plane is opened, they can come through to torment the sufferer.

Therapy. How to arrest the lower psychic powers.
a. Lower psychics who are Atlantean in consciousness.

Encourage the cultivation of a spirit of true humility. Train the intellect to think. The powers should not be used and all contacts or messages that feed the ego and sense of being superior or special should be rejected. This will eventually close the solar plexus centre and the door to the astral plane. It will also atrophy that part of the inner mechanism that has made these powers available and cause them to die out. True disciples and mystics are mentally polarised and vision is free from the deluding reactions of the solar plexus centre and astral plane.

If the door is open because of inherited activities from previous lives and an over-active solar plexus centre, focus should be on building a strong and healthy physical body and emphasising higher goals and a life of service. Wearing and surrounding oneself with the colour yellow that stimulates mental activity will help. Where there is a violent fight against psychic activity, a nervous breakdown and loss of mental control, the person needs protective seclusion, rest and a light diet. The trouble is not mental but is related to the solar plexus and should be treated as such.

b. Lower psychics who are Aryan (mental) in consciousness.

If the astral door has been opened due to certain practises (such as "sitting for development"), these should be stopped and contact with those teaching them terminated. Focus should be on everyday, physical matters - work, family, social obligations and responsibilities. All devotional practices should be left alone until the psyche has stabilised.

If the person is intelligent and has esoteric knowledge, the work can be more scientific and focused on balancing the chakras to quieten the over-active solar plexus chakra.

1. Problems with the Development of Mystical Vision. [1]
Devitalisation, Delusion and Delirium.

> The impact of the higher spiritual forces upon mystically motivated people is producing serious and widespread trouble, breaking down protective etheric barriers and throwing the doors wide open on to the astral plane. [2]

Mystical vision is the process of sensing the goal, of contacting the ideal and of visioning the many symbols that veil the soul. Mystical literature is full of these visions - seeing the Virgin Mary and Jesus in particular.

Those affected. 6th ray emotional mystics who are deeply religious.

How the problem arises. The mystic lives entirely in the world of aspiration, is devotional and adoring of God/ Jesus/ the Virgin Mary. This and the yearning to be with God or have his attention, the constant lifting of the heart upwards to that which is idealised, over-empowers the emotional body and unbalances the nature.

This occurs when spiritual imaginings, wishes and longings completely absorb a mystic's attention to the detriment of common sense. Becoming obsessed by this powerful vision or dream, they mistake it for reality.

1. Devitalisation.

How it affects the life. The constant emotional lifting-upwards, this leeches energy from the physical body, which suffers. Energies that should be vitalising the physical body feed the forces of the astral body. When devitalisation becomes excessive it leads to nervous debility, hallucinations, other pathological developments and sometimes death. The mystical approach is the right way for many, provided it does not become impractical and ungrounded and interfere with living a natural and normal life. The example of Teresa Musco in the Delusion section also fits this category. She died at the very early age of 33. Because her body was so under-vitalised, over the years, organs and systems broke down.

Therapy. Explain to the person the causal link between the devotional life and what is happening with the health of the body. Recommend that devotional practices should be stopped until the health has stabilised. Increase vitality by stimulating the etheric body through sunshine, nutrition and exercise. Balance the endocrine system.

2. Delusion.

How it affects the life. They suffer serious psychological difficulties that are induced by the ecstasy of their vision. They are victims of a hallucination that has disrupted sane and healthy living. Some even die.

> Teresa Musco (1943-1976), was born into a poor farming family in Caserta Italy. From 6 years on, she believed the Virgin Mary was her protector and comforter. So was Jesus. Her entire life was spent in rapturous yearning for union with Jesus and to suffer like he did. She wrote in her diary, "Jesus appeared with a cross on his shoulders and showed me his scourged back full of open wounds. I used my handkerchief to wipe off the blood which flowed from his face and wounds."

---
1 Bailey, Alice. Esoteric Psychology II, 598-606.
2 Bailey, Alice. Esoteric Psychology II, 487.

From an early age - for love of Jesus, Teresa agreed to take on whatever suffering God sent her. Her health suffered and she accepted this as God answering her pledge to assist Jesus in his mission of suffering. And people around her aided and abetted her delusion. As the years passed there were many illnesses requiring hospitalisation and operations (over 100). She had holes, wounds and scars all over her body. Before she died, during a vision in which she was crucified, stigmata appeared on her hands. Teresa died on in 1976 with her arms outstretched as if she was on a cross – like Jesus. She was 33 years old. [1]

Unfortunately, instead of recognising that this condition is psychologically unhealthy, many religious people consider people like Musco to be holy, saintly and very spiritually advanced. Thus, they enable and perpetuate the unhealthy condition.

Therapy. The psychologist should gently develop in the mystic a cycle of doubt, leading even to a temporary agnosticism. The result would be a rapid establishing of the desired equilibrium. Encourage a normal physical life with its ordinary interests, fulfilling obligations and responsibilities.

3. Delirium (modern term is "schizophrenia").

How it affects the life. When delusion and devitalisation are chronic and there is no inner control or sense of right-proportion, then this dangerous condition could develop. Outer expression becomes abnormal ranging from fanaticism to sadism and insanity. The mystic is obsessed by his own peculiar thoughtform of truth and reality. He has only one idea in his head. His mind is not active for his brain has become the instrument of his astral nature and registers only his fanatical devotion and emotional obsession.

Therapy. Frequently, there is little that can be done except care for the patient. The mystic has, for this one life, done himself irreparable damage.

2. Problems with the Revelation of Light and Power. [2]

Those affected. The advanced man, aspirant or disciple. Especially R2 types.

How the problem arises. The problem of the light in the head occurs when the spiritually advanced person is meditating and has learnt to focus mentally. The inflow of soul-light brings the brain cells into functioning activity and sometimes this can be seen.

How it affects the life. The unified magnetic field can become so brilliant it is seen with the eyes closed or sensed as a diffused misty light inside or outside the head. Sometimes, if the presence of this light is unrecognised and the person is not engaged in creative work or service activities it can affect the eyes and optic nerve producing poor sight and in extreme cases, physical blindness.

This is a physiological and not a psychic power and is quite different to clairvoyance. Not all occult students see this light. It depends upon temperament, the person's rays, the quality of the physical cells of the brain (body), the nature of the work and the extent of the magnetic field.

Therapy. Make no effort to see the light in the head. If spiritual practices are being followed, excessive energy can be safely released through selfless service.

---

1   Full text of this article is on: https://www.mysticsofthechurch.com/2012/01/teresa-musco-stigmatic-mystic-victim.html
2   Bailey, Alice. Esoteric Psychology II, 605-615.

C. THE PROBLEM OF DIRECTED GROUP THOUGHT.

1. The problem of Group Criticism.

Those affected. People who have not yet developed group consciousness and want to dominate the group. The ego is still strong and so is ambition and the urge to be "at the centre."

How the problem arises. People may covet the position of the leaders. They may be jealous and believe they can do a better job. In every case, it leads to criticism, a virulent poison.

> This criticism is usually rooted in jealousy, thwarted ambition, or pride of individual intellect. Each member of any group is prone to sit in judgment. The responsibility is not theirs; they know not the problems as they truly exist and criticism is, therefore, easy. Criticism is a virulent poison. [1]

The central figures in the group pay the price for this weakness.

> From every side and in every group there streams in on the group leader directed criticism, poisonous thoughts, untrue formulated ideas, idle gossip of a destructive kind, the imputation of motives, the unspoken jealousies and hates, the frustrated ambitions of group members, their resentments and their unsatisfied desires for prominence or for recognition by the leader or leaders, their desires to see the leader superseded by themselves or by someone else and many other forms of selfishness and mental pride.

When criticism is voiced, the negative stream is strengthened by those who have been influenced. Unvoiced criticism is also very dangerous. It issues continuously and as a steady stream, sent forth on the wings of jealousy, ambition and pride.

Group-directed criticism can physically undo and disrupt the physical body of the leader or leaders - the projected poison lodges wherever there is a physical weakness. In such a case, group leaders must continue the work, retreat within, speak the truth with love and refuse to become bitter.

Therapy. Draw the attention of the group to the disastrous effects of criticism. Recommend the practise of "silence". It may be necessary to eject an instigator from the group.

2. The group problem of "Smothering".

This is the reverse of the previous problem. A few emotional and devotional people attach themselves to the leader by a sort of umbilical cord. Through this link they can smother the leader with adoring personality devotion, or drain the life of the leader. Or, if aroused to hate or dislike can violently disrupt the tie, causing suffering. Group members must remain independent and when training instruction is complete, the cord must be cut.

> § *This completes this study of Soul Psychology and the various problems that arise as we journey towards enlightenment. Now our attention turns towards Raja Yoga, to the obstacles which prevent spiritual union and the spiritual practices recommended by the great teacher Patanjali, to remove them.*

---

1 Bailey, Alice. Esoteric Psychology II, 617.

CHAPTER 4. RAJA YOGA SPIRITUAL PRACTICES.

The goal of all spiritual work is to expand consciousness until union is achieved with the wisdom of the universe that some call God. In previous chapters, the evolution of consciousness was studied and psychological problems that occur during this process. In this Raja Yoga chapter, we study obstacles that prevent union, spiritual practices to overcome them, and the results when successful. This chart gives an overview of our study.

The goal of Raja Yoga is Union.			
Preventing Union are the lower (psychic) nature and the undisciplined mind.			
The 4 Impediments to Union:			
1	2	3	4
4 wrong ways of thinking (mind modifications). Incorrect knowledge, Fancy, Sleep, Memory.	**The 9 Obstacles:** due to evolution & the undeveloped state of our bodies (mind, emotions, physical).	**The 5 Hindrances:** wrong attitudes to life. Ignorance, hate, attachment, egoism, clinging to life.	**The 3 Gunas:** the tamas, rajas, sattvic qualities of matter that bind the soul, then release it.
<u>*The 8 Means of Raja Yoga*</u> 1. The Commandments (Yama) 2. The Rules (Niyama). 3. Posture (Asana). 4. Right control of the Life-force (Pranayama). 5. Abstraction (Pratyahara). 6. Concentration (Dharana). 7. Meditation (Dhyana). 8. Contemplation (Samadhi).			

RAJA-YOGA is the Kingly Science of the Mind.

Raja Yoga is a method of spiritual development presented by the great Indian initiate Patanjali, thousands of years ago. The system trains those who are on a search for union with God to achieve this.

This is not a detailed study of Raja Yoga. For that, students are referred to "The Light of the Soul," by Alice Bailey. This study covers the impediments preventing union with the soul, and the spiritual practices Patanjali gave to overcome them - Book 1, Book 2 and the beginning of Book 3. Most of Book 3 and all of Book 4 are for initiates.

Yogas for the 3 Major Root-races in Humanity.

To help soul evolution, the Yogas or methods of union were given - one for each of the three major human races (Lemurian, Atlantean and Aryan).

1. Yoga of Lemuria: Hatha Yoga.

The Lemurian root-race existed millions of years ago. The physical body was being coordinated and controlled and *Hatha Yoga* was given to help this process. In its popular form as taught by western teachers, it is a healthy practice for body and mind. However, the extreme form of this yoga - to gain conscious control of the various body organs which normally operate autonomously, is a forbidden and dangerous practise.

Laya Yoga, Kundalini Yoga and *Kriya Yoga* are related. They involve intense meditations and breathing exercises on the chakras to hasten spiritual development. This is fine when taught by a spiritually advanced teacher to students who have earned the right to this knowledge and training because of their evolutionary status. Otherwise, the premature rising of kundalini fire is highly dangerous and will destroy health.

2. Yoga of Atlantis: Bhakti Yoga.

The Atlantean root-race also existed millions of years ago. It developed the emotional nature and *Bhakti Yoga,* the yoga of devotion and love for God, was given to aid this process. In the practice, all smaller loves are given up or denied until only divine love exists. *Bhakti Yoga* provides the foundation for Raja Yoga.

3. Yoga of the Aryan Race: Raja Yoga.

Raja Yoga, the yoga of the mind or will, is related to the mental plane and the development of mind. It is the great science of our Aryan civilization. It offers a comprehensive method of controlling the mind through concentration and meditation so that in consciousness, we can pass from the human kingdom to the Kingdom of Souls.

Jnana Yoga, the yoga of knowledge, is compatible with Raja Yoga. The mind is used to study all the ideas of men. Those that do not lead to wisdom are repudiated - "Not this -not that," until only Brahma is left or found.

> Raja Yoga coordinates the entire lower threefold man, forcing him into a position where he is nothing but the vehicle for the soul, or God within. It includes the other Yogas and profits by their achievements. It synthesises the work of evolution and crowns man as king. [1]

---

[1] Bailey, Alice. Light of the Soul, 120.

BOOK 1 - THE PROBLEM OF UNION

The first three sutras in Book I, set the goal of Raja Yoga. UNION, how to achieve it and the nature of consciousness once this has been achieved.

1:1. AUM. (OM). The following instruction concerns the Science of Union.

1:2. This Union (or Yoga) is achieved through the subjugation of the psychic nature and the restraint of the chitta (or mind).

1:3. When this has been accomplished, the Yogi knows himself as he is in reality.

-----

§ *Immediately after emphasising the goal of Union, Patanjali points to the two things that prevent Union - the lower (psychic) nature and the mind.*

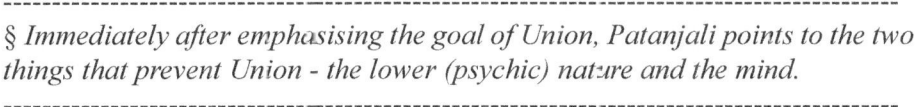

Analysis of Sutra 2.

1 problem. The Psychic Nature.

The "lower" psychic nature refers to all existing lower reactions of the mind, astral and physical bodies, stemming from everything that we have experienced in all past lives. These forces must be subjugated because they delude the soul and bind us to the past. The goal of Raja Yoga is to neutralise these impulses and replace them with the considered intelligent actions of the soul or spiritual man.

2 problem. Chitta, mind-stuff.

Chitta is not only associated with the mind, but is much more. It is the intelligent thought substance from which the manifested universe in its entirety arises. Here are 2 quotes.

> Chitta underlies and is the very substance of manifestation itself. It has, by its own nature, all knowledge. God, the planetary Life or Logos works with the higher correspondence of this mind-stuff and the forces of the mental plane are the densification of this higher mental substance. [1]

> The chitta has, by its own nature, all knowledge. It is made of sattva particles, but is covered by rajas and tamas particles. Vivekananda. [2]

When we incarnate, we take our own allocation of universal chitta, which our mind uses. When we think, it agitates chitta and thoughtforms that conform to that train of thought rise. Untrained, chitta is like the sea whipped into a frenzy in a howling gale. The average mind is like this. Chitta is in constant flux and motion. This is why those who have little control over their chitta have an over busy and perpetually chattering mind (and mouth). Sometimes this is called the chattering, monkey-mind.

Raja Yoga trains the mind so that chitta stops its aimless and mindless ramblings. When chitta is restrained, it is calm and serene, a media which enables wisdom to be accessed, and true knowledge to be attained.

---

[1] Bailey, Alice. Discipleship in the New Age I, 68.
[2] Bailey, Alice. Light of the Soul, 228. Swami Vivekananda (1863-1902) was an Indian Hindu monk and philosopher. He was a chief disciple of the 19th-century Indian mystic Ramakrishna.

The Vrittis - the modifications of the mind and mental perceptions.

The *vrittis* ("whirlpools" in Sanskrit), are waves of chitta or thought, which are generated when we think. Indirectly, the emotions are the major influencers of chitta. When a strong emotion is experienced, the mind investigates to find out what is going on. Then *vrittis*, waves of thought related to the emotion rise up. For example:

> A feeling of fear arises and mind investigates why. The *vrittis*/ train of thought could go like this: "Oh, I am afraid and it is that scary man who is causing my fear."

Mental Perceptions.

Waves of thought, *vrittis,* combine to form our mental perceptions, the way we look at the world, rate it and judge it. Our senses gather information about the world and send this information to the mind - via the *vrittis*. When we say, "I see, I taste, I hear, I touch, I smell," it is the activity of the *vrittis* that enable us to recognize the fact.

The goal is to train the mind, the chitta, the *vrittis*, so that we become deaf to non-essential information coming from the outside world. Developing lower-mind silence is the ultimate goal. Only then will we hear the soul speak.

Here is how the great occultist Helena Blavatsky describes the notion of mind-silence (in her book the Voice of Silence).

> *These instructions are for those ignorant of the dangers of the lower Iddhi (lower psychic powers).*

He who would hear the voice of Nada, "the Soundless Sound," and comprehend it, he has to learn the nature of Dharana (has to discipline the mind, train it to concentrate).

Having become indifferent to objects of perception, the pupil must seek out the king of the senses, the Thought-Producer, he who awakes illusion.

The Mind is the great Slayer of the Real. Let the Disciple slay the Slayer.

For: —

When to himself his form appears unreal, as do on waking all the forms he sees in dreams;

When he has ceased to hear the many, he may discern the ONE — the inner sound which kills the outer.

Then only, not till then, shall he forsake the region of *Asat*, the false, to come unto the realm of *Sat*, the true.

Before the soul can see, the Harmony within must be attained, and fleshly eyes be rendered blind to all illusion.

Before the Soul can hear, the image (man) has to become as deaf to roarings as to whispers, to cries of bellowing elephants as to the silvery buzzing of the golden firefly.

Before the soul can comprehend and may remember, she must unto the Silent Speaker be united just as the form to which the clay is modelled, is first united with the potter's mind.

For then the soul will hear, and will remember.

And then to the inner ear will speak — THE VOICE OF THE SILENCE

THE 4 IMPEDIMENTS TO UNION.

In these sutras Patanjali describes the four ways the psychic activities of the lower bodies impede self-realisation and union.

Impediment 1: Wrong ways of Thinking (modifying Chitta)

There are five ways we think or modify chitta. Only the first way - "correct knowledge," is the correct way to think.

1:6. These modifications (activities) are correct knowledge, incorrect knowledge, fancy, passivity (sleep) and memory.

When we perceive life clearly, without the distorting effects of emotionalism and the misinterpretation of what has been seen, then truth is seen - "correct knowledge" is obtained. This is what Raja Yoga trains us to do. When perception is correct, so is our analysis of a situation. "The basis of correct knowledge is correct perception, correct deduction and correct witness (or accurate evidence)." 1:7.

When we succumb to wrong ways of thinking, we swing between the opposites of pleasure and pain (1:5). But mostly, we are stressed and unhappy. The ego strives to get things and have experiences that are pleasurable. When each attempt to do so fails, it experiences pain. This swinging between the opposites is the way most people move through life. This is because they are still identified with the material world and the wants and needs of their bodies (wrong-thinking). Once we correct this, think correctly, the cause of pain is removed and we find happiness.

The four ways we wrong-think.

1. "Incorrect knowledge" - observing only the appearance of things.
Patanjali explains that man mis-thinks because he judges by what he sees on the surface, by the appearance of things and does not consider underlying motives and causes or the spiritual aspect of people or life.

> 1:8. Incorrect knowledge is based upon perception of the form and not upon the state of being.

The average person sees the form, what is happening in the immediate, and accepts the surface presentation as the truth. Such a mind does not weigh what is seen or heard against the inner world of causes, so wrong conclusions are reached. Consequently, the knowledge attained is distorted and erroneous. This problem is quite natural on the earlier stages of the Path.

2. Fantasising to avoid to avoid living in the present ("Fancy").
Fantasising, creating mind-movies, twisting reality and facts to create a more desirable outcome is another problem. Not liking the world as it is, life-events are re-arranged in this imaginary word.

> 1:9. Fancy rests upon images which have no real existence.

A future happier state is visioned or an unhappy event is reset so that the ego comes out the victor, the one who is the victim, the one who is right while others are wrong. This is a very common way that life events are distorted and is a real problem when people accept this imaginary world as truth and make life decisions based upon such misperceptions. People can become trapped by the delusory worlds they create in their minds. Such worlds can seem more real than what is happening in outer life.

3. "Passivity" - withdrawing from the world to avoid living in the present.
Another way the mind is misused is to psychologically "blank out" and stop thinking.

> 1:10. Passivity (sleep) is based upon the quiescent state of the vrittis (or upon the non-perception of the senses.)

The thinking processes are clamped down upon by force of will. This may happen if a person has been seriously traumatised and the will stops unhappy images playing through the mind. Sometimes the same thing is done during meditation, a potentially dangerous technique. If this habit is extended over a long period, the *vrittis* that relay information from the senses to the brain can stop functioning. If so, the mind no longer receives information from the senses and this isolates the person into their own inner world.

> Right activity of the mind and its correct use is the goal of yoga, and "a blank mind" with the sense relations cut off or atrophied, is not part of the process. The sleep here referred to is the putting to sleep of the vrittis - the senses are making contacts and connections with the outer world, but the mind is not supervising their activities. In this condition of sleep, a man is open to hallucination, delusion, wrong impressions and obsession. [1]

4. "Memory" - living in the past to avoid living in the present.
In this case, the mind lives in the past, in memories. The person holds onto that which has been known and continually relives past experiences, painful or joyful.

> 1:11. Memory is the holding on to that which has been known.

Living in the past retards our evolution. It strengthens negative psychological and unconscious patterns and attitudes to life. It renders a person susceptible to depression and to other health problems. The remedy is to practice living "in the now."

Remedial action to overcome the Modifications.

These negative modifications are simply bad-habits and can be changed by applying self-discipline.

> 1:12-13. The control of these modifications of the mind, is brought about through tireless endeavour to restrain the modifications of the mind and non-attachment.

It really helps if the desire to overcome wrong-thinking is valued and appreciated. This can be assisted by visualising how joyful life will be, how serene and blissful, when the mind is clear and untroubled.

> 1:14. When the object to be gained is sufficiently valued, and the efforts towards its attainment are persistently followed without intermission, then the steadiness of the mind (restraint of the vrittis) is secured.

Fixing the mind immovably upon a new and higher goal has a steadying influence upon the mind and chitta. Taking the mind off the lower desire and striving towards something aspi-

---

1 Bailey, Alice. Light of the Soul, 22.

rational instead, this is the vital and important practice of non-attachment or detachment. The key is to aspire towards something higher.

> 1:15. Non-attachment is freedom from longing for all objects of desire, either earthly or traditional, either here or hereafter.

When the mind-body has been steadied and freed from desiring attractions in the material world, it no longer hinders the soul from seeing clearly and accurately into the world of form (sutra 1:16). Now it is a clear and steady "eye" for the soul, it is an organ that registers accurately all that it observes in the world. No longer does the mind tell the soul what its conclusions are. It can be silent, allowing the soul to ponder and consider.

Impediment 2: Obstacles in our Bodies

The "obstacles" are the deficiencies and limitations in our psychology and the physical body which prevent progress on the Path. Patanjali lists 9 obstacles.

> **1:30. The obstacles to soul cognition are bodily disability, mental inertia, wrong questioning, carelessness, laziness, lack of dispassion, erroneous perception, inability to achieve concentration, failure to hold the meditative attitude when achieved.**

As long as we are hindered by the obstacles and perceive life erroneously (as the ego and not the soul), it results in pain, despair and a backlash of remorse, disgust and despondency.

> 1:31. Pain, despair, misplaced bodily activity and wrong direction (or control) of the life currents are the results of the obstacles in the lower psychic nature.

"Misplaced bodily activity" refers to wasted effort, the intense and violent seeking for answers or for solace from our disappointments, when we have no clear plan or idea of how to proceed. This results in turmoil in the etheric web ("wrong direction of the life currents"), problems in vitalisation to the physical, resulting in health problems.

<u>How to overcome the Obstacles.</u>

Patanjali, tells us that the obstacles are overcome by diligently applying one of the following remedies. "To overcome the obstacles and their accompaniments, the intense application of the will to some one truth (or principle) is required." 1:32.

Obstacle	Remedy
1. Bodily disability	Wholesome, sane living. (1:33)
2. Mental inertia	Control of the life force. (1:34)
3. Wrong questioning	One pointed thought. (1:35)
4. Carelessness	Meditation. (1:36)
5. Laziness	Self discipline. (1:37)
6. Lack of dispassion	Correct analysis. (1:38)
7. Erroneous perception	Illumination. (1:39)

But a theoretical understanding of what should be done is useless as long as the intense application of the will is omitted. Only the constant, steady, enduring effort of the will - functioning through the mind, to make the changes permanent in daily life, will bring success.

1. The obstacle of Body disability.

The first obstacle is a weak or sick body - not only for obvious reasons, but because it impedes service work and spiritual growth.

Remedy. Good health must be cultivated through right diet, adequate exercise and by using the body for wholesome purposes. Additionally, the right use of physical energy - such as by being kind, has a most beneficial effect on body health. It positively affects brain vibration, and this in turn removes physical body limitations to the spiritual life.

> 1:33. The peace of the chitta (or mind stuff) can be brought about through the practice of sympathy, tenderness, steadiness of purpose and dispassion to pleasure or pain, towards all forms of good or evil.

Anxiety, fearfulness, anger and other negative emotions all have a detrimental effect on health. If instead, we extend sympathy and tenderness towards those people or creatures in need, this positivity nourishes and benefits health.

We are also asked to be dispassionate towards pleasure and pain and good and evil. What we are essentially being asked is to stop swinging between the opposites and walk the middle path. A poised perspective and moderate lifestyle benefits health.

2. The obstacle of Mental Inertia (a lazy mind).

This obstacle is caused by a lazy mind, which does not want to expend energy on meditation or other spiritual practices. There is insufficient momentum.

> 1:34. The peace of the chitta is also brought about by the regulation of the prana or life breath.

Remedy. Patanjali recommends Pranayama to vitalise the brain and body cells and harmonise chitta. (See Pranayama, Means III). Pranayama practice also includes the science of rhythmic living and we are instructed to organise daily life so that it is simple, rhythmic, efficiently organised with time allotted for a period of spiritual observances and study.

3. The obstacle of Wrong Questioning.

"Wrong Questioning" refers to a mind that is so attached to its authoritative or theological beliefs, to its own conclusions about life, it dismisses and rejects the eternal truths. It asks questions only to validate its point of view. Hence, "wrong questioning."

Remedy. The remedy (sutra 1:35), is to detach from these rigid points of view. It is fortunate that by the time we reach the Path, increased soul illumination encourages us to doubt all thoughts and concepts that are limiting, judgmental and divisive. To assist this work, we are asked to practice detachment, dispassion and discrimination.

- Through *detachment*, the brain consciousness or state of awareness is withdrawn from the things of the senses and from the calls of the lower nature. Detachment imposes a new rhythm or habit reaction upon the cells of the brain so that consciousness remains unaware of lower attractions.
- Through *dispassion*, the emotional nature is rendered immune from the appeal of the senses and lower desire.
- Through *discrimination*, the mind learns to select the good, the beautiful and the true, and to substitute these for wrong concepts.

4. The obstacle of (Mental) Carelessness.

In this obstacle, the mind cannot focus, is light-minded and careless, and flits about. It is a superficial, untrained mind that is unable to think things through to a satisfactory conclusion. It is interesting that Patanjali recommends meditation as the remedy for this problem, - meditation upon spiritual topics such as Light and Radiance.

> 1:36. By meditation upon Light and Radiance - knowledge of the Spirit can be reached and peace achieved.

Remedy. The steady practice of concentration and meditation overcomes this obstacle. Meditation upon light and radiance leads us to that which radiates the light, God-within. Eastern scriptures say that at the centre of the "heart chakra" dwells Brahma, and He reveals Himself in the light. There is a heart centre in the crown chakra which is the higher counterpart found between the shoulder blades. Visioning Brahma seated at the centre of the crown chakra, radiating light, is a powerful meditation.

5. The obstacle of Laziness.

This obstacle concerns slothfulness of the entire lower nature which prevents the person from measuring up to intellectual recognitions and inner aspiration. This because material desires and earthly passions are still more attractive and interesting than the wisdom teachings. The person is too lazy to expend energy on the latter, although the desire to do so is present. Instead, the lower passions are indulged.

> 1:37. The chitta is stabilised and rendered free from illusion as the lower nature is purified and no longer indulged.

This is the major correction given for those in whom the passions dominate the life. It refers to the sacral centre and sexual desire. However, this is not an instruction for celibacy, although those who are in such a position because of life circumstances or because they live only in the higher chakras; will benefit from the instruction. For the masses, a healthy sex-life in a monogamous relationship is recommended.

Remedy. The remedy is detachment - from the desire-thoughts as they arise. They must be negated. Instead, energy should be channelled into higher creative interests. Keeping thoughts clean is the key. Energy follows thought and whatever we think, we desire and pursue. Instead, apply the technique of thinking an opposite thought.

As the organs of perception and sense contacts are continually negated, as we no longer identify with them, we free ourselves from passion (which transmutes into spiritual aspiration). When successful, we stand free from the lower sense nature. This results in a corresponding mental stability and an ability to concentrate because mind stuff is no longer subject to the modifications produced by the senses - either good or bad.

6. The obstacle Passion, or a lack of Dispassion.

This obstacle and the previous one are closely linked. Passion or desire are problems of the emotional body and of the lower chakras and of the throat chakra. We are driven by our desires through most of our history and detaching from lower passion, developing dispassion, is the most challenging task we face on the Path.

When true dispassion is developed, we can see situations as they are and not be influenced by any of our prejudices or beliefs of the people involved or the subject in question. If we are painfully affected by a revelation, it indicates a basic lack of dispassion and that we are still attached to the personality and to the opinions of others. Our goal is to strive for spiritual indifference, founded on spiritual detachment and dispassion.

Remedy. This is to purify the lower nature and no longer indulge its "wants." All the information in this book so far will assist the student in this work. Pratyahara (Means 5) - particularly thinking an opposite thought, is the basic practice.

> 1:38. Peace (steadiness of the chitta), can be reached through meditation on the knowledge which dreams give.

There are two ways to interpret "dreams." First, *dreaming* can refer to physical plane life that is chaotic and there is no clear plan for the life and no time for spiritual practices. Living life this way, disconnected from the true purpose of the soul which is to achieve enlightenment, is to *dream* the life away. But when we study what we are doing in life ("meditate on the knowledge which dreams give"), when we learn from our mistakes and make necessary changes that bring us back into line with soul-purpose, inner peace is achieved.

Second, to *dream* can refer to the use of the imagination - a powerful, manifesting faculty. To *dream* is to imagine. In a non-spiritual life, the imagination faculty is used to pursue lower desires. But when it is used deliberately to achieve spiritually, not only is inner peace achieved, but rapid gains can be made. The true use of the imagination necessitates a high degree of control and mental power and when present, the Adept can put the entire lower man to sleep and pass into Samadhi.

7. The obstacle of Erroneous Perception.

Perception will remain erroneous as long as we believe we are mortal bodies and not divine souls. Once we correct this misperception and hold the thought in our hearts that we are divine, peace will be found.

> 1:39. Peace can also be reached through concentration upon that which is dearest to the heart.

Energy follows thought and when the soul is central in the life and is enshrined in the heart, perception will be correct because the soul will be the perceiver. But ordinarily, when we focus attention on people or activities that are special to us in an unconditional, heart sense, it brings a deep sense of fulfillment, soul satisfaction and inner peace.

When the Obstacles are Removed.

As we understand ourselves more completely, so are we better able to understand and identify with others - with man and nature. The perfected seer, by consciously embracing "the entire field of knowledge", is one with all.

> 1:40. His realisation extends from the infinitely small to the infinitely great, and from annu (the atom or speck) to atma (or spirit) his knowledge is perfected.

> 1:41. To him whose vrittis (modifications of the substance of the mind) are entirely controlled there eventuates a state of identity with, and similarity to, that which is realised. The knower, knowledge and the field of knowledge become one, just as the crystal takes to itself the colours of that which is reflected in it.

The yogi sees that though forms are diverse and many, all souls are identical, and are one with the Oversoul. Complete knowledge of just one soul, puts one en rapport with the One Soul, of which all little souls are a part.

BOOK 2 - THE STEPS TO UNION.

> Love melts. Love heals. Love unites. Love forgives. A Divine Union that goes beyond time and space, that's what I'm looking for —
> Nityananda Das.

Book 2 contains the final two impediments to union - the Hindrances and the Gunas, and it starts the practical part of the work - the eight "means of Yoga." These are the eight kinds of activity which will bring about the needed results. The first sutra in Book 2, is a summary of the past and present yogas.

2:1. The Yoga of action, leading to union with the soul is fiery aspiration, spiritual reading and devotion to Ishvara.

a. *Karma Yoga*, the Yoga of action, was the development exercise of the Lemurian Race. It awakened the four centres below the diaphragm and coordinated the physical body. It did its work. *Fiery aspiration* refers to the soul's domination of the physical man so that every atom of the body is afire with zeal and endeavour.

> "We seek the fire of the spark that is already within us."
> — Kamand Kojouri.

b. Next came *Bhakti Yoga*, which opened the heart and throat chakras in the Atlantean Race. Consequently, the emotional body developed and lower mind was awakened. The emotional body of the mystic (and occultists are mystics functioning on the mental plane), is *Devoted to Ishvara* - has a heart that pours out love to God and to all living things.

c. We are currently in the Aryan Race stage of development in the human kingdom and *Raja Yoga* is the science that brings the mind under the control of the soul. It synthesises all the forces of the body in the head and from there distributes and controls them.

d. *Spiritual reading* refers to the mind's ability to see the subject or truth that lies behind the object. It is the first step to Raja Yoga, overcoming the appearances of the material life and seeing to the soul beneath.

The work of these three Yogas eliminates the obstructions so that the soul can be contacted and visioned.

2:2. The aim of these three (fiery aspiration, spiritual reading and devotion to Ishvara) is to bring about soul vision and to eliminate obstructions.

> Opened are the gates of immortality,
> you that have ears to hear, release your faith.
> Do not accept any of my words on faith,
> Believing them just because I said them.
> Be like an analyst buying gold, who cuts, burns,
> And critically examines his product for authenticity.
> Only accept what passes the test
> By proving useful and beneficial in your life.
> — Gautama Buddha.

Impediment 3: The Five Hindrances/ Perceptions of Life

In this important section we examine the Hindrances, wrong attitudes and wrong ways we perceive the world that delay our spiritual progress.

The Hindrances are five wrong ways of thinking, patterns of perceiving ourselves and the world, which have developed across time. Entrenched in the nature, rooted in the unconscious, when triggered, they shape our present and future life circumstances. The Sanskrit word for this root-seed is *samskara*. It equates to the psychological "negative core belief". Whenever a *samskara* is triggered and we succumb to its influence, it predetermines how we think, feel and act. This strengthens the power of the *samskara* and subjects us to the Law of Karma. For aeons these wrong perceptions prevent us from realizing that we are sons of God. They cause us to identify with the lower and material. They can be brought over from a previous life, sown in this life, or belong to the family or race we are born into.

> 2:3. These are the difficulty producing hindrances: avidya (ignorance) the sense of personality, desire, hate and the sense of attachment.

Hindrance 1: Ignorance.

Ignorance is the "mother-breeder" of all the hindrances.

> 2:4. Ignorance is the cause of all the other obstructions whether they be latent, in process of elimination, overcome, or in full operation.

Ignorance is the result of an unawakened consciousness - which is normal and natural in undeveloped young souls. Evil and selfishness exist because of ignorance. The human soul, ignorant of its pure and blissful true nature believes it is impure, painful and suffers because of this. Ignorance is the root cause of suffering.

Remedial work. For most, ignorance is overcome by the evolutionary process. There are higher forms of ignorance (such as of the wisdom teachings) and aspirants and disciples overcome them through esoteric study and meditation.

Hindrance 2: Egoism - the sense of being a Personality.

The mind has three basic uses: to gather information about the external world, to transmit ideas from the soul to the brain, and to be an organ of vision for the soul. But as long as we identify with the mind and what it thinks, we retain our non-spiritual identification.

> 2:6. The sense of personality is due to the identification of the knower with the instruments of knowledge.

We find self-definition in "labels". ""I am a mother," "I am a businessman," "I am fragile and easily hurt," "I am an aristocrat." We devote all our resources to feeding and defending this identity. As long as we believe in our social identity and in the permanency and solidity of our interpersonal relationships, we will fear the loss of this self.

Remedial exercise. To overcome the sense of egoism, being a personality, we must train the mind to perceive differently. Here is a mantram which will help. Use it regularly.

> There is only one Source of Life and Light.
> All living things emanate from this Life, like sun-rays emanating from the Sun.
> I am One with that Light which is in all - That self of Light, I am.
> I am one with the Self in All - that Self, I am!

Hindrance 3: Desire - for objects of pleasure.

2:7. Desire is attachment to objects of pleasure.

Desire is a generic term covering the outgoing tendency of spirit towards form life. Life is all attachment in some degree or another. This hindrance concerns our desire for objects of pleasure - a desire that keeps us swinging between the opposites of pleasure and pain. A very important task is to gradually let go of the sense of: "I have to have that (object) to be happy." This does not mean giving away treasured items or relationships, or that we should not enjoy having them around us. The correct attitude is to enjoy them in the moment, but to realise that all things are impermanent and all objects will go at some point and to be content with that. This helps to let go of any sense of covetousness.

Detachment remedial exercise. Think of something you own, and which you really value. This may be a house, a car, a book, a computer etc. Then think of giving this away to others. Visualise yourself doing so. Then think: "I can survive the loss of that if I have to. I am an immortal soul." By aspiring to detach and by visualising that we are doing so, we can begin to train the fearful mind to let go. Expand this to include giving away food, shelter, clothing, money to the world's millions, the loss of a loved one, etc.

Hindrance 4: Hate.

2:8. Hate or aversion is that which dwells on pain.

The true yogi neither feels aversion or desire. He is balanced between these pairs of opposites. Hate is the feeling of repulsion and leads to a withdrawal from the hated object. Hate is the reverse of brotherhood. It negates unity, and causes barriers to be built which separate us from others and from life. Hate in some degree, aversion to some extent, is present in every human heart. Only when hate is entirely overcome by love or the sense of unity will death, danger and fear pass out of the consciousness of the human family.

Remedial exercise. Ponder the thought that God is unconditional love and you are a child of God. If you have been wronged and wounded, it is unnatural to your true nature that you should feel hate. It is damaging to your spiritual growth.

> Visualise yourself stepping into the heart of God and feel your heart being healed. Forgive the soul of the person who hurt you, for the frailties of the personality. This does not mean forgiving the bad action. Align with your soul, visualise that one you dislike, and affirm: "I ask a blessing Holy Child of God, that I may see you through the eyes of Christ." Endeavour to look at that soul, act "as if" you were looking through the understanding eyes of Christ. Repeat this mantram as required.

This affirmation helps to free ourselves from unhealthy psychic links to people we hate or resent.

Hindrance 5: Attachment - desire for sentient existence.

Desire stems from the fact that our solar Logos is in incarnation. The great opposites of Spirit and Matter, Father and Mother - having been divided, are now desirous for unity. This affects all of us. The intense desire for sentient existence, to survive, is the most powerful primeval desire in the body.

> 2:9. Intense Desire for sentient existence, for form life, is attachment. This is inherent in every form, is self-perpetuating, and known even to the very wise.

As long as this is so, desire remains - though it is more limiting in those who are still ignorant of the higher mysteries, than in those who have developed wisdom.

Remedial work. Hold the thought that you are a spiritual Divine ray, here on earth for learning and service, but that this is not your true home. Imagine what your destiny would be if you stayed stuck in that body forever, while every other soul moved on (as they will). See yourself letting go, as a free spirit returning to your spiritual Father/ home. Use the mantram given for Hindrance 2 - "There is only one Source of Life and Light, etc."

<u>Major remedy to overcome the Hindrances</u> - "Think an Opposite Thought."

2:10-11. These five hindrances, can be overcome by an opposing mental attitude. Their activities are to be done away with, through the meditation process.

1. Identify the negative thought.
2. Find an opposing and unifying thought.
3. Continuously offset the energy of the old thought by using the new one. Take time to 'feel' the new effects in your astral field. Feel good about it.

It is the fire of mind - concentrated mind power, that destroys the five wrong perceptions of life, the Hindrances. Just as a burnt and dried up seed is no longer capable of propagation and becomes infertile, so the seeds of the obstructions to the life of the Spirit are similarly rendered infertile by the blow torch of the focused mind. And a mind such as this, directed as it is by the soul, is acquired through the ongoing practise of occult meditation.

Eliminating the Hindrances is a dual process. The technique of holding an opposing thought is vital. But it must also be accompanied by a concerted effort to stop the physical body from acting out the hindrance.

Much that we do is automatic and the result of patterns embedded in the emotional brain. But every time we indulge a negative core belief (that is rooted in one of the hindrances), allow it to take over our minds and emotions and act this out on the physical plane; the pattern is strengthened. These external 'acting-outs' must also be suppressed. The two techniques should be applied simultaneously.

The Triangle Technique.

Use the technique when you are in turmoil. Remember you are dealing with energy.

1. Visualise yourself standing in the bottom middle point of a triangle. On one side is a violated expectation and the hurt and pain that generated - on the other side, what you would have liked to occur.
2. Ask yourself "As a soul, what can I learn from this situation?"
3. Then appreciate what each opposite can contribute to your growth and wisdom. What you have learnt from the pain and disappointment.
4. Then affirm: "It is, what it is" or "What happened has happened. I accept what life has brought me."
5. Lift up to your soul, to the apex of the triangle, and sound a word or mantram to help stabilise the higher perspective. For example: Serenity, Wisdom, Beauty, etc.

1. The Hindrances are the causes of Karmic Retribution.

2:12. Karma is rooted in the 5 hindrances and fruits in the current or a later life.

Whenever we succumb to a wrong way of thinking, it subjects us to the Law of Karma, which demands that we harmonise the negative currents we have created in Universal Mind.

> Karma is the popular name for the Law of Cause and Effect. It is simply the working out of the universal Law of Rhythm, which governs the cycles and seasons of all life. If this harmony is disturbed, nature will try to restore balance, bringing consequences of a similar nature to the original action. A good action brings good karma, an evil action brings evil karma.

Karma can be personal, racial, national and global, affecting millions of people. The warlike aggression of man, collective emotional and mental turmoil, hatred and greed; these affect nature. Natural disasters such as earthquakes, tidal waves and hurricanes, which devastate affected communities, this is karma at work in a neutral and global sense.

An example of wholesale retributive karma occurred at the close of World War II. When Berlin burned, it was the direct result of the many horrors caused by Nazis misusing the element of fire - harming with weapons and bombs and burning people in concentration camps.

Amongst the casualties of an inferno such as this, or as a result of a natural disaster, will be people innocent of the karmic backlash. But all souls in a country, even the innocent, "own" the karma created by the majority. The teachings tell us that those who are innocent are recompensed in the future (which may be a future life), with good karma. Under the Law of Karma, the "books are balanced" in the long term.

2. However, Karma caused by the Hindrances can be warded off.

2:16. Pain which is yet to come may be warded off.

When we are unmindful and act contrary to the teachings, the karma we experience is negative. Most of the acts we have committed to create such karma, is in the past. It brings pain, sorrow and misery to be worked out in the present.

One of the very important things that Patanjali points out is that it is possible to prevent any further pain-producing causes to be set in motion, by being mindful in the present. As consciousness expands and the senses are gradually brought under control, in the lighted intelligence and wisdom of the soul we develop the insight and power to make wiser, selfless decisions. This leads to right-action in the world, attracting good karma.

> I am the owner of my actions, heir to my actions,
> born of my actions, related through my actions,
> and have my actions as my arbitrator.
> Whatever I do, for good or for evil,
> to that I will fall heir.
> - Gautama Buddha.

> All that we are is the result of
> what we have thought;
> what we think we become.
> - Gautama Buddha.

Impediment 4: The Three Gunas.

In this section we examine the nature of substance and its binding effects. It is a vital section because in the Eastern teachings we are told repeatedly that our erroneous identification with our bodies - with the thoughts our minds create, with our emotions and with the physical body; this is the cause of our pain. Further, this misperception keeps our souls bound to matter. In this first quote, the Sanskrit word for substance - "prakriti" is used. It introduces the topic of the gunas.

> According to the Sankhya philosophy, prakriti is considered to possess three basic qualities, namely sattva (substantial reality), rajas (inherent activity), and tamas (inertia), popularly rendered goodness, passion, and darkness; or virtue, foulness, and ignorance. Theosophical Glossary.

Here are definitions for prakriti and the gunas.
- *Prakriti.* It is defined as "original or universal substance" from which all forms - visible and invisible arise. Prakriti has three qualities or gunas - sattva, rajas and tamas.
- *Gunas.* The word guna literally means "strand" or "fibre" and implies that, like strands of a rope, the gunas are woven together to form the objective universe. The gunas are the three qualities of matter, the three effects produced when the life of God energizes substance.

Most human souls are controlled by the activities of the gunas – the density of tamas and the wild activities of rajas. The goal is to be consciously free from their control, by purifying the bodies so that sattva material dominates.

> Even then, sattva is merely a harmonious combination of the existing rajas and tamas and is not anything apart from them.

Different teachers give varying attributes for the gunas. But the basic attributes are "inertia" for tamas, "mobility and action" for rajas, and "harmony" for sattva. Here is a chart which includes these qualities and which also relates each of the gunas to one of the aspects of the Trinity.[1]

1. Sattva	2. Rajas	3. Tamas
Energy of Spirit	Energy of Soul	Energy of Matter
Monad	Soul	Personality
Father	Son	Holy Ghost
harmonious vibration	mobility or activity	inertia

2:18. That which is perceived has 3 qualities, sattva, rajas and tamas (rhythm, mobility and inertia); it consists of the elements and the sense organs.

This sutra draws our attention to the fact that our sense organs (including the mind), which enable us to be conscious, these are inherent in the gunas. At first the undeveloped gunas/ the undeveloped senses, they imprison the soul. They allow him to recognise that he exists, but not who he essentially is. All memory of, and identification with Spirit, is blocked off.

---
[1] Bailey, Alice. Light of the Soul, 32.

Through incarnation after incarnation - under the impact of spiritual force, the gunas (the senses, brain, nervous system and the mind) develop. They take the soul through all life experiences and levels of identification, until finally - when they have been fully developed and refined, they stage the soul's liberation. The seed-soul inherently contains all the qualities of its spiritual source - the Monad. Through the evolution of the gunas and of consciousness, the soul eventually realises this.

Sutra 18 concludes with:

... The use of these (the gunas) produces experience and eventual liberation.

The soul's identification with the body is the cause of our pain, our anxiety and craving after happiness. The way we perceive the world and the negative attitudes that arise when we do not like what we see (the pain, sorrow, anger and rage), these are not attributes of the soul but arise from the tamas and rajas guna. For a long period form is a prison because consciousness identifies with the activities of the rajas and tamas gunas.

2:15. It is the gunas (qualities of substance), which create consequences, anxiety over the anticipated loss of happiness, or fresh craving for future happiness.

The Raja Yoga goal is to detach ourselves from the kingdom of the senses (from the gunas) and stand apart as the divine perceiver and actor. Then we can use the gunas, the forms, as we desire to gain certain ends and not be deluded by them in the process.

1. Tamas – inertia, density.

When the atoms of the body are predominately tamas (more inert and denser as they are in all young souls); consciousness cannot pierce through this density to any great extent in dealing with the world. The body is too heavy for the soul, causing lethargy, darkness, apathy, delusion, drowsiness and a dull and inert mind. At this level, the soul identifies completely with its physical body and the material world that it perceives. Tamas induces a love of ease and pleasure, indolence, procrastination, a desire to let things be, to rest, and to take no thought of the morrow.

The heavy, gross tamasic form needs many violent contacts to stir up the atoms in the body and over time, across lives, they become more active (rajas). Due to these violent impacts and the life consequences they cause, the five sense organs become more sophisticated and consciousness - man on the physical plane; becomes more alert and aware to what is going on around him.

2. Rajas - activity, mobility.

Rajasic activity is full of fire and emotion - passion, desire and ambition. People whose vehicles are dominated by rajas are full of ambition, greed, lust, and have a strong desire to use power for personal gain. This drives them out to compete for spoils on the stage of life. As a result of the wide variety of life-experiences which rajas' people have, the sixth sense - the mind, develops along with a more sophisticated brain and nervous system.

The frenetic activity and mobility going on in the world, the constant change, rank ambition, greed and aggressiveness - from this we can see the rajas guna is vying for equal footing with tamas. Hypothetically, the world is reaching the point where there are as many souls working through tamas-predominant bodies as there are in rajas-dominant bodies. This balance allows souls who have sattva-dominated bodies to come to the fore and this is to be welcomed, although in the short term it leads to more aggression in the world.

3. Sattva – harmony.

The sattva guna harmonises and unites. In the Bible, we are instructed to live in harmony with each other.

> Live in harmony with one another. Do not be haughty, but associate with the lowly. Never be wise in your own sight. Repay no one evil for evil, but give thought to do what is honourable in the sight of all. If possible, so far as it depends on you, live peaceably with all. Bible, Romans 12:16-18

Sattvic substance is light and luminous and balances tamas and rajas.

> Rajas is activity and Tamas inertia. Sattva is the balance of these two, for only consciousness can balance kinetic (rajas) energy with potential energy (tamas). Robert E. Svoboda.

Those on the Path should strive to harmonise their lives and one area of life to concentrate on is the meditation period. Endeavour to make it Sattvic. As Swami Sivananda said:

> For purposes of meditation, everything must be rendered Sattvic. The place of meditation must be Sattvic. The food must be Sattvic. The wearing apparel must be Sattvic. The company must be Sattvic. Talking must be Sattvic. The sound that you hear must be Sattvic. Thinking must be Sattvic. Study must be Sattvic. Everything must be Sattvic.

When it is dominant, Sattva permits the light of Buddhi – the love and wisdom of a Christed consciousness to shine through the lower nature. This allows for clarity of mind, lightness of being, perception of wisdom and acquisition of knowledge. Light represents wisdom.

> Jesus said, "I am the light of the world. Whoever follows me will never walk in darkness, but will have the light of life." Bible, John 8:12.

Bodies composed predominantly of sattva enable the yogi to identify with his spiritual nature and to be in harmony with all around him. His manifestation is rhythmic and in tune with the greater whole. He looks on at the spectacle of life and because the forms through which he is active in the world are lighted and harmonised, all his activities are in harmony with the great plan. Such people are spiritual leaders, teachers, and healers of the race. Eventually, our spiritual task is to free ourselves completely from the gunas.

> Our important duty on earth is to increase sattva and to control the senses and the mind. Other duties are secondary. When there is increase of sattva, there is brightness and brilliance in the face, lightness in the body, joy, purity, strength, peace and illumination. Swami Sivananda.

Detachment from the Gunas.

Non-attachment to the gunas is what we are striving for and Patanjali addresses this in Book I, sutra 16, when expanding upon the benefits of non-attachment.

> 1:16. The consummation of this non-attachment results in an exact knowledge of the spiritual man [the Monad] when liberated from the qualities or gunas.

Monadic awareness occurs when the spiritual man applies the art of detachment and has finally freed himself from manifested substance, from the three gunas. We are told that Gautama Buddha and the Christ have reached this union in consciousness. This is the level that Raja Yoga urges us to strive for.

1. The 4 Divisions of the Gunas.

The Specific, the Unspecific, the Indicated and the Untouchable.

We have previously analysed the three qualities of substance, of the gunas - tamas, rajas and sattva. Now we look at the four divisions of the gunas, and the bodies of consciousness they build on the 5 planes of human endeavour - the atmic, buddhic, mental, emotional and physical planes.

2-19. The divisions of the gunas are fourfold; the specific, the non-specific, the indicated and the untouchable.

The 4 Divisions of the Gunas

Logoic plane	Logoic Consciousness	
Monadic plane	Monad	The Monad is bound to the gunas "like an animal" during objective manifestation, yet is entirely free from them.
Atmic plane	Spiritual will	UNTOUCHABLE GUNAS (Tamas-Rajas-Sattva). the great Existence who is the sum total of all these.
Buddhic plane	Spiritual love	THE INDICATED GUNAS (Tamas-Rajas-Sattva). Primary substance...the tattvas, atomic matter
Mental plane (higher)	Spiritual Mind SOUL	NON-SPECIFIC GUNAS (Tamas-Rajas-Sattva). The senses, force reactions, the tanmatras
(lower)	Concrete mind	SPECIFIC GUNAS (Tamas-Rajas-Sattva). They give access to the external world
Astral plane	Emotions	5 senses - ears, skin, eyes, tongue, nostrils. 5 organs of action - voice, hands, feet, excretory, generation.
Physical plane	Physical	The Mind, the 6th sense.

Each plane has its own arrangements of the gunas. The substance of the atmic plane is the finest. It has more sattva and less rajas and tamas. The physical plane is the densest plane and has more tamas and less rajas and sattva. The intermediary planes have combinations of the these three, with rajas dominating in the astral world and lower mental.

1. Gunas that give us access to the external world (the Specific).

This dense group of gunas form the apparatus and organs which enable basic expression with the external world. They consist of the:

Five sense organs - the ears, skin, eyes, tongue, nostrils.
Five organs of action - voice, hands, feet, excretory and generation.
The Mind which is the 6th sense.

People functioning at this basic level are not self-conscious identities. They are totally focused on the external and objective life. Survival is foremost.

2. Gunas that give us self-awareness (the Non-specific).

Buddhi, the love and wisdom aspect of God, the Spiritual Soul, it directs the gunas to build the apparatus it needs (in the specific and non-specific groups), so it can express itself through the personality.

In Hindu books this group of gunas are called tanmatras. They are very subtle structures of matter, and are the non-physical aspects of the sense organs and that which is sensed. Vivekananda likens them to streams of light. They provide the apparatus necessary to allow a man to recognise "himself", that he is an "I", that he is a separated unit of consciousness, a personality. Then later, to recognise that he is a soul, a spirit and God.

3. Gunas that give us Buddhic Consciousness (the Indicated).

In consciousness, once intelligent discrimination has been developed and applied, the atoms of intuition start to awaken. This triggers the "Indicated" gunas to build the Buddhic vehicle. It permits the emergence of Buddhic consciousness, synthetic reasoning. Buddhi is defined as:

> Buddhi, or pure reason, the intellect apart from the lower mind, sometimes called the intuition, whose nature is love-wisdom, this is the Christ-life or principle, which in the process of taking incarnation or form, as we know it, manifests forth as the specific and the unspecific. [1]

A person functioning at this level is still strongly aware of form life and the identity of objects, but these are seen as parts of an indivisible whole. This stage of growth is far in the future for most people, so for aeons its presence is only 'indicated' or hinted at.

4. Gunas that build the body of Brahma, Universal Consciousness (the Untouchable).

This fourth division of the gunas, permits complete expression of the untouchable or unknown God in manifestation - Brahma (Universal Spirit - Atma [2]), the third aspect of the Divine Trinity. This is Universal Mind (Manas), the intelligent thinking process of the Logos, the great form of existence in which all our bodies are a part.

The yogi who has attained this immortal level, is no longer bound to the constant activity engendered by the gunas, now he beholds the process as a whole. Rather than being subject to the transformations of the world, he is the Perceiver (Purusha), utterly unaffected by the passing show of phenomenal Nature (prakriti). This is complete emancipation, and supreme peace (nirvana).

2. Pure Perception results when the Gunas are transcended

This important sutra describes how the liberated spiritual man interacts with the world. We may not be at this level yet, but we can act "as if" we were, which will help develop the higher perspective.

2:20. The seer is pure knowledge (gnosis). Though pure, he looks upon the presented idea through the medium of the mind.

There are three factors in this sutra:
1. The Seer: who looks on and considers (from his divine standpoint) the world of effects.
2. The mind: used by the seer as his medium of search and interpretation.
3. The presented idea. Every form in life is a "presented-idea," an embodied thought of some kind. The seer perceives first the forms in the 3 worlds, then that which caused them, the type of force which brought them into being, later the idea which they embody.

---
1 Bailey, Alice. Light of the Soul, 159.
2 Bailey, Alice. The Soul and its Mechanism, 109.

The experience of being a Seer and seen, only begins when a degree of non-attachment is achieved. As this process continues, gradually we pass out of the realm of objectivity, out of the mental, emotional and physical worlds into the realm of the true soul, the subjective cause of manifestation. When this process is complete, the conscious Seer is aligned with Purusha (Cosmic Self, Cosmic Consciousness, the Universal Principle). This perspective is held while simultaneously looking into the phenomenal world. Everything the Seer sees is viewed as an idea being presented to him to take up or discard as he wills.

---

§ This sutra is powerful and if stated as an affirmation and used constantly, it will help readers rapidly achieve this elevated life-perspective. The man or woman who has attained this level has realised the injunction, to "Be in the world, but not of the world."

---

3. Discrimination, Dispassion, Detachment free us from the Gunas.

Discrimination is the important way of looking at life, the attitude of mind that must be cultivated, if liberation from the three human worlds is to be achieved. Patanjali raises the topic again in sutra 26.

2:26. The state of bondage (to the gunas) is overcome through perfectly maintained discrimination.

Discrimination is based on a realisation of the spirit-matter duality and that we have to learn to discriminate between them, between the unreal and real, and the higher Self and not-self.

The average person spends his whole life swinging back and forth between the opposites. But it is only when we step onto the Path of conscious spiritual development, that the conflict really makes its presence felt. We wish to change, to overcome old hungers and appetites, to rise above the pain which this oscillation causes. But without proper esoteric training we find we cannot, no matter how hard we try.

> Conflict rages between two forces, and the student cannot move on until he finishes the battle and stands detached from emotional complications, instead of losing his ship's helm and floundering upon the stormy sea. [1]

The basis of Gautama's teachings are based on these three actions and that when applied, they enable us to find our pathway home, to find where the opposite forces meet and counterbalance each other at the central, balanced, still point. This is the razor-edged path, the narrow line between the pairs which we must find and tread, turning neither to the right nor to the left but move straight ahead. The instrument we use to gain release from the lower worlds is the discriminating mind. It enables us to ignore what is happening outside of the immediate moment, and to make decisions and choices based on truth, on reality and for the greater good. When discrimination begins to develop in earnest, then the great process of liberation is progressing well.

- Through *Discrimination*: the mind learns to select the good, the beautiful and the true,
- Through *Dispassion*: the emotional nature becomes immune from the appeal of the senses/ desire.
- Through *Detachment:* awareness is withdrawn from the senses and calls of the lower nature.

---
1 Saraydarian, Torkom. The Science of Becoming Oneself, 28.

To help develop Discrimination.

1. Study your motives, analyse why you do what you do. Make this an intellectual exercise, avoid descending into the emotions or trying to justify your actions. Look for facts.
2. Continually scan yourself and others, and look for those differences when:
    There is more soul in a person, or when there is more ego.
    If you at any time may be expressing more soul, or ego.
    Whether an outcome is better for just you, or for all concerned.
    In organisations - if there is more soul because a concern for good is
    being demonstrated, or there is more self-serving, predatory behaviour.
3. From this point on, try to assume the attitude of the Soul, continually discriminating between the form and the life, between soul and body, between right action and wrong action, between higher and lower values. Cultivate the real and negate the unreal in all your relationships and affairs.

The practice of the three D's will gradually lead us into an entirely new dimension and result in an identification with higher consciousness. This distinction will at first be theoretical, then intellectual, but later it will assume more reality and deeply affect the life.

4. Freedom from the Seven Desires.

When discrimination is developed and dispassion and detachment is being applied, they are used to satisfy and quieten seven cravings which arise from the desire nature.

   2:27. The knowledge (or illumination) achieved is 7-fold, and is attained progressively.

1. Desire for knowledge: this dies down when one is sure the Truth has been found, resulting in mind satisfaction.
2. Desire for freedom: this quietens when correct spiritual disciplines for release are found, and successfully followed.
3. Desire to do one's duty: the need to serve the personality life is transformed into serving the greater good, and this becomes a natural impulse.
4. Sorrow: this ends when longing for liberation is so great, all pain ends.
5. Fears (of the mind, based upon memory): freedom from the chitta is only overcome by the Soul itself, by becoming soul conscious.
6. Doubt: this quietens as one learns to go beyond mind for the Truth.
7. Desire for happiness: this quietens when we realise we have always been blessed, omnipresent, pure, perfect, and require nothing else to be happy, for we are happiness itself.

All the developments covered so far, enable us to gradually free ourselves from desire on all levels.

This ends this introductory section to Raja Yoga and the four impediments to union. Now we go through the 8 steps that will lead us to spiritual freedom.

THE EIGHT MEANS TO YOGA

> Yoga does not just change the way we see things, it transforms the person who sees. B.K.S Iyengar

At some time or other - depending upon our level of spiritual advancement, we all have to undergo Raja Yoga mental training. There is no choice. All must return to the sacred Source of Life and this is achieved through mind control. The masses do not feel the urge to aspire spiritually because they are not yet receiving adequate spiritual inspiration. Only when the cup of pleasure and pain is tasted and a life lived entirely for the lower self is found unsatisfying, is the inner attraction strong enough. Then the inspired man or woman turns towards higher things and begins to practice Yoga.

All the previous instructions on the impediments and how to clear them, and the spiritual disciplines to be applied, all these need to implemented into the life somewhat, before the serious one-pointed work of Raja Yoga transformation can be undertaken.

Then, if we practice the 8 Means of Raja Yoga diligently and apply then to our thought, words and actions; the substance in our bodies will purify and become filled with lighted sattva atoms. Consciousness will automatically merge with the light, love and wisdom which is the true nature of the soul, enabling us to achieve full enlightenment.

> Yoga is a light, which once lit will never dim. The better your practice, the brighter your flame. B.K.S Iyengar.

2:29. The eight means of yoga are: the Commandments or Yama, the Rules or Nijama, posture or Asana, right control of life-force or Pranayama, abstraction or Pratyahara, attention or Dharana, meditation or Dhyana, and contemplation or Samadhi.

1. The Commandments or Yama
2. The Rules or Nijama
3. Posture or Asana,
4. Right control of life-force or Pranayama
5. Abstraction or Pratyahara
6. Concentration or Dharana
7. Meditation or Dhyana
8. Contemplation or Samadhi.

Sutra 28 reminds us of the goal and reward which lies ahead for those who diligently attend to these instructions - enlightenment.

2:28. When the means to Yoga have been steadily practised and when impurity has been overcome, enlightenment takes place leading up to full illumination.

> To enjoy good health, to bring true happiness to one's family, to bring peace to all, one must first discipline and control one's own mind. If a man can control his mind he can find the way to Enlightenment, and all wisdom and virtue will naturally come to him. Gautama Buddha

MEANS I YAMA: "THE COMMANDMENTS."

There are five wrong ways that most people use to engage with the world. In Means I, we are commanded to change them. These five "sins" are:

- Harmfulness
- Falsehood.
- Theft.
- Incontinence (misuse of the sex function).
- Avarice.

There are no circumstances or justifications in life that permit us to use them. If we violate these spiritual commands, it will call down upon us painful karmic consequences. This is clearly laid out for us in sutra 34.

2:34. Thoughts contrary to yoga, whether committed personally, caused to be committed or approved of, whether arising from avarice, anger or delusion (ignorance); whether slight in the doing, middling or great. These result always in excessive pain and ignorance.

Then we are told how to make the change. For each wrong way of thinking, we must think a contrary and higher thought. When applied rigorously, the energy of the higher thought will counter-balance and over-write the old energy pattern expression.

2:33. When thoughts which are contrary to yoga are present there should be the cultivation of their opposite.

It is much like over-writing an existing file in our computer. However, these wrong patterns of expression have rooted themselves deeply into the unconscious aspect of the mind and are not so easily eliminated. They will keep surfacing again and again if we are not vigilant.

Then Patanjali lists the 5 commandments that will counter-balance these wrong ways of thinking and their associated actions.

2:30. Harmlessness, truth to all beings, abstention from theft, from incontinence and from avarice, constitute yama or the five commandments.

- **Harmlessness** instead of harmfulness,
- **Truth** instead of falsehood,
- **Abstention from theft** instead of stealing,
- **Self-control** instead of incontinence,
- **Contentment** instead of avarice or covetousness.

We are commanded to develop and express these virtues. They are the basis of good and decent character. There is no ambivalence or choice. They must be cultivated irrespective of circumstances. There are no situations that could arise in life where the Commandments do not apply. It is our universal duty to follow them irrespective of race, place, time or emergency. They are Yoga's equivalent to the Bible's Ten Commandments.

These commandments are broken all the time by the average person and it attracts karma. But when we are at the point that we can actually realise these ideals, then karma is more strictly applied to any violation.

▲ Commandment 1: be Harmless, not Harmful.

This sutra demonstrates the working out of a great law, "Whatever you see in yourself, you will see in others." If opposition and hatred is being experienced from others for example, it is because these seeds are present in our nature. If one is not the recipient of this antagonism, these traits are not present in the nature.[1]

> Becoming harmless is an aspect of universal love and its cultivation is essential in order to be at-one with all beings.

Harmfulness is based on selfishness, and on an egocentric attitude. Such people try to enforce, self-aggrandise and self-gratify. They speak words which damage, think thoughts which are poisonous and spew these onto others in ways that result in harm. Our thoughts, speech and actions need to be continually monitored to ensure we are observing this rule. The most common way we commit daily violence is by being critical of ourselves. If we stop this inner criticism and learn to be kinder to ourselves, we will be naturally kinder to others and reap the karmic rewards of that.

Remedial Spiritual Practice 1: Ahisma/ Harmlessness.

Ahisma is nonviolence, non-killing, non-harm. It is the practice of loving kindness and compassion. Harmlessness is the outstanding quality of the advanced soul. A harmlessness that speaks no word that can damage another person, that thinks no thought which could poison or produce misunderstanding, and which does no act to hurt even the smallest of God's creatures. Harmlessness is the main and outstanding virtue that will enable us to tread with safety the difficult path of spiritual development.

> § Harmlessness is the expression of the life of the man who lives consciously as a soul, whose nature is love and whose method is inclusiveness.

Harmlessness brings about prudence, right speech, ability to refrain from impulsive action, and the demonstration of a non-critical spirit. When this level is reached, free passage is given to the forces of true love, and to spiritual energies which vitalize the personality, leading to right action.

- Try to be more patient and understanding. Listen more. Develop a sensitive awareness of the wholeness of life and rein in any impulse to react and criticise. Consider the underlying cause that is behind the negative things people do; rather than judge the action. Be kinder and more generous to yourself.
- Do an evening review on harmlessness. Identify any harmful thought you may have created during the day, then think a kindly opposite thought, to neutralise the negative energy force you created. Identify any harmful emotions you generated, then send out love or compassion instead. Identify any harmful action, then how you can act more kindly and wisely, in the future.

Remedial Spiritual Practice 2: Silence.

Our thoughts and speech become more potent as we evolve, and as a result, our capacity to harm others through wrong thinking and wrong speech is greater. So is our capacity to heal and help people through right thinking and right speech. Cultivating silence trains us to right-think and right-speak and to become harmless.

---
[1] This point needs to be qualified. Sometimes, when a higher teaching or principle is presented, it attracts group anger and hatred from people who hold an opposite belief. Such people harbour these traits within them and they are reacting to the lighted principle being presented (through resentment and fear), and not to the character of the presenter.

In earlier times, novices in the Ancient Wisdom temples were taught the lesson of harmlessness by not being allowed to speak for a few years. This so they would learn to value speech, appreciate the impact that would be made by any words spoken, and to carefully consider what to say before speaking. Spiritual training is different today, and is self imposed. But we all need to copy the example of the temple novice and speak only when necessary - and when we do speak, to speak wisely.

Modern life conspires against this. People are busy, tense, ambitious, conflicted, hyperactive and thoughts and words are often used as a weapon. It is easy to get caught up in this melee and aspirants must break free and learn to be silent and still.

The silence required is not just the cessation of speech, but inner quiet. Constant internal chatter overflows onto the physical plane as mindless chatter, just as when a dam is full water will overflow. True silence also requires that judgmental thoughts stop. Apart from the fact that this is a requirement of harmlessness, if a critical thought is present and is not being voiced, it will bank up and lead to a still more violent display of words at a later date. It may also bring about serious conditions within the astral body - energy blocks, manifesting as physical and psychological illness.

Most people have not appreciated the enormous value of silence for its own sake, and that a quiet mind is the key to spiritual growth and achievement. A mind which is able to reside in true inner silence enables the owner to reach a state of total love and oneness or communion with God. This is why traditionally, monks, priests and nuns have observed silence.

- Physically, silence conserves energy, and lengthens the period of our life. There is a close connection between the tongue and the brain and the more the tongue can be kept relaxed, the clearer the brain, the quieter the mind, the longer the life.
- A busy, chattering mind is always in "send mode"; a quiet mind receives, hears and listens. Silence enables us to see more clearly any issues involved. As a consequence, one is better able to bring the interpretative light of expressed goodwill, upon any topic.
- We are imprisoned on the planet by what we say and do. Each time we stop thinking a negative thought or speaking wrong words, little by little those ties that hold us are severed.
- Silence helps sanitise the substance of our lower bodies, and keeps away psychic germs - unwholesome entities from the astral plane.
- When the mind and emotions are quiet, the soul can illumine consciousness. True inspiration comes when the mind is calm and listening.

Points to Observe:

1. Strive to eradicate negative habits of thinking by applying the "Think an opposite thought" technique. Remember that thought habits are just the energies of the mind which have developed a certain pattern, a path of least resistance, a short cut, because the route is used so often. We have to build a new and higher pathway of thought, and when used enough, it will replace the old habit.

2. Do not use the creative imagination in an unwholesome manner. There are many ways we manage to transgress this instruction, from imagining ourselves as the victim of circumstances, indulging in violent mental onslaughts against a person who has offended us, or in unhealthy sexual fantasies, etc.

3. Be "in the now". Every day, as often as you remember, determine that "in this moment" you will step out of the stream of thought and enter into quietness. Bring your whole attention into the current moment. No thinking, just observing, feeling, listening and noticing what is going on within and without you. Notice and feel the sensations in your body. Notice and listen to the activities and sounds in your environment. Look at the vibrancy of nature around you, the colours, the growth. Gently and silently be with yourself, and with whatever you observe. When you mind begins to wander, pull it gently back to the present moment. Accept that whatever is at that moment, is.

When anger and hatred are absent, having been eliminated, then peace and harmony exists within and that is what is seen by people.

2:35. Harmlessness being perfected, in his presence all enmity ceases.

Developing harmlessness is the first stage of universal love, the practical work in becoming one with all beings. When the seeds of harmfulness are eliminated, the cause which produces enmity in others is likewise eliminated. In the presence of the Seer who has developed harmlessness, all become peaceful. Even wild beasts become still and peaceful in the Seer's presence.

▲ Commandment 2. Be Truthful, do not Lie.

Truth is relative whilst evolution proceeds, and can be defined as the demonstration on the physical plane of as much of the divine reality as the stage in evolution and the medium employed permits. Meaning, that a less evolved consciousness sees less truth and therefore speaks more falsehoods (but also attracts less karma); than the more evolved consciousness who sees more of the truth and attracts more karma if the same lies are told.

The ego builds up a false mental world filled with injustices, victimisation, distortions, and lives there. Stretching the truth, shrinking it, covering it up, embellishing it, pretending it has done something it has not - this is all falsehood. In this world there are complexities, game-playing, avoidances, denials and untruths. In contrast, *the world of spirit is stark*. It is clear truth and reality. Life is lived in the open. All is revealed for others to see. It leads to a life lived more simply.

In her autobiography, Alice Bailey recounts an episode regarding truth and dishonesty. Here is an abridged version. "When I was about fourteen, I was furious with my governess. I went to her room and collected valuables - wrist watch, brooches, rings, etc., and flushed them down the toilet. My governess kept a self-examination book in which she analysed her words and actions in the light of the question: "What would Jesus have done?". I read it and found out that she knew that I had taken the jewellery. But in order to help me, she was not going to say anything until my own conscience prompted me to confess. At the end of three days I told her what I had done, only to discover that she was more distressed at my reading her private papers than she was over my destroying her jewellery. That reaction of hers gave me a new sense of values. It made me think, and for the first time I began to differentiate between the spiritual values and the material. To her, it was a greater sin to be dishonest than it was to destroy material things."

Remedial Spiritual Practice: Truthfulness.
Truthfulness is simple, clear, factual, and has a clear motive. Aim to be scrupulously honest about yourself and all you do. With honesty, comes fearlessness. When there are no lies, the entire life becomes an open book. Communicate the truth without underrating or overrating. However, be mindful that vulnerable souls may shatter if they hear a truth they cannot handle. In such cases we should moderate what is said or be silent.

Regularly scrutinise your actions, your motives, and do not gloss over one fault, nor excuse yourself along a single line. Affirm constantly, "I must to my own Self be true."

2: 36. When Truth is perfected, the effect of this is immediately seen.

When truthfulness has been perfected, people feel this, they recognise it. When the yogi thinks and speaks only that which is truth, then his words carry great power. For example, if he says to a sick person "be healed", the patient will be healed immediately. This is why Jesus was so influential. He only had to speak and people knew they were hearing eternal truths, he only had to touch and people would heal.

▲ Commandment 3. Abstain from Stealing.

The major sin of the Atlantean people was theft. The seeds of aggression and of personal acquisitiveness grew, warping the consciousness of the race, until great evil stalked the planet, culminating in a great war. Today, all nations are guilty of greed and theft, of separativeness, of pride and prejudice, as well as national and racial hatreds. If we fall prey to these sins, we contribute to the problem of world greed.

If we feel empty inside, if we compare ourselves to others and want what they have (physical ability, beauty, youth, material wealth, fame, power, love and spiritual attainment,etc); this leads to mental, emotional and physical stealing.

Buddha's Second Noble Truth states that suffering is caused by craving after material things. Emotional craving for love is the root of much discontent. But true love cannot be given from an unhealed mind and heart, which is the state of the average human being. Unhealed souls are actually in love with a collection of beliefs about "the ideal person". But these are not real.

An important task is to clarify what you want and then what you really need to survive. Wants are endless - a bottomless pit. Rather than constantly struggling to get what we want; we are asked to modify our wanting. Wanting deprives us of contentment and happiness.

Remedial Spiritual Practice: The practice of Contentment.
When all manipulation or craving is abandoned, peace and contentment follows. The key is to learn to be content with what we have

> Ask yourself, "what do I really need?" If I were living in a country where there was war, or poverty, or natural disasters, what would I and my loved ones really need in order to be okay? Do we have physical safety, and a safe place to stay? Do we have enough food to eat? Do we have warmth and adequate clothing? Can we access affordable health care? Are human rights being respected in our environment?

If you have all that you need to be safe - especially when you think of the situation of people living in dire poverty or in war-torn regions; relish the fact. Give thanks for living in a safe place. If you also have the time and means to develop your creativity and to pursue the spiritual life, give thanks for being truly privileged and blessed.

The true cause of discontent is the sense of being separated off from the Oneness of Life, separated from our originating Spiritual Source, from universal and unconditional love. As long as this sense exists, we remain discontented and look for something external to explain why we feel that way. This is why the teachings of yoga, of union, were created. To eliminate this sense of separation.

Another practise to develop contentment is to give to others. Contentment and charity go hand-in-hand. Helping people who are disadvantaged helps us feel good and appreciate what we have. Set aside a portion of your time or income, to help others. Through meditation, send love and healing to individuals and to the world. At the end of every day say, "I give thanks for all the blessings in my life."

> Because one believes in oneself, one doesn't try to convince others. Because one is content with oneself, one doesn't need others' approval. Because one accepts oneself, the whole world accepts him or her. Lao Tzu

When the disciple has learned to desire nothing for the separated self, he can then be trusted with the riches of the universe. When we ask nothing for the separated self, then all is given to us. Such is the law of karma.

2:37. When honesty is perfected, the yogi can have whatever he desires.

▲ Commandment 4. Balance the sex function.

Remember, these instructions are for disciples, not for the masses. In this context, incontinence refers to wasting our energy or potency through the *misuse* of sexual force. This misuse of the sex-function has created most of the problems we have today. These range from "free love", general promiscuity, widespread prostitution, a heritage of diseased and over or undersexed physical bodies, the narrow and bigoted Christian teaching that sex is sinful, or that priests "must" be celibate.

These have resulted in legalised prostitution, ill-health, seeking of illicit relations outside the home, neglected and unwanted children, the friction produced by wrong mating and divorce, paedophilia and other sex crimes. In the lives of those who avoid marriage, there is often discontent, a hidden sex life, ill-health as a result of sexual repression, illegitimate children, an unhealthy psychology and sexual perversions. All this has resulted in:

1. The development of complexes, psychoses, psychological disruptions and inhibitions, which have seriously undermined the health and serenity of hundreds and thousands.
2. A threatened family life due primarily to promiscuity, sterility and birth control.
3. An enfeeblement, loss of vitality and virility, and anaemia.

Many people consider sexual license as "sophisticated", and a right This is fed by advertising, magazines, movies, etc. In one part of the world a woman may have many husbands, in another, a man is legally entitled to several wives. In the West, a man has legally one wife, but through his promiscuity has many 'wives', and today women are little better. This is something the masses have to work through.

Disciples are required to work through their higher chakras and not indulge the sexual sacral chakra. A normal and monogamous sexual life in marriage is recommended for both the masses and disciples. However, at an advanced stage of the Path when the nature is balanced and the soul is expressing through the head and heart centres, celibacy then is a normal, natural and healthy expression. But not before.

Remedial Spiritual Practice: Be sexually responsible
Be monogamous. Abstain from lustful thoughts. Remember, "energy follows thought." If you do not allow sexual thoughts to enter the mind and instead, think of other things, lust dies down. Celibacy is not demanded, but self-control is. Sometimes aspirants are required to spend a life celibate in order to learn sexual control. If this is your situation then remember that desire must be expressed. Do not try to repress it. Expressing it through the throat chakra via a higher creative outlet such the arts, scientific investigation or in service, is vital. This will help disperse sexual demand. The right use of the sex principle along with entire conformity to the law of the land is characteristic of every true aspirant.

2:38. With right sexual control, tremendous energy is acquired.

A true celibate is not troubled by sexual discontent. There is tremendous energy, a clear brain, gigantic willpower, bold understanding and a retentive memory.

▲ Commandment 5. Be Content instead of Avaricious and Covetous.

Theft on the mental plane is avarice - mind force craving after desirous things. It leads to physical plane sins - theft on the physical plane originates from avarice. The key is to stop hungering after what other people have. All material forms dissolve and die. If we get what we crave, in time we lose interest in it and discard it. Then a new cycle of craving arises. So what is the point?

Remedial Spiritual Practice: The Spirit of Generosity.
1. Give material things to others, such as food or shelter.
2. Give the gift of fearlessness - help others who are afraid.
3. Help people overcome the darkness of ignorance.

Learn to be content. Ponder the thought that you are a soul and your primary purpose is to realise this as a fact. All the glories of earth are given to those who ask for nothing in return. Pursue the goal of enlightenment. Crave this. Make this your first priority. Dedicate yourself to your spiritual practises, and you will find that craving for material things begins to fade. The more you let go in all areas of life, the more life and its wonders and glories will unfold.

39. When contentment is achieved, there comes an understanding of the law or rebirth.

In other words, when abstention from avarice is perfected, chains which bind us to the wheel of rebirth drop away, and memories of past lives are gained. When desirelessness is present, then the three worlds can no longer hold the yogi.

By overcoming thoughts contrary to Yoga, Soul Powers are developed.

When the ego looks out at the world it sees itself as being separative from others. It also sees in others what it harbours in itself. So, if it is angry, it will see anger and people will be angry back. If it sees deceit, this trait will be seen and people will be deceitful back, and so on.

On the other hand, when the Seer looks at others, it sees the soul and its perfect relation with God. This is because it has achieved this in its own nature. And, because the Seer has eliminated the modifications, hindrances and obstacles; when he looks at others, he sees them in a state of grace or in the process of becoming so. This has an immediate transforming effect on those in his presence. This capacity to see God's presence in others is at the root of the supernatural powers (siddhis) which the Seer wields.

MEANS 2: NIJAMA, "THE RULES."

In Means II, Patanjali gives 5 rules which must be kept along with the Commandments. Only when these are being observed can we safely proceed with the following steps of Yoga. But not until then.

> 2: 32. The five rules (Nijama) are:
> - Purification, internal and external.
> - Contentment.
> - Fiery aspiration.
> - Spiritual reading.
> - Devotion to Ishvara.

▲ Rule 1. Purify yourself, internally and externally.

We are all familiar with ways and means to purify the body and life externally. In Book I we studied ways to attend to internal purification. As we work through them - begin to straighten out our internal functioning and disengage from material attachments, the way we engage with life changes. There is a gradual turning away from objects and things that seemed so important in the past.

> 2:40. Internal and external purification produces aversion for form, both one's own and all forms.

The factor of time must be taken account when considering this sutra. The aversion referred to, is the natural reaction of our evolving soul-self as purification proceeds and we remember our spiritual Source and home. Gradually, all remaining external attachments become repugnant and from these our soul seeks to disengage.

Another tremendous benefit which emotional purification in particular brings about is inner peace and insight.

> 2:41. Through purification comes also a quiet spirit, concentration, conquest of the organs, and ability to see the Self.

<u>Exercises to Purify and control the Emotional Nature.</u>

Endeavour to become familiar with what is happening on an emotional level. This field registers whatever arises from the unconscious part of our natures, so its responses are a barometer to what is occurring deep in our nature. This work is especially important for those who have become disconnected from their feelings. Spiritual growth requires that we integrate our fields before the soul can work through them.

1. Emotional cleansing exercise.

Routinely cleanse and quieten your emotional field every day through the use of this exercise or one that is similar.

> Whenever a strong emotion arises, say mentally "Peace be still." Imagine Jesus saying those words when he was on a boat in the ocean and a storm arose. Immediately the waters became still. Likewise, imagine your astral nature becoming calm and still like a serene ocean. Finish the exercise by sending white light through your astral nature. Sound an OM, remembering that you are a sacred soul.

140 - Soul Psychology & Raja Yoga: Spiritual Practices for Enlightenment.

2. Emotional Observing exercise - the practice of Dispassion.

This is an exercise in being dispassionate, dis-identifying from unruly emotions as they play through the body. In the exercise, you are no longer the emotion, you are experiencing an emotion which you name. Recall an emotional incident from your past to work with.

> Focus firmly in your mind and imagine yourself disengaging from the incident. Look at it as if it were a movie playing out on a screen in front of you. You are no longer an actor in the movie, you are an observer. Emphasise this by affirming, "I am observing." Examine your reactions and name each emotion you see being expressed. Do not suppress the emotions. Just name them.

Then cleanse and quieten your emotional field by using the emotional cleansing exercise. Use this observing exercise whenever a strong emotion rises. Start to observe your emotions, scanning your emotional field daily, and naming any emotion which may be present.

3. Standing on the Bridge exercise - the practice of Dispassion.

This exercise is suitable for dealing with powerful emotions such as anger, rage and grief. Practice it first, then use it whenever a powerful emotion is evoked. It can also be used for incidents that happened in the past which still evoke powerful emotions in the present. Find a quiet place, close your eyes, quieten your breath, relax.

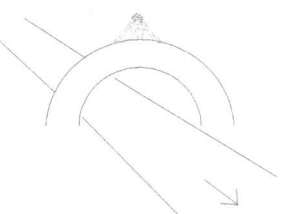

> Close your eyes and see a small river with a bridge over it. You are standing on the bridge holding firmly to the guard rail.
>
> a. Think of an episode which generates emotions. Let the feelings arise again and let them sweep through you.
>
> b. Bring to mind the river and bridge scene. You allow your emotions to pour through your solar plexus area like that river, running from behind you away to the front.
>
> c. But you are standing on the bridge, holding firm. You look down as the torrent of energies as they pour through. You let them run until they begin to be exhausted and you feel better. Keep affirming, "I am observing."
>
> d. Do the emotional cleansing exercise.

▲ Rule 2. Be Content.

Worry, doubt and despair cloud the issues of life. Accepting one's lot, wasting no time in vain regrets, frees all energy for the perfect fulfilment of dharma, or obligatory work.

> 2:42. As a result of contentment, bliss is achieved.
>
> > The Master said: "A mind at rest results in contentment. It produces a state of mind where all conditions are regarded as correct and just, and as those in which the aspirant can best work out his problem and achieve the goal for any specific life. This does not entail an acquiescence producing inertia, but a recognition of present assets, an availing oneself of one's opportunities and letting them form a background and a basis for all future progress." [1]

Note that contentment does not mean being lazy and making no effort to change, grow and to improve things. Be patient, learn to be content with what you have. Embrace the Law of

---

[1] Bailey, Alice. Light of the Soul, 189.

Karma, acknowledge its fairness and that all is correct and just - that you are in the right place, at the right time to learn your lessons and achieve your current spiritual goal.

Affirm continuously "I give thanks for all the blessings in my life."

▲ Rule 3. Evoke Fiery Aspiration.

Aspiration towards God, towards the higher spiritual realities lights every atom in the body with zeal and endeavour. Aspiration (transmuted lower desire), is the fuel that propels us forwards on our spiritual search and should be cultivated.

2:43. Through fiery aspiration and through the removal of all impurity, comes the perfecting of the bodily powers and of the senses.

Aspiration rises naturally as we centre our alignment with the soul through meditation and other disciplines. Reading about the lives of the Masters and other inspirational figures also calls in this fire. When we charge the whole nature with spiritual fire, it pours through all the atoms in the body, purifying and motivating them with the Life of God. This fire gives us the strength and perseverance required to move through the trials and tribulations of the Path. Fiery aspiration also destroys the seeds of the Hindrances, which hinder soul vision and the free play of spiritual energy.

▲ Rule 4. Develop the technique of Spiritual Reading.

Every object we see around us is a symbol veiling a divine thought, idea or truth - and behind all forms God is to be found. Spiritual reading is the art of looking behind the obvious, to the truth behind. This must become the normal way life is viewed.

2:44. Spiritual reading results in a contact with the soul (or divine One).

This technique is powerful. When we do this, we are aligning our life perspective with that of the soul. It changes the way we normally view people.

Exercise in Spiritual Reading. The next time you feel irritated, angry or repulsed by someone, knowing that Christ sees all peoples - including sinners, as souls who are in the process of becoming enlightened.

a. Affirm, "I ask a blessing holy child of God, that I may see you through the eyes of Christ."

b. Visualise that person as a free, beautiful and unblemished soul, standing in the lighted presence of Christ.

This exercise breaks the cycle of negative thoughts being directed at others and helps strengthen the link between a person's soul and personality. Seeing someone as a soul does not excuse wrong behaviour and if it is appropriate, the person should be held accountable.

Realise that we are all in the process of becoming enlightened and we all make mistakes or sin on the Path. But this is normal and natural. It is how we learn. We are baby souls learning the rules of the road. It is the blinded soul, the personality, who commits the error - not the spiritual soul.

Study your motives, the causes, thoughts and ideas which lie behind your own expression. Do the same with others. This will train the mind to probe beneath surface appearances. When you know you are Divine in fact as well as in theory, you will see the same in all other human beings, creatures and forms. We all are a part of the One Universal Life and are in the process of realising this factually in waking consciousness.

▲ Rule 5. Cultivate Devotion to Ishvara.

The Spark of God (Ishvara) is anchored in the heart. It is the seed of our Divine nature and heritage, our connection to God, into which we are growing - just as the seed of a tree grows into a model of its parent tree.

> 2:45. Through devotion to Ishvara the goal of meditation (or Samadhi - contemplating with God), is reached.

Being devoted to our personal Ishvara in the heart - the impulse of unconditional love and wisdom, develops a correct attitude towards universal Ishvara. This purifies the astral nature, clearing obstructions so that the whole heart can pour out love to God - God in one's own heart, God in the heart of sister and brother souls, and God as seen in every form. This is devotion to Ishvara, the practice of Bhakti Yoga. Djwhal Khul said:

> There is much importance attached to the necessity for establishing direct egoic contact (with Christ in the heart), via the (antahkarana), for only in this way can the aspirant ascertain the causes lying at the back of the present manifestations of his life, or begin to deal with the samkaras or seeds of his future activities. [1]

The real Master, claiming attention and subsequent obedience, is the Master in the Heart, the spiritual soul, the indwelling Christ.

- This Master first makes His presence felt through the "still small voice" of conscience, prompting us to higher and more unselfish living, and sounding a quick note of warning when there is deviation from the strict path of rectitude.
- Later this comes to be known as the Voice of the Silence, the guiding direction that comes from the "Word incarnate," which is ourselves.
- Later still, we call it the awakened intuition. The student of meditation learns to distinguish accurately between these three.

Every time we meditate, pray or revere great Lives such as Jesus Christ and Buddha, or read the writings of those who have pioneered esoteric philosophy in the west such as Helena Blavatsky, Alice Bailey, Geoffrey Hodson, Annie Besant, Vivekananda, Paramahansa Yogananda, etc; our connection to our Spiritual Self is enhanced. We are clearer about what we need to do to grow spiritually, and the aspiration to do the needed work is strengthened. This work ignites a spiritual fire within which burns away dross within our natures.

> Bhakti is a series of succession of
> mental efforts at religious realization
> beginning with ordinary worship
> ending in a supreme intensity
> of love for Ishvara.
>
> - Swami Vivekananda.

---

[1] Bailey, Alice. Light of the Soul, 144.

MEANS III: ASANA (RIGHT POISE).

The Vedanta master Swami Vivekananda recommended daily physical exercises to help build a healthy physical body and nervous system, which is required to take the brunt of the higher vibrational forces that are invoked in meditation and other spiritual practices.

2:46. The posture assumed must be steady and easy.

To this end, Hatha Yoga exercises are ideal. The Salute to the Sun exercise has a double benefit - it trains the physical body and can also be a devotional practice.

Salute to the Sun exercise.

Traditionally done at dawn facing towards the rising sun. While doing the exercise, hold the thought that you are adoring Ishvara and solar-fire flowing from the Sun is burning out impurities and blockages in the nadis so that prana can circulate freely. One complete exercise involves two cycles, each with alternative leg work. Do what you are comfortable with.

1. Prayer Pose. Stand, feet together, hands in prayer position, even out the breath.

2. Upward Salute. Inhale. Lift arms up, arch back.

3. Standing Forward Bend. Exhale. Tuck hands into the body as you forwards bend. Place hands or fingertips to the floor, shins, or ankles.

4. Low Lunge. Inhale, lift head up to look forwards, ground hands, and step right foot back behind. The left front foot stays grounded and the (left) leg bends.

5. Plank Pose. Exhale. Ground both hands, send left leg back. The body is held up by straight arms, palms down. Hold breath before going to the next pose.

6. Downward-Facing Dog. Inhale. Spread palms and soles, raise bottom, stretch the torso.

7. Four Limbed Staff. (a). Exhale, slowly drop knees to floor. (b). Hug elbows in, drop chest and chin to floor, gaze forwards or down. (c). Tuck arms into your sides, and lift stomach, thighs and shins. [Alternatively, go into child's prayer pose. Keeping hands in the same position, bend knees, sit back on legs, brow to floor, back and arms stretched out].

8. Cobra. Inhale. Straighten arms, swing head and torso forwards and up and rest the rest of the body on the floor. Bend elbows, drop shoulders away from the ears, body lowers slightly; arch head and neck up and back.

9. Downward Facing Dog. Exhale. Go back into Downward Facing Dog.

10. Low Lunge. Inhale. Back into low lunge by stepping right foot forwards.

11. Exhale - Standing Forward Bend.

12. Inhale - Upward Salute.

13. Exhale - Prayer Pose.

One or two full breaths before repeating with the other foot.

The Five Tibetan Rites.

It is beneficial for health. Start by doing each step 7 times and gradually build up to 21 counts.

1. Spin clockwise breathing deep and slow. Practitioners say spinning restores the speed and balance of the vortex in the chakras.

2. Lie down. Raise head tucking chin against chest, inhale, lift legs, hold for a breath. Exhale, lower head and legs.

3. Kneel, hands against thighs. Tuck chin into chest. Inhale while tilting head back, arch spine. Exhale and return to start position.

4. Sit, legs straight out, palms on floor by buttocks. Tuck chin into chest, inhale while tilting head backwards and raising hips off the floor. Exhale and sit.

5. Downward Dog - Upward Dog. Lie with stomach on the floor, palms face-down beside or just in front of your head. (a). Push yourself up, raising your chest, head and eyes looking up. (b). Tuck chin against chest, exhale (opposite to yoga) swing the backside up so the body is in an arch. Inhale, returning to original position.

Asana and Meditation.

A physical body which is in a comfortable meditation posture, is able to concentrate better.

2:47. Steadiness and ease of posture is achieved through persistent slight effort and concentration of the mind upon the infinite.

The best physical position to adopt in meditation is the one in which you can soonest forget that you possess a physical body. But in general, the recommended posture for westerners is an upright position in a comfortable chair, spine erect, feet crossed naturally, hands folded in the lap, eyes closed, and the chin down a little. If you sit cross legged, then ensure the buttocks are higher than the knees.

Although the physical asanas of Hatha Yoga are very beneficial for the body and also aids this work, the important message addressed in Means III is to attain right-balance within, in all relationships and in life generally.

When mind and body are correctly focused and rightly adjusted, when poise on the physical plane and one pointedness on the mental plane is attained, when the mind can concentrate on the spiritual realities ("the infinite"); then the deeper goal of Means III is attained. The outer, physical poise is but a symbol of this inner, balanced, spiritual alignment.

When achieved, the pairs of opposites on the astral plane, emotional disturbances, will no longer impede the mediation process (sutra 2:48). Gaining control of the astral nature is the most formidable task facing the aspirant and physical poise assists this.

All these endeavours lead to right-control of the breath.

2:49. When right posture (asana) has been attained there follows right control of prana and proper pranayama.

MEANS IV: PRANAYAMA (BREATH-CONTROL).

It is not possible nor right to give in a book intended for the general public those rules, practices and methods which enable the trained disciple to bring his dense physical vehicle into instantaneous synchronization with his etheric body, to densify and irradiate his aura so as to produce certain magnetic results in his environment, and to awaken his centres so that certain psychic powers are displayed. [1]

Pranayama is the yoga practice of focusing on the breath. In Sanskrit, *prana* means "vital life force", and *yama* means "to gain control". Untamed prana disturbs the mind and causes unstable, flickering thoughts that obscure spirit. It is this constant, restless motion that must be tamed and Pranayama helps. By controlling prana, restless thoughts are restrained.

§ The important goal in Raja Yoga step 4, is to use the basic Pranayama technique to balance the energies of the mind and quieten the mind modifications.

1. The basic Pranayama breathing technique.

2:50. Right control of prana (the life currents) is external, internal or motionless.

There are three motions of pranayama - drawing in the breath (internal), expelling it out (external), then either holding the breath in the lungs, or stopping it from entering (motionless or balanced).

Adopt a meditation pose. Keep the mouth and eyes closed, the shoulders and jaw relaxed. Establish a quiet, rhythmic breathing cycle. Imagine the process as being like the gentle, steady, uninterrupted pouring of water from a glass. Aim for ease and flow.
Breathe in, a smooth continuous flow (4 counts).
Pause all breathing action (4 counts).
Breathe out, a smooth continuous flow (4 counts).
Pause all breathing action (4 counts).

The 4-beat is very grounding and balancing. If you are able to comfortably do this, you may choose to raise the count to an 8-count. If not, try a 2-count.

Mastering the pause between the breaths leads one into deep interior silence, makes one a conqueror of the forces of time and grants ultimate mastery over death.

Benefits of Pranayama.
Rhythmic pranayama (in its triple process of internal, external and balanced), if practised correctly (with meditation) brings the entire lower nature into a rhythmic response with the soul and then into complete quiescence or stillness. In this latter condition of receptive waiting, a fourth stage to the process occurs. The soul imposes its higher rate of vibration on the lower and sounds forth its note, producing beneficial effects in the mind, emotional and physical bodies (sutra 51). This has a refining and transmutative effect upon the substance of these bodies allowing the illuminating light of the soul, of God, to shine through the nature (sutra 52).

When this process is mastered and the soul can grip the mind and transmit knowledge, light and wisdom to the brain via the mind. This is the ideal preparation for meditation (sutra 53) and for the remaining steps or Means in Raja Yoga.

---
[1] Bailey, Alice. Light of the Soul, 221.

2. Thoughts to keep in mind.

1. Using a mantra to time the breath.

Start with counting to time the breath until you find your own rhythm, what suits you and your body. Then find a mantram you like which has the same number of words as the breath-count you are using. For instance, for a 4-count, use the mantram *Om Mane Padme Hum* (the jewel in the lotus, spirit residing at the heart of our nature). Using a spiritually beneficial mantra causes the vibration of that mantra to bring about positive changes within the nature.

2. Thinking during Pranayama.

If while practising Pranayama, no clear train of thought is held in the mind, the practise could be detrimental. The ego could be strengthened, because undirected energy goes to centres below the diaphragm, feeding the lower nature and deepening glamour. The physical appetites could be strengthened, making the task of the aspirant much harder as he seeks to sublimate the lower nature and focus in the centres above the diaphragm.

So, begin the practice with a clear understanding of what you want to achieve in the practice (for example, improved health, energising the body, spiritual enlightenment, etc). Then hold this thought throughout - especially while the breath is being paused.

3. Dangers of Pranayama.

There is danger in the practice of pranayama. Prana is fire energy. The most serious danger - and that which the inexperienced student should avoid, is using pranayama to force-develop the chakras. This could overstimulate the nervous system. But the greater danger is that it could lead to the premature awakening of the chakras and the rising of the fiery forces of the body called kundalini. If so, this would result in the most serious damage - physically and psychologically. The fires of the body literally go wild.

> There is extreme danger attendant upon the premature awakening of the fire, and the consequent destruction of certain protective structures in the etheric body and the breaking down of the barriers between this world and the astral world, before the pupil is properly "balanced between the pairs of opposites.[1]

3. Safe Breathing Exercises.

1. Exercise to assist correct breathing.

Breath is Life, and Life is God. Deep breathing brings in more Life and God. First the bottom (of the lungs) is filled, then the middle, finally the upper portion.

> Gently push the stomach forwards as you begin to breathe in, then the ribs sideways.
> Let the mid, then top sections of the lungs fill with air while still breathing in.
> Hold for a few seconds.
> Allow the entire chest and ribs to relax - the air will go out automatically.
> When the air seems to be out, push the stomach in slightly to expel remaining air.

This last action is important because it eliminates poisonous matter which often remains in normal breathing. Keep a smooth, continuous rhythm. Avoid any jerky movements.

---

[1] Bailey, Alice. Light of the Soul, 221.

2. Alternate nostril breathing.

The technique is safe to use any time and was recommended by the great Vedanta Master Shankaracharya. In Sanskrit, it's known as *Nadi Shodhana Pranayama,* which translates as "etheric channel purification through pranayama." The etheric channels referred to are the spinal channels *Ida* and *Pingala* that are located on either side of the physical spine. The negative and positive forces of the body flow up and down the body via these channels and nostril breathing helps balance this flow.

In the very advanced man, when the energies of *Ida* and *Pingala* are equilibrized, the forces can ascend and descend by the central channel *Shushumna*, to and from the brain, passing through the centres up the spine without hindrance. When this is the case, we have perfected soul expression in the physical man.

But generally, the technique calms the mind, soothes anxiety and stress, balances the left-right hemispheres of the brain, improves lung function, lowers the heart rate and promotes clear thinking.

Sit comfortably, right hand up to nose.

1. Exhale completely, then use right thumb to close the right nostril.
2. Inhale through left nostril, then close left nostril with fingers.
3. Open right nostril and exhale through right nostril.
4. Inhale through right nostril, then close right nostril.
5. Open left nostril and exhale through left nostril.

This is one cycle. Continue the cycles for a few minutes. Always end with an exhale on the left side. Aim for ease and flow.

3. Mindfulness in Breathing.

Prepare as for meditation. Calm, even count breathing. Repeat the cycle a few times.

(Breath in) I am breathing in calmly. (Breath out) I am breathing out calmly.

(Breathe in) My physical body is quiet. (Breathe out), my physical body is quiet.

(Breathe in) My emotions are still. (Breathe out), my emotions are still.

(Breathe in) my mind is still. (Breathe out), my mind is still.

(Breathe in) I accept all that is. (Breathe out) I accept all that is.

(Breathe in) Peace, be still. (Breathe out), Peace be still.

4. The Manifesting Breath Technique.

This technique adds visualisation to the basic Pranayama exercise. Its goal is to empower a thought, so it (whatever is envisioned), can manifest in the physical life. This is a powerful manifesting technique when mastered.

1. Clearly identify the idea or thought that you are seeking to make real. For instance, "My body is strong and healthy," or "I am illumined with the light of the soul."

2. Hold this thought or image clearly during the entire in-out breath cycle, but particularly on the in-pause period. On the in-breath, the thought is built and vitalised. On the out-breath, it is sent forth into manifestation.

MEANS V: PRATYAHARA - ABSTRACTION - DETACHMENT.

Once outer conduct is corrected, inner purity is arrived at, right attitude towards all things is being cultivated and the life currents are being controlled - then is the time to begin the serious work of subjugating the outgoing tendencies of the five senses. To bring under control the psychic nature, which is the emotional body tinged faintly with mind (kama-manas).

> By the practice of dispassion and of non-attachment, and by the strenuous control of the desire nature it becomes possible for the man to re-orient himself so that his attention is no longer attracted outward by the stream of mind-images but is withdrawn, and fixed one-pointedly upon reality. [1]

In detachment work we train the mind to stop slavishly following the demands of the senses. When the senses are no longer tied to external sources, one can concentrate without being distracted by externals and all sense perceptions perform their legitimate functions. This results in "correct analysis" - seeing things correctly through vision that is uncoloured by the distorting effects of the mind or emotions. As we progress, external forms will gradually lose their hold until eventually we are liberated from their control. We become masters of our senses and of all sense contacts. This is very advanced spiritual work.

2:54. Abstraction (or Pratyahara) is the subjugation of the senses by the thinking principle and their withdrawal from that which has hitherto been their object.

In average man, the mind appears to be 'fused' to the senses. Whenever a sense becomes attracted to an external object, the mind follows, and so does the man.

> For example, a man is hungry and thinks of a steak. He can taste its juiciness and salivates after the steak. So out comes the frying pan and in goes the steak. As soon as the steam is turned on, the engine runs. As soon as things are before us, we respond.

The mind modifications respond automatically. The yogi must prove that he is not a machine, that nothing controls him. Controlling the mind, and not allowing it to join itself to the centres so that the senses and desires are stirred up, is Pratyahara.

> 2:54. Pratyahara is the turning of the mind inwards, and restraining it (them) from going outwards.

By applying an appropriate technique, consciousness is prevented from surging outwards along the five senses - the senses are dominated by the sixth sense, the mind. Consciousness and the perceptive faculty are synthesized in the head, and turns inward and upward. This subjugates the lower psychic nature and the mental plane becomes the field of focused activity.

1. (Right) Detachment is not a cold and insensitive attitude to people and a withdrawal from normal human interactions. In detachment work we separate the real Self from the inertia of the body, from the glamour of the emotions and from the illusions of the mind. With detachment we dis-identify, not separate. We see objects as they are, free from personal, mechanical reactions and from the imposing, forcing will of the lower self. With success, soul love increases, our light becomes brighter, our will stronger, our joy deeper.

---

1 Bailey, Alice. Light of the Soul, 399.

2. In detachment work, it does not mean we do not care about people or things, just that we understand that they inevitably change and eventually go away. What we detach from is the neurotic attempt to make things permanent or to selfishly have them go just the way we want.

Definitions for Detachment.

> Detachment is not self-protection or of self-immunisation or aloofness, but that soul detachment which works from soul levels and - seeing all life in the light which streams from the soul - regards everything from the standpoint of eternity. You will then see the real values involved and the true perspectives of the picture. [1]

> The process of abstracting one's mind from all imposed thoughtforms—imposed by one's background, one's tradition and one's social group - is a very difficult and subtle undertaking. It must definitely be learned, prior to mastering the science of thoughtform building. The disciple has to stand free from mental impression and mental concepts before he can successfully create under direction of the Ashram. [2]

> Detachment is the freeing of the soul from the thraldom of the form life, and the subordination of the personality to the higher impulses. It is detachment from the lower ego, the vainglorious ego, the dispersed and capricious ego, the plaything of external circumstances, the slave of fluctuating opinion. Above all, it is detachment from the proud ego. [3]

> Detachment is that inner, divine detachment of the Onlooker [who, because he is not] identified with aught that may happen on the physical and emotional planes, mind is a limpid reflector of truth and sees life in its true perspective. This truth is intuitively perceived because there are no violent mental reactions or emotional states of response; the vehicles of perception are quiet and therefore there is nothing to offset the correct attitude. [4]

> Detachment, also expressed as non-attachment, is a state in which a person overcomes their attachment to desire for things, people or concepts of the world and thus attains a heightened perspective. It is considered a wise virtue and is promoted in various Eastern religions, such as Hinduism, Jainism, Taoism and Buddhism. It is also a key concept in Christian spirituality (often referred to by the Greek term *apatheia*), where it signifies a detachment from worldly objects and concerns. Wikipedia.

> True detachment isn't a separation from life but the absolute freedom within your mind to explore living. Ron W. Rathbun.

> In the Bhagavad Gita, Krishna tells Arjuna that acting with detachment means doing the right thing for its own sake, because it needs to be done, without worrying about success or failure. T. S. Eliot paraphrased Krishna's advice when he wrote, "For us, there is only the trying. The rest is not our business."

---

1 Bailey, Alice. Discipleship in the New Age I, 130.
2 Bailey, Alice. Discipleship in the New Age II, 693.
3 Bailey, Alice. Intellect to Intuition, 97-98.
4 Bailey, Alice. Discipleship in the New Age I, 146.

Detachment Disciplines & Practices.

1. Practices to Detach from the Senses.

1. Restraining Sight.
   a. Look around you and realise the wonderful gift of 'sight', and how it enables you to see.
   b. Now, keep your eyes open, but stop paying attention to what they see. Think of something else which really interests you.

If you have been successful, you managed to take your mind away from the sight sense. This was the intention of this exercise, and is a simple demonstration of non-attachment to the senses. If you found it relatively simple thing to do, that is good.

True pratyahara demands an ability to detach from the senses permanently. We only turn our attention to what they convey to the mind, when required.

When we consider that the mind is a sense, and that the ultimate goal is to be able to detach from the streams of thought passing through the mind as and when required; we realise the magnitude of the task. Practise this now.

   a. Empty your mind of all thoughts and try to hold it empty for a period.
   b. Close your eyes and practise being "just being a mind". Direct your sight sense to the 'thought world'. Think of the word 'magnificent'. What images or thoughts appear before your mind's eye?

2. Restraining Smell and taste.
   a. Think of your favourite food being cooked. Imagine this, smell the aromas, salivate over the taste. Or perhaps, hold perfume or incense under your nose.
   b. Now think of something quite different - something you like, or perhaps a holiday you have had, maybe something that you will be doing in the near future.
   c. If you were successful, you took your mind away from your taste and smell senses, and directed it again into the thought world.

3. Restraining Hearing.
   a. Listen to the sounds around you: a clock, birds, the wind, people outside, an aeroplane. Let yourself enjoy the wonders of hearing.
   b. Now decide that these sounds are no longer going to activate your thoughts. They are unimportant. Let them flow over you in mass, without trying to pick out the individual noises.
   c. Remember a sound you have enjoyed, perhaps music or the sea.

4. Restraining Touch.
   a. Sit in a comfortable chair. Feel the seat of the chair, the floor, your lap under your hands. Get yourself comfortable, scratch or wriggle if you need to, breathe easily.
   b. Now try to sit still for five minutes. Tell your body to ignore any little itches and prickles while you spend a few minutes thinking of something in which you are keenly interested. For example, think of meeting your Master, who gives you advice about your training.

2. Dispassion: practices to detach from the Emotions.

The best discipline to start with is the 'Think an Opposite Thought' technique given in the Hindrances section. In this technique, the mind is used to control emotional reactions.

  a. Whenever you are having a negative reaction or emotion to something. Find an opposing, unifying or strengthening thought or visualisation.
  b. Continuously offset the energy of the old thought by using the new one. Take time to feel the new effects in your astral field. Feel good about it.

Example 1: Visualisation for inner strength.
  a. Someone has been aggressive and you feel weak and afraid.
  b. You imagine that you are a mountain or a redwood tree, impervious to any insult.
  c. Hold this image and thought until you feel stronger.

Example 2: Standing on the Bridge.
You are aware you are in conflict or turmoil.
  a. Identify that you are emotionally upset and briefly what has upset you.
  b. Apply the "Standing on the Bridge" technique (given in the Rules section). You are standing on the bridge, holding firmly to the rail, while the emotions pour through you and away.
  c. Hold the visualisation until the emotions settle down and you feel at peace.

Example 3: Wash away the disturbance with Light.
This is a powerful, effective and easy to use technique.
  a. Align with your soul, Master or God and keep your eyes fixed on your soul (Master or God), through the entire exercise.
  b. Affirm, "The soul pours white light through me to wash away disturbances."
  c. See your soul pour a stream of white light through you and through the solar plexus chakra. Breathe steadily in and out as you do so.
  d. Keep this going until you feel the disturbance fade and you can regain balance.

3. Practices to Detach from the Mental Nature.

The emotional world is like the ocean and the mind is like the atmosphere above. Any motion in one affects the other. Men move in the direction of their thoughts. If thoughts are greedy, a person becomes greedier. An impure mind surrounds itself with impure things, a pure mind with pure things. Once we have begun emotional purification, extending this to the mental level is the next step.

1. Detached Observation of the Mind.

In this technique, we turn the mind back on itself to observe itself. We use the mind to understand what is going on in our own psychological field.

  Whenever you think of it, ask yourself, "What have I been thinking?" Then, try to recall the train of thoughts you have been thinking.

Monitor your mind. Try to be mindful of the thoughts you are thinking, especially if they are critical, judgmental or dark thoughts. If you catch yourself thinking such thoughts:
a. Immediately apply the Think an Opposite Thought technique.
b. Say the mantram usually used at noon, "O Lord of Light and Love I know about the need. Touch my heart anew with love, so that I too may love and give."

2. The Mind must be trained to be quiet, still and serene.

This is the immediate goal - to develop a quiet, silent, attentive mind. A silent mind is beautiful. It hears more and sees more. Silence is not only the end of noise but is the complete cessation of all movement of chitta. Normally the brain is active all the time. The task is to quieten the everlastingly active, chattering, brain cells. This is basically all that is required. Our job is to hold the quiet observation until mind disturbance fades away.

Sky Mind exercise.
a. Centre your consciousness high in the head.
b. Imagine you have come thorough a dark night of the soul experience. As dawn breaks, the clouds (all trauma) roll away. There is only peace and stillness. Enjoy the sensation of stillness.
c. In your mind's eye, you look up and see blue sky, no clouds (no traumas).
d. Allow the limits of your being to melt into that blueness. Identify with that wholeness, that quietness and stillness of the Mind of God.
e. Now thoughts scurry across mind, like clouds across the sky. Let them flow until they disappear.
f. Settle back into the peace of clear sky mind. Enjoy the sensation of stillness.

Shiny Sea Mind.
a. See Eternal Mind stretched out before you like a pure, still and silent cosmic sea of pure gold.
b. Merge your mind into Eternal Mind and feel the blissful silence quieten every sound in your nature. Rest in that.
c. Now thoughts disturb the peace, like bubbles rising up from the depths and breaking on the surface.
d. Let the disturbance settle and mind settle back into the eternal, gold stillness. Enjoy the sensation of stillness.

Points to Observe.
a. Do not let your mind run free. Practise mind control. Select one area to start with, perhaps sexual imaginings, or angry thoughts. Every time you find your mind starting to think those thoughts, think an opposite, positive or healthier thought.
b. The mind needs to be cleansed, emptied of dark thoughts. Continually pour in good thoughts - like clean water, until all the filth has been washed out and the mind is clean. Pour the thought of God into mind. Or use a favourite mantram such as:

When the mind is pure, joy follows like a shadow that never leaves. Buddha
With a pure mind and an honest heart, there is nothing to fear. Gurudev.
For those pure in mind, everything is pure. Georg Feuerstein.

c. Make a castle of your mind. Decorate it with thoughts that are good, beautiful and true. Fiercely guard your mind and protect it against evil or coarse thoughts.
   d. Take responsibility for the consequences of your actions. An empowered person does not act like a victim and blame others. Do not make choices based on fear. Choose to be a student of life.
   e. Train yourself to think only good about others, even in the face of adversity, temptation and abuse. Choose words with care, for you will affect people by what you say - for good or ill. Never speak ill of others. Speak truth with harmlessness and kindness.
   f. Energy follows thought. Constantly visualise your mind as being soul illumined and your thoughts loving, generous and kind. Use the Manifesting Breath Technique.

4. Practices to Detach from the Personality.

1. A Simple Detachment Meditation.
It is good to do this at the beginning of your morning meditation.
   a. In your mind's eye, observe your physical body. Sound the OM through it as you silently affirm, "I have a body but I am not my body." Visualise and feel your physical body as being relaxed.
   b. Observe your emotional body. Sound the OM through it as you silently affirm, "I have emotions but I am not those emotions." Visualise and feel your emotional body as being serene and still as a glassy lake on a windless day.
   c. Observe your mental body. Sound the OM through it as you silently affirm, "I have thoughts but I am not those thoughts." Visualise your mental body as being quiet and still as an unflickering candle flame.
   d. Affirm "I am the Self of Light, the Soul."

2. "I am pure gnosis".
   a. You realise you are thinking negative thoughts, your emotions are disturbed.
   b. Lift your point of observation out of the ego, up into the soul. This can also be done through a mantram or sutra such as 2:20. "I the seer am pure knowledge (gnosis). Though pure I look upon the presented idea through the medium of the mind."
   c. Then, clinically examine what is going - a steady, cool, analytical observation through the lens of the mind. Remind yourself, that whatever is going on in the world, you stand detached from any turmoil. That this is a presented opportunity to detach from any drama so you can make a decision from clear mind.

Generally.
1. When this work begins, it may seem the character grows worse. Horrible thoughts and distractions may arise. Everyone experiences this. As clean thoughts pour in the subconscious mind is disturbed. It is like a lake with a layer of mud at the bottom. If you stir up that mud, the whole lake becomes muddy for a time. Distractions, evil thoughts, wicked desires, will rise. Let them come up and then get rid of them with light.
2. Prevent the mind from trying to rewrite what is going on, to justify or make excuses. If emotions start to rise, it means your point of view is slipping down into the astral plane.

Break the connection and restart, or do the "think an opposite thought" technique. Tell yourself, "I am observing", or reconnect with the Light of your soul.

3. One of the hazards in the early stages of detachment work occurs when the student tries to observe an emotional situation while holding an impartial, detached perspective. This is what we are instructed to do. But often, it is impossible. We energise with our eyes whatever it is we look at. In this situation, the emotional drama when gazed upon, sucks the observing student back into the turmoil. If this happens, then use one of the techniques that counter-balance what is happening, such as Think an Opposite Thought.

4. In the first few months in this detachment work, the mind will have a great many thoughts. Then as these disciplines are applied, it will begin to calm down. Each day as desires and thoughts are reduced, it will become less restless, and less violent. Eventually, you will be able to entirely separate yourself from the mind and actually know it to be apart from yourself.

5. Practise patiently every day. It is a tremendous work, not to be done in a day. Only after a patient, continuous struggle for years can we succeed and control the mind at will.

When the work of the first four means of Raja Yoga are successful - in particular that of Pratyahara; then sutra 55 is achieved.

2:55. The result of the (previous four means, and pratyahara) is the complete subjugation of the sense organs.

As pratyahara is steadily practised, the senses will become quiescent, consciousness will cease its outward surge, the psychic nature will be controlled. This is a major step forward in our spiritual growth.

> *Those who have succeeded*
> *in attaching or detaching*
> *their minds at will*
> *have succeeded in Pratyahara,*
> *which means gathering towards,*
> *checking the outgoing powers*
> *of the mind, freeing it*
> *from the thralldom of the senses.*
>
> *When we can do this,*
> *we shall really possess character;*
> *then alone we shall have taken*
> *a long step towards freedom.*
>
> *Before that, we are*
> *mere machines.*
>
> Swami Vivekananda.

BOOK 3: UNION AND ITS RESULTS.

The first three sutras in Book 3 (sutra 3:1 Concentration, sutra 3:2 Meditation, and sutra 3:3 Contemplation or Samadhi) complete the Eight Means of Raja Yoga. The two following sutras (3:4 and 3:5), describe the effects of the successful practice of these Means. The study of Raja Yoga in this book stops at sutra 3:5. The rest of Patanjali's work (in Book 3 and Book 4), are for initiates. Those who wish to study the entire manual can do so in Bailey's book, "The Light of the Soul."

MEANS VI DHARANA - CONCENTRATION.

3:1. Concentration is the fixing of the chitta (mind stuff) upon a particular object. This is dharana.

Dharana can be translated as "holding steady". Concentration is the power to focus the mind on a given subject and to hold it there as long as desired. The mind should be conscious only of itself and the object. The physical body, emotions, surroundings, and all sounds and sights are lost sight of and the brain is conscious only of the seed object. Then the mind's true function comes into play - to be an intermediary between the soul and brain, to transmit to the brain that which the soul has become aware of. If we are to master the science of meditation we must learn to concentrate. Occult meditation is based upon being able to concentrate upon a chosen "seed thought."

Average man does most things unconsciously. He eats unconsciously, drinks unconsciously and talks unconsciously. He is either completely or partially unaware of the afflictions (negative thoughts) rampaging through his mind, influencing everything that he does. Aspirants must learn to stay focused in the present moment. This starts with concentration.

The best way to harness the mind's attention is to become really interested and focused on whatever is being done in the moment. This will make the mind one-pointed. Avoid daydreaming and that half-alert state of mind when the mind is allowed to drift. In daily life, focus steadily on what you are doing and saying. Be mindful.

Correctly practised, Dharana causes a particular kind of mental wave to arise, which gradually becomes more prominent because it is not being swallowed up by other waves that have been triggered by distractions. When the multiplicity of these waves recede, just the meditation wave is present. When the whole mind has become one wave, this is Samadhi. Until concentration is achieved, true meditation is impossible. Meditation is extended concentration. So, the student needs to diligently develop concentration.

Concentration exercise 1: on an External Object
Choose an object. For instance, a triangle, square, circle, cube, sphere, cup, apple, flower etc. You can use a different object each time. Place it before you. Go into meditation pose. With the eyes closed take a few deep breaths.
1. Open your eyes and look at the object you have chosen. [Eg. apple.]
2. Think of nothing except the apple for 1 - 3 minutes. This is long enough for a beginning. Note its shape, its colour, the stalk and any other details such as the number of circles,

lines and shapes, etc. If your mind wanders to other objects, come back again to the apple. You are interested only in the apple. Do not drift into a dreamy state. You are looking at the apple and this is your great interest, your sole interest.
3. Close your eyes and continue to visualize the apple, to think about it. It is at this point that you may find thoughts wander. Come back to the apple. When thoughts wander again, come back to the apple.
4. Stop before the brain gets tired. Do not strain so that you get a headache or get bored with the exercise. At the end of the exercise, take a few deep breaths, open the eyes and look around, feel bright.

Concentration exercise 2: on an Internal Object
1. Select an object that is part of yourself such as the tip of the tongue, nose, a central point on the top of the head, the area between the eyebrows or the little finger.
2. Feel your consciousness withdraw from the rest of the body to the spot chosen, say the little finger. Wriggle it so that you feel its movement. Hold it still but keep your consciousness there. Think about it, its shape, the three parts with two joints, the fingernail, the sensitivity at the tip.
3. When you decide to stop, do this by allowing consciousness to flow back into the whole hand and to the rest of the body.
4. Focus either on your nostrils, or your abdomen.
5. With each breath, observe the effects - the subtle sensations as the breath enters and leaves the nose; or the in-out movement of the abdomen.

Concentration exercise 3: Sequential Thinking.
In meditation, this technique helps to keep the mind focused on a seed thought. It requires that you use intense concentration to stop the mind from wandering when you come to the end of a train of thought and before you move to the next thought.

For this exercise we will use the *Lord's Prayer*, since many have memorised it. Or use the Great Invocation, a favoured poem, etc. Close your eyes and starting from the beginning, silently recite each word, concentrating on just one word at a time as you proceed. If you are visual, see that word in your mind's eye. Do not race through the process but set a steady pace. Be careful when you come to the end of a sentence or phrase, because that is when restless mind will try to flick away. Work through the prayer step by step, word by word, concentrating to your utmost, until you come to the end. When successful, congratulate yourself. Practice on other mantrams, prayers or poems.

> Our Father, who art in heaven, hallowed be thy name;
> thy kingdom come; thy will be done on earth as it is in heaven.
> Give us this day our daily bread; and forgive us our trespasses
> as we forgive those who trespass against us;
> and lead us not into temptation,
> but deliver us from evil. Amen.

There are many other exercises to do such as counting exercises, Sudoku, etc. Try to do daily mental gymnastics to keep the brain young - especially as you age.

MEANS VII. DHYANA - MEDITATION

[The Master said] Now comes to all of you the most important series of lives to which the previous points of culmination were but stepping stones. In the lives immediately ahead of those upon the Path will come final achievement through the instrumentality of the ordered occult meditation, based on law. For some few may come attainment in this life or the next; for others, shortly in other lives. Master Djwhal Khul.

1. Occult Meditation.

3:2. Sustained concentration (dharana) is meditation (dhyana).

The method of meditation taught by Patanjali and used in this book is Occult Meditation. It teaches us to identify with our soul and to become in outer manifestation what we are in inner reality - a sacred Being. It facilitates our union with the Divine by developing and merging our consciousness with Universal Mind.

Occult meditation hinges on the mind - it is a strictly mental process that trains the mind to observe eternal states. This mind becomes an instrument for illumination, because through it, the soul or Self transmits its wisdom to the physical brain (body).

> Through meditation, spiritual knowledge grows up within the mind, and from the basis of ordinary knowledge, we steadily expand our understanding of the term, until knowledge merges into wisdom. This is direct knowledge of God by means of the mental faculty, so that we become what we are, and are enabled to manifest our divine nature. Thus, meditation brings about union, or at-one-ment. [1]

a. Meditation without and with Seed.

There are two types of Occult Meditation - with a "seed" (judicial reasoning), or without.

1. In meditation without an object - or seedless meditation; the rational mind and its ability to concretise is not used. The experienced meditator immediately bypasses the mind and enters directly into the realm of ideas and of causes. This is pure contemplation, free from forms and thought. This is a very advanced technique and is not for beginners, who should start by using a seed-thought.

> 3:42. When the perceiver blends the words, the idea (or meaning) and the object, this is called the mental condition of judicial reasoning.

2. Meditation with an object or seed uses the rationalising judicial mind with its concretising faculty and its ability to create thought forms. This is the recommended method to use and only when it has been mastered, should the disciple try the first method. There is a danger for the unprepared student in seedless meditation. If the will is used to force the mind

1 Bailey, Alice. From Intellect to Intuition, 80-81.

to be still, or the mind is allowed to drift, it is damaging for health and counter-productive for the meditation process.

But both methods have the same goal in mind, to reach the realm of pure ideas and of causes. Just the means to get there is different.

Through Meditation:
1. We discover our relation to the universe, that our physical body and vital energies are part of the outer garment of Deity or Universal Mind.
2. We find that our ability to love and feel puts us in touch with the love that pulses at the heart of all creation.
3. We discover that the mind is the key that unlocks the door of wisdom and when enlightened, it enables us to enter the purposes and plans of Deity.
4. We eventually arrive at the Source of all. Knowing that we are divine, we find that the whole is equally divine.
5. The powers of the soul unfold, new states of consciousness register and a new phenomenal world is seen.
6. We transform from being a selfish and unhappy person who is attached to outer material life, into a blissful, free and spiritually powerful soul.

2. Dangers of Occult Meditation.

1. Overstimulation of the nervous system.
Care needs to be taken because activity takes place on the mental plane, the plane of fire. Flooding an unaccustomed nervous system with this fire is dangerous and overstimulation of the nervous system is a common problem. Early signs are excitability, an inability to relax, increased irritability, twitching, depression and low vitality. In the early stages, keep meditation under 15 minutes to avoid this problem.

2. Depleting the energies of the physical body to a dangerous level.
People who constantly dwell in a state of excited emotional rapture, yearning for a blissful connection with the divine, can starve the physical body of energy. In extreme cases, people have died from this.

3. Impairment of sense perception.
Another highly dangerous practice is forcing the mind to be still by either using the will to force the mind to be still or going "into the void," or by simply by "spacing out." In these states, the mind is held in a state of blankness. This can cause permanent damage to the senses, so that contact with life on the physical plane is impaired. In meditation, you must stay alert. If you feel yourself losing consciousness or drifting, refocus in your mind.

> [Patanjali said] By withdrawing from active sense perception, by no longer utilising the "outward-going" consciousness, by abstracting that consciousness from the periphery to the centre, he can bring on a condition of passivity - a lack of awareness, which is not the samadhi of the yogi, nor the achievement of one-pointedness such as the student of yoga aspires to, but which is a form of trance. This self-imposed quieting is not only a detriment to the achievement of the highest yoga but is excessively dangerous in many cases. [1]

---
1 Bailey, Alice. Light of the Soul, 21-22.

Watch the brain function for any dulling of its normal activities such as difficulty thinking or focusing, or a deep mental lethargy as if the mind is in a heavy fog. If so, check to ensure you are not blanking out. Stop all meditation work until the situation heals. Instead, practice physical forms of meditation such as Hatha Yoga or Tai Chi.

4. Emotional and sexual overstimulation.

To ensure the sexual nature is not being overstimulated, avoid meditating immediately after sexual intercourse. If your mind is continually being excited by sex thoughts, there is a danger that in meditation, instead of consciousness lifting into the higher self, attention will be drawn to the sex-region because the in-coming energies pour straight down there rather than being arrested in the heart, ajna or crown chakras as they should be. If this occurs, all meditation should cease until the situation reverses itself. More physical forms of meditation such as Tai Chi or Hatha Yoga should be practiced instead.

5. Raising kundalini fire.

Violent meditation or focusing on the chakras to stimulate progress may cause kundalini fire to rise too soon, before the body can handle it. If so, it will destroy body and brain tissue, and this can impede further occult work for several lives. The occult rule is to never focus on kundalini - it will rise normally if the Raja Yoga disciplines are correctly followed.

6. Dangers from subtle forces

Would-be magicians who successfully use mantrams to summon unintelligent members of the deva kingdom, can be attacked by these elemental forces. Additionally, unpleasant and sometimes dangerous denizens may emerge from the astral plane if the doorway to that plane has been opened through practices such as "sitting for development," past life regression, dream retrieval, astral travelling, etc.

To overcome meditation problems.

Stop meditating immediately. Take steps to strengthen the physical body through exercise, sunshine and by bathing the etheric body with violet light. Nourish the emotional body with inspirational music, beauty in nature and by thinking positive thoughts. Strengthen the mind with mental exercises and concentration. Do not meditate again until health is restored and the mind is alert, strong and able to focus. Observe the following points.

1. Be clear about your limitations and your strengths.
2. Proceed slowly and with caution and study effects, realising that eternity is long and that which is slowly but soundly built, endures.
3. Aim for regularity.
4. Realise that psychic phenomena is regressive and does not indicate successful meditation. True spiritual effects are seen by an expansion of wisdom and a life of selfless and compassionate service.

Quiet the mind and the soul will speak. – Ma Jaya Sati Bhagavati.

Meditation is not about stopping thoughts, but recognizing that we are more than our thoughts and our feelings. – Arianna Huffington.

Learn to be calm and you will always be happy. – Paramahansa Yogananda.

3. Preparation for Meditation.

Around sunrise is the best time for meditation - in a quiet spot. Make the meditation space beautiful and fragrant. Use incense, flowers, a photograph or statue of an enlightened Master. Burn a candle to purify the atmosphere.

The goal is to forget about your body during meditation. Sit comfortably, spine erect, on a chair or floor, hands gently clasped together in your lap. Balance your head comfortably on your neck, the chin slightly down and ensure there is no tension in your jaw or body. Breathe two or three breaths, relaxing as you out-breathe. Eyes are normally closed, though may be opened slightly (looking downwards) to help stay alert if necessary.

For beginners, fifteen minutes is ample time to meditate. The point is not how long you meditate, but whether the practice brings a certain state of mindfulness and presence. Five minutes of wakeful alertness is of far greater value than twenty minutes dozing.

1. Selection of a seed thought.

It is important to pick a "seed" that is beautiful, inspiring and spiritual. From the seed a "tree" will grow and we want it to be helpful for the spiritual journey. The meditation process starts by concentrating on the seed, then moves forwards as a new thought rises from the seed, then another thought rises, and so on. Each subsequent thought should take us closer to the light, love and wisdom of God. It is like a spiral of thoughts that raises consciousness from the seed to God. Here is an example given by Alice Bailey. The seed thought was "Thou God seest me" and it is included so students can see how sequential thoughts can arise in the mind of a practiced meditator.

> Thou God seest me.
> This God is the divine in me, the indwelling Christ, the Soul.
> For long ages this soul has perceived and observed me.
> Now for the first time I am in a position to see God.
> Up till now, I have been negative to this divine Reality.
> The positive relation is becoming possible.
> But — this seems to involve the idea of duality.
> But I and God are one.
> I am God, and have been all the time.
> Therefore I have been seen by my Self.
> I am that Self, That Self am I.

2. The sacred word "OM".

The OM is the sound or word of the soul. When correctly sounded, it attracts finer matter into our various bodies and casts out that which is coarse. Sounding the OM mindfully, helps to release the soul from its entanglement with the world of glamour. It assists alignment with the soul and helps to hold the lower bodies steady. To gain maximum benefit, sound the OM inaudibly within the head, then hear it reverberate there recognising that this sound is part of the original Sound of the Most High.

> The Sound is the name of the One in Whom we live and move and have our being and when it is the dominating note, the initiate is identifying with the Whole. [1]

---

[1] Gathered from AAB. The Rays and the Initiations, 52-53.

A. The Basic Occult Meditation Method.

There are five steps in the Raja Yoga meditation method. Each step leads sequentially to the next. Keep these five steps in mind and endeavour to practise them in meditation and in daily life.

Stage 1. Basic alignment.

1. Body relaxed, eyes closed.
2. Go within. Disconnect attention from the outer world and focus high in the head. Hold focus there throughout the meditation.
3. Align with your soul. Visualise the soul sending light down through your physical body, cleansing and purifying. Simultaneously sound an OM (silent or out loud).
4. Visualise the soul sending light down through the emotional vehicle. OM.
5. Visualise the soul sending light down through the mind. OM
6. Refocus in your head, "look" upwards at the soul and feel its enfolding presence.
7. Sound an OM, attuning your whole nature to the love and wisdom of the soul.

Stage 2. Meditation with Seed.

1. [Concentration]. Select a seed-thought and hold the words before your inner eye and commit them to memory. Slowly repeat-read the words a few times to impress it on your mind and to more clearly understand what the phrase means.

2. [Meditation]. Then move to the first associated thought that rises, then to the next and so on. Remember to concentrate so that mind does not wander off as you step forwards. Use the Sequential Thinking or Flower methods.

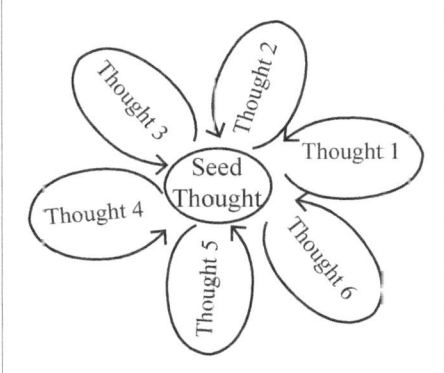

The Flower method of Meditation.
1. From the seed-thought, step forwards to investigate thought 1.
2. Then go back to the seed-thought, and repeat it.
3. Then step forwards to investigate thought 2, etc.

Finally, there comes a point in meditation, when you sense that your investigation of the seed has come to an end. You have gained a deeper comprehension about the seed and its relation to the whole and to the eternal Realities. The data-gathering has given you a clearer and more insightful understanding. This is the stage when - once practiced and accomplished in the meditation process, consciousness slips past mind into the contemplation stage.

Stage 3. Contemplation.

1. Allow consciousness to rise into the contemplation stage and soul impression. Be receptive to Divine inspiration and imagine receiving it.

> *At the beginning, you may have to act "as if" you are contemplating (which is the process when you connect with ideas in the Mind of God, and they come streaming towards you). You are not using the mind. It is still. You are using the intuition, the "pure reasoning" faculty. You see and absorb what the universe is imparting to you.*

2. See a soul inspired thought or symbol drop into your consciousness.

This may not happen at once but keep trying and in time it will. You may have to imagine a symbol dropping into your mind.

Contemplation is the high-point of the meditation, one in which we become one with God or with our spiritual source. This is what we should always aim for. (See Means VIII, Samadhi, for more information on contemplation).

Stage 4. Illumination.

1. At the end of the contemplation stage, consciousness drops back into the mind and it begins to analyse what was seen and touched. At this stage, the soul will try to illumine the mind with its wisdom, to help us understand what was touched upon in the contemplation period. Our job is to use the mind to receive this data, to sort, memorise and absorb what we saw or heard during the contemplative stage.

2. Then summarise in a few sentences the main impressions and understandings gained in the entire meditation. You may choose to write these in a spiritual journal. [1]

3. Close the meditation by sounding the Great Invocation, sending the accumulated light, love and will-to-good to humanity.

> THE GREAT INVOCATION
>
> From the point of Light within the Mind of God,
> Let Light stream forth into the minds of men,
> Let Light descend on Earth.
>
> From the point of Love within the Heart of God,
> Let Love stream forth into the hearts of men,
> May Christ return to Earth.
>
> From the centre where the Will of God is known,
> Let purpose guide the little wills of men,
> The purpose which the Masters know and serve.
>
> From the centre which we call the race of men,
> Let the Plan of Love and Light work out,
> And may it seal the door where evil dwells.
> Let Light and Love and Power restore the Plan on Earth.
> OM ... OM ... OM. [2]

Stage 5. Inspiration

Impressed with light, love and inspiration received in the meditation period, this changes our atomic makeup and we take these higher lighted energies and use them to live a more inspired life.

---

[1] A spiritual journal. Students are advised to keep such a journal and record only those thoughts and impressions that have to do with their spiritual endeavours.

[2] The Great Invocation. This invocation is a potent invocation designed to bring about needed spiritual adjustments in humanity. Its evocative power is increasingly attracting the forces of Light, Love and spiritual Power into humanity.

B. Other Meditations.

------------- 1. Solar Meditations at the Full Moon period -------------

The periods around each full moon are awash with spiritual energies, which pour into earth space because of the more refined atmosphere that prevails at that time. The Sun, radiating the power of spirit, dominates the Moon, which represents the forces of evil. To take advantage of this, the Guides of the race hold rituals to invoke higher spiritual forces from the astrology sign the Sun happens to be passing through (from the earth perspective). Djwhal Khul said that a new world religion would arise based on celebrations held at this time.

We can all assist the healing of humanity and the spiritual evolution of the planet by meditating at each full Moon, using the astrology sign and theme which the Sun happens to be in. Each sign has its own quality and vibration. These are given later. Aries, Taurus and Gemini are the most important festivals. They build the divine qualities of Will, Love and Abstract Intelligence into the collective consciousness.

> The two major Full Moon Approaches will be those of the Wesak Full Moon (consecrated to the Buddha Who embodies the wisdom of God) and the Full Moon of June (consecrated to the Bodhisattva - known to Christians as the Christ) Who embodies the love of God. [1]

------ Solar Meditation at the Scorpio Full Moon period ------

This is a meditation format which can be used at any full moon. This meditation is for Scorpio. The leader reads through the meditation, line by line, pausing when necessary.

Welcome to this Scorpio Solar Fire Celebration.
We have come together to send healing into earth-space and to all the kingdoms in nature. Close your eyes. Let us bathe in the spiritual energies pouring into our space today, using our creative imagination to see the golden light surrounding and pervading us. Feel the heightened vibration. Sense the increased light and love. Let us give thanks for this land we are upon and all the creatures we share it with, and the First Nations people who call it home.

1. Dedication.

a. Let us see ourselves surrounded by our family and loved ones and all sentient beings.

b. Today, in the name of Christ, I dedicate our group work to the glory of God, to the upliftment and healing of humanity, to the healing of all sentient beings and to the healing of the planet.

c. I invite all those on the other side of the veil and the deva angels, those who wish to join us in this group work, to do so now and step into the group.

d. I call upon the Archangels to assist us in our work and ensure it supports the Plan for humanity.

> Before us stands Raphael, behind us stand Gabriel,
> to the right stands Michael, to the left stands Uriel;
> Around us flames the pentagram.
> And in the centre we take our stand, beneath the blazing Star of Christ.

---
1 Bailey, Alice. The Externalisation of the Hierarchy, 55.

2. Alignment.

a. Disconnect your awareness from the outer world and turn within.

b. Align with your soul, your source of light, love and wisdom – OM.

c. Let us align invoke the light and love of the soul, to purify our natures.
   - Send soul light through the physical body – OM
   - Send soul light through the emotional body – OM
   - Send soul light through the mind body – OM
   - Send soul light through the group – OM

3. Group fusion.

Let us integrate as a group:

a. From your heart chakra, send love to the right and to the left, so we are bonded in a circle of love. OM

b. Visualise our solar angels hovering just behind each of us, and all others who have joined our group seated in the greater group circle. As we sound the OM, see all sound the OM from their hearts, sending it to the right and left, building and integrating the larger group. OM

c. Let us observe the network of the New Group of World Servers – a network of inter-linked lighted triangles that surrounds the planet. All individuals and groups in the world whose hearts are open to the love and light streaming in from the One Soul of Humanity and who work for world goodwill; are part of this group. The NGWS mediates between Hierarchy and humanity. Let us see our group as one point in this lighted network. Feel the connection with the worldwide group - the light flowing from the network to us, and our light flowing out to them.

d. Say the Mantram of the New Group of World Servers

> May the Power of the one Life pour through the group of all true servers;
> May the Love of the one Soul characterise the lives
> of all who seek to aid the Great Ones.
> May we fulfill our part in the one Work through
> self-forgetfulness, harmlessness, and right speech. OM.

4. Alignment.

a. We project a line of lighted energy towards the spiritual Hierarchy of the planet, the planetary heart, and towards the Christ at the heart of Hierarchy. OM.

For a few moments, let us feel the energy of the Christ permeate our group.

b. Extend the line of light towards Shamballa, the centre where the Will of God is known and to the Lord of the World, Sanat Kumara. OM.

c. We now have alignment between Shamballa, the Hierarchy, the New Group of World Servers of which we are a part, and humanity.

d. We are now open to the cosmos and the energies of light, love and spiritual power pouring in. Let us visualise this energy stream flow from The Great Bear, Sirius and the Pleiades (forming a triangle), through Scorpio to our Sun; and flowing out via Mars, Pluto and Mercury to Earth.

5. Meditation.

a. The meditation keynote for Scorpio is: "Warrior am I and from the battle I emerge triumphant". The lighted power we work with is the yellow ray, the 4th Ray of Harmony through Conflict.

b. In our meditation, let us strengthen with our thoughts, the one soul of humanity. Let us see all human souls merging and rising as a spiritual warrior to fight intelligently against injustice. Let us see harmony being created from conflict. Our weapon is light, the light of clear mind and the love of the One Soul. "Warrior am I and from the battle I emerge triumphant." [A period of silent meditation]

5. Precipitation.

Our group now acts as a channel for the spiritual energies pouring in from the cosmos and from the Lord of Scorpio into our planet. We use the pathway of light established from

- Shamballa
- Hierarchy
- the Christ
- the new group of world servers
- men and women of goodwill everywhere in the world
- physical centres of distribution (London, Darjeeling, Tokyo, Geneva, New York)

The pathway distributes into humanity as a whole. Consider that Christ is using this channel to come closer to humanity. In focused silence, let the group be an unobstructed channel for the light and love streaming in from Scorpio, into humanity, into all sentient beings and into the planet.

6. Distribution.

Let us seal this work by sounding the Great Invocation. Simultaneously visualise Light, Love and Power pour through the five planetary inlets of, Darjeeling, Geneva, London, New York and Tokyo; thereby irradiating the entire consciousness of the human race.

> THE GREAT INVOCATION
> From the point of Light within the Mind of God,
> Let Light stream forth into the minds of men,
> Let Light descend on earth.
> From the point of Love within the Heart of God,
> Let Love stream forth into the hearts of men,
> May Christ return to earth.
> From the centre where the Will of God is known,
> Let purpose guide the little wills of men,
> The purpose which the Masters know and serve.
> From the centre which we call the race of men,
> Let the Plan of Love and Light work out,
> And may it seal the door where evil dwells.
> Let Light and Love and Power restore the Plan on earth.
> OM ... OM ... OM

1. The three major full moon festivals.

Aries: Easter, Festival of the Risen Christ.
Keynote: "I come forth and from the plane of mind - I rule".
In this festival, the forces of restoration flowing from the Mind of God stimulate the mind of man, inspiring him to initiate a new and higher World Order based on Christ principles. These energies affect governments and politics in particular.
Energies available to work with are: R1 of Will and Power (the colour of this ray is red), and R7 of Ceremony, Order and Magic (violet). Planet rulers Mars, Mercury and Uranus.

Taurus: Wesak, Festival of the Buddha.
Keynote: "I see and when the eye is opened, all is light".
In this festival, the forces of enlightenment flowing from the Heart of God stimulates hearts and minds, urging mankind to develop a wiser understanding of all men and women.
R4 Ray of Harmony through Conflict (yellow). Planet rulers Venus and Vulcan.

Gemini: Goodwill Festival of the World Teacher - Christ, World Invocation Day.
Keynote: "I see my other self and in the waning of that self, I grow and glow."
This is the festival of the Spirit of Humanity aspiring towards God. Christ, standing before the assembled Hierarchy and representing humanity, "preaches again the last sermon of the Buddha." [1] This invokes the forces of reconstruction and promotes world unity and peace.
R2 of Love-Wisdom (indigo blue). Planet rulers Mercury, Venus, the Earth.

2. The nine other full moon festivals.

Cancer.
Keynote "I build a lighted house and therein dwell."
This festival cleanses the collective mind of man of negativity, emotionalism and separativeness. See dark clouds of fear dissolving under spiritual force and the mind of man becoming radiant and translucent. Vision the one family of man.
R3 of Intelligent-Activity (green), and R7 of Ceremony, Order and Magic (violet). Planet rulers the Moon and Neptune.

Leo.
Keynote "I am That and That am I."
This festival helps to integrate the various nations and races into a unified whole and brings humanity under the influence of the Spiritual Hierarchy. See humanity respond to love flowing from the Hierarchy and will-to-good permeating political and power institutions.
R1 of Will and Power (red), and R5 of Concrete Mind and Science (orange). Planet rulers the Sun, Vulcan, Neptune and Uranus.

Virgo.
Keynote "I am the mother and the child, I God, I matter am."
Virgo symbolises the birth of the Christ child [soul]. This festival purifies the lower nature so that the beauty of the soul can shine through. See human consciousness evolving into Christ [group] consciousness.
R2 of Love-Wisdom (indigo blue), and R6 of Devotion-Idealism (pale blue). Planet rulers Mercury, Vulcan and Jupiter.

1 Bailey, Alice. The Externalisation of the Hierarchy, 480.

Libra.
Keynote "I choose the way which lies between the two great lines of force."
This festival helps to restore balance in all departments of human life, but particularly in relations between people, groups and nations. See spiritual order and right human relations manifest throughout the world.
R3 of Intelligent-Activity (green). Planet rulers Venus, Uranus, Saturn.

Scorpio.
Keynote "Warrior I am and from the battle I emerge triumphant."
This festival urges man to fight the dark side of his nature. See light destroying hatred, separativeness and cruelty in all human departments. See the human spirit soaring victoriously, like an eagle.
Scorpio expresses R4 of Harmony through Conflict (yellow). Planet rulers Mars, Pluto and Mercury.

Sagittarius.
Keynote "I see the goal, I reach that goal and then I see another."
This festival inspires man to manifest his higher ideals, to search for higher understanding, to find and walk the Spiritual Path. See humanity re-orienting itself towards higher ideals such as peace and goodwill.
R4 of Harmony through Conflict (yellow), R5 of Concrete mind and Science (orange), and R6 of Devotion-Idealism (pale blue). Planet rulers Jupiter, the Earth and Mars.

Capricorn.
Keynote "Lost am I in light supernal, yet on that light I turn my back."
This festival urges man to give his resources and sacrifice his life for the greater good. See governments, power institutions and leaders, transformed by spiritual Light and serving the needs of the masses.
R1 of Will and Power (red), R3 of Intelligent-Activity (green), and R7 of Ceremony, Order and Magic (violet). Planet rulers Saturn and Venus.

Aquarius.
Keynote "Water of life am I, poured forth for thirsty men."
This festival promotes universal brotherhood and the urge to give where the need is greatest. See spiritual love and light wash away prejudice from the collective consciousness, stimulating cooperation between all nations.
R5 of Concrete mind and Science (orange). Planet rulers Uranus, Jupiter and Uranus.

Pisces.
Keynote "I leave my Father's house and turning back, I save."
This festival promotes an urge to help heal and save the suffering masses. See the collective consciousness imbued with Christ light, all suffering alleviated and humanity saved and light-filled.
R2 of Love-Wisdom (indigo blue), and R6 of Devotion-Idealism (pale blue). Planet rulers Jupiter, Neptune and Pluto.

2. The Yoga of Light Meditation

Geoffrey Hodson (1886-1983) was an occultist, Theosophist, Co-Freemason, mystic, Liberal Catholic priest, philosopher and a leading light for over 70 years in the Theosophical Society. He recommended this meditation, which he received from the Indian sage Ramana Maharshi. Here is what he said about the meditation.

To the permissible aspiration for psychic awareness and cell-enfiring yoga, leave room for the yogic experience of One-ness.

As the yogi develops, he or she continuously gains deeper and deeper realisations that the idea of "others", of oneself as a separate entity, are erroneous. They have been necessary for the successful passage through phases of human life, for the mental experience from personal to impersonal. But in the Universe there is only a Vast Unitary Identity, a ONE, a UNIT - not separate because there is nothing else in existence from which to be separated.

Like all Sun-Rays and other radiances physical and superphysical emanating from the Sun, each human "Ray" (Monad) is an indivisible part of the Sun or Source.

In the quietude of your own mind as you meditate, dwell upon this extraordinary and wondrous Truth that ONLY ONE EXISTS and there are not any others anywhere. Then affirm in your meditative consciousness and seek ever to know "I am that all inclusive ONE, THAT am I."

The Yoga of Light Meditation

1. Place your consciousness in the middle of your head.
2. Try and hold it there and then whilst your consciousness is in or near that position, repeat contemplatively and yogically the aphorisms on ONENESS as follows:

    i. There is only one Vast Unitary Identity, a ONE, A UNIT.

    ii. All are like SUN-RAYS and other radiances emanating from the SUN.

    iii. Each human "RAY" (Monad) is an indivisible part of the Sun or SOURCE.

    iv. The extraordinary and wondrous TRUTH that ONLY ONE EXISTS and there are not any others anywhere. I seek ever to know and affirm: "I AM THAT ALL INCLUSIVE ONE, THAT AM I."

    v. I ENTER INTO this knowledge of ONLY ONE-NESS: I AM THAT ONE, THAT ONE AM I."

3. Let exaltation fill your mind as you contemplate this splendour, glory, truth that Only One exists, I am that One That am I." Sink into mental silence, contemplating the ONE ALONE in quietude.

Experience this at sunrise and at noon.

> If a person is truly on the yogic line of development there is no more direct form of guided meditation than "A Yoga of Light." Geoffrey Hodson.

-------------- 3. Meditation on Gautama Buddha --------------

1. Seated around me are family/ friends/ all sentient beings who just like me, want to find happiness and avoid suffering.
2. I see Buddha seated on a throne facing me.
His body is of fine golden light. His face is peaceful and beautiful. He smiles at me with love and compassion. I feel strongly that I am in His presence, that He wants to help me reach enlightenment.
3. See rays of light emanating from the Blessed One's body,
reaching all parts of the universe.
4. (From the heart) "I ask for your blessing, Lord Buddha,
that I may be free from all negative energy and misconceptions
and develop all realisations of the path to enlightenment."
5. Feel the request is granted - a stream of purifying white light flows from Buddha's heart and enters the crown chakra.
Feel that all negativities are dispelled.
Affirm "I am filled with blissful white light."
6. Chant Buddha's Mantra: "Tayata Om Muni Muni Maha Muniye Soha."
7. (From the heart) "Lord Buddha, I ask for your blessing, so that I can develop all your enlightened qualities for the benefit of all sentient beings.
8. Feel the request is granted.
A stream of purifying golden light flows from Buddha's heart,
it enters the crown chakra,
bringing all qualities of enlightened body, speech and mind.
See the body filled with this golden light.. feel great bliss.
9. Chant Buddha's Mantra: "Tayata Om Muni Muni Maha Muniye Soha."
10. Buddha comes to the crown of my head (facing forward with me).
11. I generate love and compassion for those surrounding me
"Tayata Om Muni Muni Maha Muniye Soha."
See light rays of wisdom and compassion radiate to them, to all,
bringing all the qualities of enlightened body, speech and mind.
- Feel strongly that all their negativities are purified and that they become perfectly enlightened, experiencing great bliss and wisdom.
12. Buddha melts into pure golden light, which absorbs into me.
I dissolve, become one with Buddha's enlightened body, speech, mind;
one with Buddha's blissful, omniscient mind in the vastness of Space.
13. I rest in that.
14. I rejoice in having done the meditation, assisting the process of my own and other's enlightenment.
15. I dedicate any benefit I have gained from doing this meditation to attaining a perfect state of mind, so that I can benefit countless others.

----- 4. Meditation to align with one's Spiritual Nature -----

This meditation given by Djwhal Khul is from Letters on Occult Meditation. He said, "There is a direct relationship between the two twelve petalled centres (the heart centre between the shoulder blades and the other at the heart of the crown chakra). This visualization leads to synthesis, to causal development and expansion, and eventually conducts a man into the presence of the Master." [1]

1. The Basic Alignment.
2. Meditate on the heart centre, picturing it as a closed golden lotus.
3. Sound the Sacred Word OM and see the lotus slowly expand until the inner centre or vortex is seen as a radiating whirlpool of electric light, more blue than golden.
4. Build there the picture of the Master, in etheric, emotional and mental matter. This entails the withdrawing of the consciousness ever more and more inwards. OM.
5. When the picture is fully built then gently sound the Word again, and using the will withdraw still further inwards and link up with the twelve petalled lotus in the head centre, the centre of causal consciousness. OM.
6. Do all this very slowly and gradually, maintaining an attitude of perfect peace and calm.

----- 5. Garden Meditation -----

This meditation is very healing on all levels.

1. Basic Alignment.
2. Imagine you are entering a landscape on the inner planes and your task is to create an imaginary garden, one that will become a place of healing for you and for others.
3. For several minutes, create your garden. Fill it with flowers, trees, add rocks and water features - whatever, to maximise its beauty.
4. Then for a few minutes, bathe in the fragrant beauty of your garden. Feel the healing energies of nature, the gentle play of the Sun, and the magic of the garden heal you.
5. Finally, send a blessing of peace and love to the world.

----- 6. Meditation on Silence -----

1. Basic Alignment.
2. You are standing on a busy street in the heart of a busy and noisy city.
3. See yourself enter an ornate doorway. Immediately, you step into a far distant spiritual temple, located high on a sacred mountain. It is silent. The view before you is of mountain tops. There is no one else present. You sit in silent contemplation, looking at the view. Rejoicing in the silence, you listen to what silence sounds like.
4. Then you move your awareness inwards - imagining that you are moving ever deeper into the Spiritual Light and Silence within. Dwell there a while.
5. Send a blessing of peace and goodwill to the world.

---

[1] Bailey, Alice. Letters on Occult Meditation, 84.

7. Meditation to open the Heart Chakra

1. Basic Alignment.
2. Align with your Monad, the "Greatest Light."
3. See a clear cool stream of spiritual love, flow from the Monad into the love petals of the egoic lotus, energising and opening them.
4. Into the astral body, energising all astral matter; then briefly
5. Into the solar plexus, purifying and energising it, then up to the heart centre.
6. See and feel the heart centre expand and radiate love through your whole being.
7. Radiate spiritual love to the world.

8. Breathing with God

You imagine that you are breathing with God, drawing in the light and love of God on each in breath, and on the out-breath, God draws in and transmutes any negativity you exhale.

1. Do the Basic Alignment.
2. As you breath in, God exhales and you breath in the light and love of God.
3. As you breathe out, God inhales your breath.
4. You breathe in God's breath - light and love.
5. You exhale and God breathes in your breath, and so on.

9. Healing Meditation

This can be used at any time including in the first part of the Solar Meditations.

1. Let us imagine that we are seated in a temple of healing high in the sacred Himalayas. The temple is crystalline white and the atmosphere is filled with the sacred energies of the great ones, it is still and serene. We breathe in this serenity and stillness. Pause.
2. In the centre of the temple, we see suspended - partway between the roof and the floor, a large, sacred, white rose. It represents the Heart of God and radiates divine healing light and love into the room. We breathe in this light.
3. Let us open our minds, hearts and body to Universal Healing as it flows through the Rose. Let us breathe in this flow of light and love, and on the out-breath, send it through our bodies. Let us do this with several slow breaths.
4. Let us now ask for healing for our friends and loved ones and for all sentient beings. As we name each person, see that person appear in the centre of the temple under the Rose. We also include in our request, healing for all sentient beings and see them surround us. (The leader begins, then go around each person in turn). "I ask for healing for …"
5. May all our loved ones and friends be made whole in Light and Love.

10. Mantrams and Affirmations

1. *OM Mane Padme Hum,* "the jewel in the lotus", referring to the energy of spirit that is anchored in the egoic lotus and at the central point in the seven major chakras. Sound this mantram daily. It is "the most sacred of all the Eastern mantrams given out as yet.

2. *The Gayatri:* is widely used - mostly at dawn to salute the rising Sun (God rising within). The Gayatri is a plea for enlightenment so we can better help others.

> Oh Thou, Who givest sustenance to the universe.
> From whom all things proceed, to whom all things return.
> Unveil to me the face of the true spiritual Sun,
> Hidden by a disk of golden light.
> That I may know the truth and do my whole duty,
> as I journey to Thy sacred feet.

3. *The Noon Mantram.*

> O Lord of Light and Love I know about the need;
> Touch my heart anew with love,
> That I too may love and give.

4. *5pm Mantram of the New Group of World Servers.*

> May the Power of the One Life, pour through the group of all true servers;
> May the love of the One Soul, characterise the lives of all
> Who seek to aid the great ones.
> May I fulfil my part in the one work,
> Through self-forgetfulness, harmlessness, and right speech.

5. *Group Bonding.*

> I am one with my group brothers and sisters, and all that I have is theirs;
> May the love which is in my soul pour forth to them,
> May the strength which is in me lift and aid them,
> May the thoughts which my soul creates, reach and encourage them.

6. *Affirmation of a disciple.*

> I am a point of light within a greater Light.
> I am a strand of loving energy within the stream of love divine.
> I am a point of sacrificial Fire, focussed within the fiery Will of God.
> And thus I stand.
>
> I am a way by which men may achieve.
> I am a source of strength, enabling them to stand.
> I am a beam of light, shining upon their way.
> And thus I stand.
>
> And standing thus revolve, and tread this way the ways of men,
> And know the ways of God.
> And thus I stand.

7. *Affirmation of service.*

> In the centre of the will of God I stand.
> Naught shall deflect my will from His.
> I implement that will by love.
> I turn towards the field of service.
> I, the Triangle divine, work out that will
> Within the square and serve my fellowmen.

MEANS VIII SAMADHI - CONTEMPLATION

> The gradual conquest of the mind's tendency to flit from one object to another and the power of one-pointedness make the development of contemplation. [1]

Contemplation has previously and briefly been touched upon. Towards the end of the meditation section, after the assembling of facts and their examination has proceeded for a period, a synthetic understanding arises from the data. A deeper and wider comprehension dawns. This is a clue that consciousness is slipping into the contemplation stage - where the mind is transcended.

> The term Samadhi derives from the roots sam-a-dha, which means "to collect" or "bring together." In early Buddhist texts, it is also associated with the term "samatha" (calm abiding).

In contemplation, consciousness transfers out of the mind into that of the spiritual man, the soul on its own plane in the world of causes. Technically, consciousness has moved from the lower mind body into the egoic lotus, [2] the soul body. Then it is the soul who contemplates. It is the high point in the meditation, when efforts to be free of the modifications of chitta are realised and consciousness has been raised into the spiritual realms - there, to calmly contemplate with the Mind of God

2:3. Samadhi (contemplation) results when chitta gives up all forms, and becomes absorbed in reality, reflecting only the meaning.

In contemplation, it is the soul that contemplates.

> The human consciousness ceases its activity and the man becomes what he is in reality — a soul, a fragment of divinity, conscious of its essential oneness with Deity. The lower or personal self is entirely quiescent and still, whilst the true spiritual Entity enters into its own kingdom and registers the contacts that emanate from that spiritual realm. The world of the soul is seen as a reality; the transcendental things are known to be facts in nature; union with Deity is realized as constituting as much a fact in the natural process as is the union between the life of the physical body and that body. [3]

Patanjali compares the experience of Samadhi to placing a transparent jewel on a coloured surface. The jewel (consciousness), takes on the colour of the surface (the Mind of God).

At this level, the source of illumination is tapped. The experience is a sense of vastness, an expansion accompanied by a sense of freedom, joy and bliss. This sense of bliss is confirmation that the contemplation stage has been reached.

> In Samadhi, that very deep state of meditation, you are given energy and long-lasting bliss. It carries you higher and higher until your very presence radiates love. Sri Ravi Shankar.

This completes this analysis of the 8 Means of Raja Yoga - Patanjali's guiding steps that lead us to enlightenment.

---

1 Patanjali.
2 Bailey, Alice. Light of the Soul, 39.
3 Bailey, Alice. From Intellect to Intuition, 137.

Sanyama.

Sanyama (also known as Samyama), is the demonstrated mastery of the three stages of meditation. The Sanskrit term "Samyama" is derived from *saṃ-yama* (holding together, tying up, binding, integration), referring to the combined simultaneous practice of Dharana (concentration), Dhyana (meditation) and Samadhi (union)

3:4. When concentration, meditation and contemplation form one sequential act, then is sanyama achieved.

The yogi - who now stands free from the lower worlds because they no longer attract his attention, can focus his attention at will and hold his mind steady in the mental world when required. He can centre himself in the consciousness of the soul, the spiritual man and look out into the world of the soul. From that level - as the soul, he knows himself to be separate from the lower instrument. He can transmit to the brain, via the controlled mind, that which he sees and can thus impart knowledge of the self and of its kingdom to the man on the physical plane.

At this level the indwelling consciousness is no longer a "human" soul or a member of the human kingdom; but now is a spiritual soul fully functioning in the kingdom of souls.

The radiation of Light.

As a consequence of Sanyama, all obstructions to soul influence are removed and consciousness has become a vessel for the shining forth of soul-light.

3:5. As a result of sanyama comes the shining forth of the light.

Light is the great revealer. Light is the quality or major characteristic of the soul in its own realm and when - through Raja Yoga meditation, all impediments to its light within the lower nature have been removed, it can shine its radiance unimpeded into the phenomenal world. On Light, the Masters said:

> Make of yourself a light. Be a light unto yourself.
> If you light a lamp for someone else it will also brighten your path.
> - Gautama Buddha.

> You are the Light of the World. Let your light shine.
> - Bible, Matthew 5:15

> Forgetting the things that lie behind let the light of your soul lead you where it will. Be the sannyasin - living in the world of men, yet having your interests in the world where the Great Ones work. You are not alone. You have found your own company of souls. You are not walking in the dark, for there is a light upon your way. Stay within the radius of that light. Master Djwhal Khul. [1]

This completes this examination of the Raja Yoga sutras of Patanjali and of the journey of the soul through its various transformations as it strives towards enlightenment.

---

[1] Bailey, Alice. Discipleship in the New Age I, 599.

THE LINEAGE OF WISDOM AND LIGHT contained in this book stems from the greatest Masters, Teachers and Sages the world has known - from Gautama Buddha, to Sankaracharya, to Jesus Christ, to Patanjali, to the Master Djwhal Khul and to many others too numerous to name. It is the author's earnest wish that the assembly of these thoughts has helped achieve the stated goal of this book, which is:

To help students gain a clear understanding of consciousness - the developments the soul makes and the problems it faces, as it journeys from ignorance to enlightenment. This information is accompanied with spiritual practices to empower students and so they know what they have to do to intelligently walk the Spiritual Path.

> *"Love and blessings to all my fellow travellers on the Path and I leave you with the Rules of the Road, which we are all urged to follow."* Leoni Hodgson.

The Rules of the Road

The Road is trodden in the full light of day, thrown upon the Path by Those Who know and lead. Naught can then be hidden and at each turn upon that Road a man must face himself.

Upon the Road the hidden stands revealed. Each sees and knows the villainy of each. And yet there is, with that great revelation, no turning back, no spurning of each other, no shakiness upon the Road. The Road goes forward into day.

Upon the Road one wanders not alone. There is no rush, no hurry. And yet there is no time to lose. Each pilgrim, knowing this, presses his footsteps forward and finds himself surrounded by his fellow men. Some move ahead; he follows after. Some move behind; he sets the pace. He travels not alone.

Three things the Pilgrim must avoid. The wearing of a hood, a veil which hides his face from others; the carrying of a water pot which only holds enough for his own wants; the shouldering of a staff without a crook to hold.

Each pilgrim on the Road must carry with him what he needs: a pot of fire, to warm his fellow-men; a lamp, to cast its rays upon his heart and shew his fellowmen the nature of his hidden life; a purse of gold, which he scatters not upon the Road, but shares with others; a sealed vase, wherein he carries all his aspiration to cast before the feet of Him Who waits to greet him at the gate - a sealed vase.

The Pilgrim, as he walks upon the Road, must have the open ear, the giving hand, the silent tongue, the chastened heart, the golden voice, the rapid foot and the open eye which sees the light. He knows he travels not alone.

Bailey, Alice A. Discipleship in the New Age I, 583-4.

And a final blessing from
the Tibetan Master Djwhal Khul.

That the Angel of the Presence may make His nearness felt and inspire you to pass courageously through the fires of the burning ground is my earnest prayer; that the fact of the Presence may be sensed by you and lead you to greater activity - once the burning ground is passed - is my deepest wish for you; and that the light may shine upon your way and bring a certain and assured consummation of all the travail and struggle which has characterised your way of life is my heart's desire for you. To more active and steady enterprise I call you. [1]

---

[1] Bailey, Alice. Glamour: A World Problem, 271-272

APPENDIX

Bibliography

Bailey, Alice A.
  A Treatise of Cosmic Fire, Lucis Publishing Press (11th printing 1977).
  A Treatise on White Magic, Lucis Publishing Press (13th printing 1974).
  Consciousness of the Atom, Lucis Publishing Press (7th printing, 1972).
  Destiny of the Nations, Lucis Publishing Press (5th printing 1974).
  Discipleship in the New Age, vol I. Lucis Publishing Press (10th printing 1981).
  Discipleship in the New Age, vol II. Lucis Publishing Press (5th printing 1979).
  Esoteric Astrology, Lucis Publishing Press (11th printing 1975).
  Esoteric Healing, Lucis Publishing Press (8th printing 1977).
  Esoteric Psychology I, Lucis Publishing Press (9th printing 1979).
  Esoteric Psychology II, Lucis Publishing Press (8th printing 1981).
  Externalisation of the Hierarchy, Lucis Publishing Press (7th printing 1982).
  From Bethlehem to Calvary, Lucis Publishing Press (4th printing 1972).
  From Intellect to Intuition, Lucis Publishing Press (6th printing 1965).
  Glamour: a World Problem, Lucis Publishing Press (4th printing 1971).
  Initiation, Human and Solar, Lucis Publishing Press (6th printing 1951).
  Letters on Occult Meditation, Lucis Publishing Press (13th printing 1979).
  Light of the Soul, Lucis Publishing Press (9th printing 1972)
  Rays and the Initiations Lucis Publishing Press (5th printing 1976).

Barborka, Geoffrey.
  The Divine Plan. The Theosophical Publishing House, Adyar. 5th Printing 1992.

Blavatsky, H. P.
  Collected Writings. The Electronic Book Edition of Theosophical Classics. Theosophical Publishing House.
  The Secret Doctrine I and II. The Electronic Book Edition of Theosophical Classics. Theosophical Publishing House.
  Isis Unveiled. The Electronic Book Edition of Theosophical Classics. Theosophical Publishing House.

Saraydarian, Torkom.
  The Science of Becoming Oneself, McCoy Printers, Los Angeles (1982).

Barker, Trevor.
  The Mahatma Letters to A. P. Sinnett. Published in 1923. The original letters are in the British Library.

Glossary

Alice Bailey books	Most of the books attributed to Alice Bailey were actually dictated telepathically to her (in the first part of the 20th Century), by Master Djwhal Khul who is also known at DK or the Tibetan Master. When referring to the books written by Alice Bailey, it refers to the writings of Djwhal Khul. As his name suggests, the last physical incarnation of the Tibetan was in the Tibetan Race and body. He is a master in Trans-Himalayan Wisdom.
Animal soul	Quote: The instinctual powers of the "animal soul," or the capacities of the aggregate of lives which form the sheaths or bodies, imprison the real man and limit his powers. [1]
	Quote: The solar plexus centre is the seat of the instinctual life, of the animal soul, and of the highly developed emotional nature. [2]
Antahkarana	The antahkarana is our conscious response to God, built out of mental essence from below upwards. It inter-weaves with the sutratma as it does so. All the wisdom we gain through our life-experiences, meditative work and the magical creative work of the soul goes into its building. When completed, it spans the gap between the higher and lower divisions of consciousness, from the brain to the spiritual Triad. Through it, information flows between the soul, mind and brain.
Arhat	One who has taken the 4th initiation and renounced the personal life for the larger whole; who is freed from the lower worlds and aligned directly with the Monad.
Ashram	A spiritual group or centre, to which the Master gathers his students for personal instruction, and which has responsibility for an area of service in the world.
Aspirants	Those who are beginning to tire of material life, who aspire to a higher and finer life and who have reached the portals of the Path of Discipleship.
Atlantis	Continent that was submerged in the Atlantic ocean, according to occult teaching. Atlantis was the home of the Fourth Root Race, the Atlanteans.
Atma	Universal Spirit, the seventh Principle, or aspect of truth to be developed by man.
Bodhisattva	One who has perfected knowledge. A very advanced soul who is able to reach nirvana but delays doing so through compassion for suffering beings. Bodhisattvas need another incarnation to become a Buddha (such as Gautama).
Buddha	A Buddha is one who is enlightened (to the Monadic level in esoteric terms) and has attained the highest degree of knowledge and wisdom possible for man in this solar system. The term is commonly applied to Gautama Buddha, born in India about B.C. 621. Buddha embodies the wisdom of God.
Buddhi	Buddhi is a synonym for the intuition. [3] The Universal Soul aspect in man. It is pure, all knowing consciousness, the Sixth Principle as Atma or Spirit is the Seventh Principle.
Causal Body	See Egoic Lotus
Chohan	Lord, Master, a Chief. Those Adepts who have taken the 6th initiation.
Christ	Christ, the World Teacher, which is at present occupied by Lord Maitreya. He is the Head of all the religions of the world, the Master of all Masters and of the

---

1 Bailey, Alice. Light of the Soul, 12..
2 Bailey, Alice. Esoteric Psychology II, 435.
3 Gathered from AAB. Discipleship in the New Age I, 69

	angels. Christ embodies the love of God.
Deva (Angel)	The deva life stream runs parallel with the Human life stream. The higher devas are called celestial beings, angels, or Greater Builders. The lower unconscious devas are the elementals of substance in all kingdoms and are called Lesser or Lunar Builders, fairies and goblins. There are many grades of semi-intelligent devas.
Disciple	One who is pledged to a Master and to co-operate with the plan of the Great Ones as best he or she may. The personal task is to take initiation and become enlightened.
Ego	In modern psychology, the ego refers to a person's sense of self-esteem or self-importance. This is how it is used in this book. Some esoteric writers such as Helena Blavatsky used the term "ego" to signify the indwelling thinker, the soul The Thinker. In many cases, a capital "E" (Ego), signifies a higher thinker such as the soul or spirit. A small "e" (ego) signifies the thinking personality or lower self.
Egoic Lotus	The Causal Body, the body of the soul. It is the centre of human or soul consciousness that was planted in animal man by the Solar Angels. All knowledge and wisdom accumulated throughout a series of incarnations is stored in the lotus. It shatters at the 4th initiation when the antahkarana has connected the brain to the Monad.
Elementals	Lower devas, the unconscious creatures of the four kingdoms, the elementals of Earth, Air, Fire and Water - fairies, goblins. They build the bodies and are the bodies. For instance, man's physical body is built by physical elementals from physical deva substance and it is called the physical elemental. The same applies for the emotional and mental bodies.
Enlightenment	Generally, consciousness infused with soul love and wisdom. In Bailey's work, enlightenment is associated with the 3rd initiation of Transfiguration, symbolised by Jesus on the mountaintop when he was flooded with spiritual light. In Buddhism, it seems to equal Monadic awareness, or esoterically, the 6th Initiation.
Esoteric	The words "esoteric" and "occult" signify "that which is hidden". They indicate that which lies behind the outer form, the causes which produce appearance and effects. They refer to the subtler world of energies. Esotericism is the scientific study and intelligent use of energies. An esotericist uses energies intelligently.
Etheric body	(Etheric double or web). Man's physical body has two parts. The dense physical body, formed of matter from the lowest three subplanes of the physical-etheric plane and the etheric body formed from the four higher etheric subplanes of the physical-etheric plane. The etheric body is the blueprint for the physical body and it receives and distributes energy to the physical.
Glamour	A psychological problem stemming from the emotional nature, which distorts the mind, perception and reality because of bias and prejudice.
Guru	A Teacher or Master in metaphysical and ethical doctrines.
Illusion	A psychology problem affecting intellectuals. Reality is distorted because of fixed attitudes and beliefs.
Initiate	Higher than a disciple in consciousness, but beneath an Arhat and Master. One in whom the soul and personality have fused and who rules the human worlds. He is a spiritual man, a blend of scientific and religious training, who is guided

	by the Monad.
Initiation	Initiation is simply an expansion of consciousness, moving up one subplane or plane on the spiritual ladder. Initiations are inner syntheses and fusions that mark specific developments and expansions of consciousness. Each initiation enables us to function consciously on a higher level than before and to express a greater proportion of wisdom.
Karma	The law of cause and effect. It is the power that controls the behaviours of all things.
Kundalini	The fiery power of matter, fire by friction. One of the forces of nature. It is centred in the base chakra and in man rises up the spine when he connects consciously with his spiritual nature.
Lemuria	The name given to a continent that, according to Blavatsky's The Secret Doctrine, preceded Atlantis. It was the home of the Lemurian third root race.
Light	Light represents the power and presence of God. "Divinity is radiance and pure white light". [1] In the Bible Christ said, "I am the Light of the World". [2] "From light to light we pass, from revelation to revelation." [3] Light plays out on various levels: For example: 　1. The light of matter itself, found in every atom of substance. 　2. The light of the intellect or the light of knowledge. 　3. The light of the soul.
Logos	Gk: "word", in Greek and Hebrew metaphysics, the unifying principle of the world linking God and man. Theology: the divine word or reason incarnate. The divine Life behind the Sun is called the solar Logos. Plural: Logoi.
Manas	Or manasic principle. Literally the mind, the mental faculty.
Mantrams	A set of words or syllables rhythmically arranged so that when sounded, a vibration of a certain note is generated.
Master	One who has taken five initiations, who has expanded consciousness to include the 3rd plane of spirit (Atma) and who is now a master over the five lower planes of the system. A Master of Compassion, a Master of the Wisdom.
Maya	Sanskrit: illusion. Physical Plane glamour. It is the unthinking, emotional mess in which most people seem always to live.
Monad	Source of Consciousness. The Monad - also known as a ray or spark of God, is our highest spiritual aspect because it is our direct link with God. The soul is the vehicle of the spiritual Triad, which in turn is the vehicle of the Monad.
Mystic	One who senses divine realities from the heights of aspiration. Who contacts the mystical vision through prayer, adoration and worship, then longs ceaselessly for the constant repetition of the achieved ecstatic state. The mystic must eventually become an occultist. Occultists are mystics (lovers of God) functioning on the mental plane.
NGWS	The New Group of World Servers. All those men and women who reach a certain level of harmlessness, who see no racial, national or religious barriers, who work to heal the breaches between people, evoke a sense of brotherliness and foster a sense of mutual inter-relation in the world through goodwill. Members of the NGWS belong to all parties, religions and races on earth - and may or

---

1　Bailey, Alice. From Bethlehem to Calvary, 55
2　Bible, John 8:12
3　Bailey, Alice. Glamour: A World Problem, 205

	may not have knowledge of the Masters and Ageless Wisdom.
Occult	The occult refers to the hidden forces of nature, "Those springs of conduct which produce the objective manifestation".[1] This is the world of energies. Occultism is the manipulation of energies. Occultists are concerned with the manipulation of those energies and forces which all outer forms veil and hide.
OM	A sacred word, sound or vibration. The word of the 2nd aspect, of the soul.
Path of Probation	Preparatory period in discipleship training, prior to becoming a fully accepted disciple.
Raja Yoga	The Royal Science of the Mind. It involves the exercise, regulation and concentration of thought.
Ray	One of the seven energy streams of force of the Logos.
Root Race	One of the seven races of man which evolve upon a planet during the great cycle of planetary existence. Humanity is currently in the Aryan 5th root race.
Shamballa	The seat of world spiritual government, the "centre where the will of God is known," headed by Sanat Kumara.
Solar Angel	Also called the Lords of Flame. One of the great Hierarchies of spiritual beings who guide the solar system. They took control of the evolution of humanity upon this planet about 18 million years ago, during the middle of the Lemurian, or third root race. From their own essence, they planted the seed of intelligence (egoic lotus) in animal man - the great act of "individualisation". Through millions of years, they hover over the developing egoic lotus in the causal body, fanning the expanding solar fire. At man's 4th initiation they leave man to return to their source - the Sun.
Solar Logos	The ensouling life of the solar system.
Soul	The consciousness aspect in all living things.
Spiritual Hierarchy	A organism formed of Chohans, Masters, adepts and initiates, working through their disciples in the world. Christ is the head of this hierarchy.
Subconscious	Signifies the entire instinctual life of the form nature. All the inherited tendencies and innate predispositions, acquired and accumulated characteristics (from past incarnations) reside here. The subconscious nature is like a deep pool from which a man can draw almost anything from his past experience, if he so desires, and which can be stirred up until it becomes a boiling cauldron, causing much distress.
Superconscious	Consists of the wisdom, love and abstract idealism which are inherent in the nature of the soul but which are not yet, and never have been a part of the equipment available for use amongst the general masses. Eventually, all these powers are recognised and used.
Triad	The expression of the Monad, its vehicle. It is the Spiritual Man, consisting of Atma, Buddhi and Manas.
Universal Mind	The collective hosts of the higher creative spiritual kingdoms (Dhyan Chohans). The divine intelligences charged with the supervision of the Kosmos.
Wesak	Buddha's birthday. A festival in the Himalayan Wesak Valley at the full moon of May attended by all members of the Hierarchy. Buddha returns for a brief period to bless humanity and all life on earth.

---

1 Bailey, Alice. A Treatise on White Magic, 10

Personality Ray Dynamics					
	Outstanding negatives	*How the call of the soul is missed*	*How the ego limits expansion*	*Selfish demands of the ego*	*How the ego self-references*
1	Too proud, dominating; too determined to do things entirely on its own, exactly as it chooses.	Preoccupied with bossing others around, getting its own way, protecting its power, place & position.	Refuses to accept the value of what others have to offer. Does things its way. Isolates itself.	Demands to be "number one," the alpha male, the one who leads.	Exaggerates its importance, its power to rule, takes charge noticeably.
2	Too timid, fearful, too permissive, too attached to its relationships and life comforts.	Preoccupied with personal wealth & comfort, to things that bring personal happiness.	Too sensitive/ lethargic/ fearful to seize the moment in case others are upset & it is rejected.	Demands to be popular, loved, universally appreciated & accepted.	By letting people know how it suffers, the sacrifices made to look after others.
3	Too busy, active, critical, vague, and impractical, devious, untruthful, manipulative.	Preoccupation with a multitude of plans, scattered projects and extraneous activities	Too busy with its external preoccupations, trying to make money, taking advantage of people.	Demands to be the cleverest, to manipulate people to do what it wants.	Brags about its superior mentality, its cleverness, skill in living & making "a buck."
4	Too temperamental, inconsistent, unstable, emotional, conflicted, combative.	Too preoccupied with its dramas, crises, battles, mood swings, emotional suffering.	By being too embroiled in fights & struggles with itself & others.	Demands freedom to do what it wants, without accepting any responsibility for its actions.	By calling attention to its suffering, or to its artistic and entertaining talent.
5	Too narrow & focused on its own mental/ technical interests at the expense of the larger picture.	Too preoccupied with being right, with the facts, with foreground considerations.	By relying only on an overly mental, rationalistic approach to life.	Demands the right to weigh, measure & judge people, with clinical objectivity.	By putting itself up as the expert with all the facts, who knows more than anyone else.
6	Too fanatical, extreme, emotional, rigid, narrow; too convinced of the rightness of its point of view.	Too preoccupied & intensely "caught up" with the passion of the moment, adoring God/ Jesus.	By holding rigidly to its own narrow vision and beliefs of life.	Demands the right to find and follow the "one true path" and insists that others follow the same path as well.	By claiming to be beloved of God, following the true teaching, the right path.
7	Too rigid, resistant to change, too caught up in externals, methods, rules; too locked into personal routines and habits.	Too preoccupied with appearances, routines, rules, being superior & perfect.	By being superficial, too rigidly formal, too quick to judge by appearances.	Demands that others follow its superior ways and methods of doing things.	By being perfect & letting others know how flawed they are in comparison. Having supernormal powers.

	Checklist for Soul Ray				
	The Experience	*Contribution*	*Soul-inspired aspiration*	*Heart's desire:*	*Vocations*
1	A dynamic charge of spiritual will and power.	To strengthen and liberate people, to impel them to find the courage to "be".	To be a dynamic, powerful, benevolent leader; to free people from oppression.	To be the One and Only.	Leaders, managers, controllers, politics, armed forces, law.
2	An inflow of: a: loving inclusiveness or b. Expansive wisdom.	To lovingly and wisely teach and help people to achieve their potential and become healed & whole.	To develop an intuitive loving understanding of people. To help people achieve self-realisation and illumination.	a. To be in love with all, one with all. b. To live in simple truth & understanding.	Health, education, religion. Study and dissemination of the Wisdom Teachings.
3	An inflow of creative, versatile and acute intelligence.	To stimulate the intellect and mental creativity of others. To solve unsolvable puzzles.	To create a philosophy explaining the truth of reality. To apply the intellectual powers to challenging enterprises	To plan along with God & manifest God's plan.	Thinker, teacher, scientist, philosopher, philanthropist, business and finance.
4	An inflow of creative artistry, an urge to create beauty or to harmonise chaos.	To help others harmonise and resolve conflict. To beautify what was ugly. To fight for the higher good.	To harmonise every aspect of life. To express the exquisitely beautiful yet painful drama of life in all its vibrancy.	To live in beauty, create beauty and become beauty itself.	Artists of all genres, fighters, protectors of the weak, peacemakers, diplomats, counsellors.
5	An inflow of crystal clear and logical thought that unravels life mysteries.	To discover new scientific truths and technology that empowers man.	To find solutions to problems through advanced scientific research.	To know the truth & reveal life's mysteries.	Science, research, technology, finding the truth.
6	An inflow of dynamic idealism, or heart-felt devotion to a master or teaching.	To inspire people to devote their lives to their highest ideals. To serve and sacrifice the life for the greatest truth.	To surrender in complete faith, devotion and adoration to the highest guidance; being loyal to one's highest ideals.	To be loved by one's Beloved; to express one's highest ideals.	Care and service industries, inspiring people to find their true Path or Teacher.
7	A dynamic surge of power and urge to bring order out of chaos, to manifest ideas in perfect form.	To help people manage and organise their lives so they realise their highest goals.	To bring order out of chaos. To provide leadership and organisation skills in order to help people bring their lives into line with divine law.	To achieve perfection in form	Managers, designers, builders, architects, organisers. Ceremonialists, workers in magic.

INDEX

Symbols

1 chart. Chakras & levels of consciousness 103
1 chart. Initiations 17
1 chart: Psychic Powers 104
1 chart. Seven Planes of Consciousness in the solar system 15
1 chart. Seven Rays and disease 46
1 chart. Seven Rays overview 31
1 chart. Three Gunas chart 124
1 chart. Tibetan's Disciples 61
1 pic. Chakra transferences 101
1 pic. Egoic Lotus petals 7
1 pic. Etheric webs 10
1 pic. Flower meditation 161

A

Abstention from theft 132
Abstraction - see Pratyahara 148
Act "as if" 121, 128, 161
Adept 118, 180
Affirmation of a disciple 172
Affirmation of service 172
Ahisma - harmlessness 133
Ajna Chakra 10, 12–13, 15, 17, 23, 100–104, 159
Alternate nostril breathing 147
Angel of the Presence 24, 177
Animal soul 104
Annan, Kofi 45
Anorexia nervosa 78
Antahkarana 7–8, 14, 16, 99, 142, 180–181
Antisocial Personality Disorder 88–89
Anxiety 65, 77
Aquinas, St Thomas 37
Arhat 26, 180
Aristotle 37
Arjuna 22, 61, 149
Aryan 11, 19, 92, 105, 110, 119, 183
    consciousness 11, 19, 92, 105
Asana - Poise 131, 143–144
Ashram 25–27, 149, 180
Aspirants 17, 20, 28, 47, 100–103, 107, 138, 140–144, 146, 155, 180
Astral 13–14
    body 10, 12, 33, 35, 37, 39, 41, 43, 45, 74, 76, 171
    field 27, 37, 43, 56, 122, 151
    maniacs 67–68
    nature 14, 80, 107, 139, 142, 144
    plane 7, 10–11, 15–17, 19, 23, 42, 66, 76, 80, 94–95, 104–106, 134, 144, 153, 159
    ray - see Emotional Ray 47
Atlantean 19, 23, 57, 75–76, 92, 105, 110, 119, 136, 180
    consciousness 19, 57, 75, 92
Atlantis 180
Atma 5, 16, 26, 118, 180
Atmic 15–17, 26, 104, 127
    plane 15–16, 104, 127
Atomic Subplane 180
Attachment as a hindrance 121
Aura 27
Avarice 132, 138
Awakening the Centres 100

B

Bacon, Sir Francis 45
Bailey, Alice 60, 135, 142, 155, 160, 180–181
Base Chakra 8, 10–12, 15, 18, 24, 100–103, 182
Basic Alignment for Meditation 170
Beethoven 39
Be in "the now" 114, 135
Berners-Lee, Tim 41
Besant, Annie 142
Bhagavad Gita 149
Bhakti Yoga 110, 119, 142
Bible 3–4, 10, 21, 23, 29, 126, 132, 174
Bipolar disorder 77
Bismarck, Otto von 33
Black Magic 23
Blair, Tony 45
Blavatsky, Helena 5, 14, 99, 112, 142, 181, 182
Bodhisattva 163, 180
Bodily disability 115–116
Body
    astral - emotional 12–14, 23, 58, 60, 62, 74–75, 94, 106, 134, 171
    emotional 9, 19, 45, 77–78, 82, 90, 96, 117–118, 148, 153, 159
    etheric 9, 16, 55, 75, 106, 145–146, 159, 181
    mind - mental 9, 13–14, 173
    physical 9–11, 16, 18, 20, 27–28, 47–48, 58–62, 66, 74–75, 79, 89–90, 93, 96, 105–110, 115–116, 119, 122, 125, 137, 143–145, 147, 153, 155, 157–159, 161, 173, 181
    soul 6, 173

Bohr, Niels 41
Borderline personality disorder 77
Borgia, Lucrezia 37
Brahma 110, 117, 128
Brain
    serious organic damage 67
    switchboard of the mind 14
Breath-Control 145–147
Breathing with God 171
Bridge of Light 8
Buddha 12–14, 26, 35, 69, 76, 95, 136, 142, 152, 166, 169–170, 180, 183
    birthday - Wesak 166, 183
    teachings 69
Buddha's Mantra 169
Buddhi - Buddhic Plane 6–7, 11–12, 15–17, 26, 38, 103–104, 180–181
    defined 16, 180
Buddhism 181
    esoteric 3
Bulimia nervosa 78–79
Burns, Robert 39
Byron, Lord 39

C

Cardinal McCarrick 68
Carelessness 115, 117
Carlyle, Thomas 33
Carter, Jimmy 43
Catholic Church 68
Causal body 7, 26, 180–181, 183
Celibacy 117
Centralisation 35
Chakras 10, 21, 24, 103
    & consciousness 100
    development 100–103
    transferences 101–103
Charlemagne 33
Chitta 111–113, 116–118, 130, 152, 155, 173
    defined 111
Chohan 26, 180–181
Christ 6, 25, 34–35, 76, 95, 121, 128, 141–142, 160, 162, 175, 183
    Christed consciousness 126
    consciousness 6
    principle 6
Christianity iii
Churchill, Winston 33
Clairaudience 104

Clairvoyance 104
Clairvoyant 10
CLEAVAGE Problem 73–81
    between one's life task or vocation 80
    between physical and etheric 74–75
    between the mind and brain 79
    between the mind & emotions 80
    between the personality and soul 81
    healing 84
    within the astral body 76–78
    with the environment 76–78
Clinton, Bill 35
Commandments (The) 132–138
Concentration - Dharana 155–156
Concentration exercises 155–156
Concrete-mind 8–9, 13, 16, 41
Consciousness
    Arhat 26
    Aryan 11, 19, 105
    Aspirational 20
    Atlantean 19
    Discipleship 22
    Evolution of 1–16
    group 8, 51, 81, 101–102, 166
    human soul 6
    Initiate 25
    Lemurian 18
    Master of the Wisdom 26
    Monadic 5
    soul 6
    spiritual soul 6
    thread 8, 16, 67, 75, 79
        connected to a foreign entity 67
        not connected to the brain 67
        Synonyms: antahkarana, bridge of light, rainbow bridge, of continuity, path of return 8
    triadic 5
Contemplation 40, 131, 155, 157, 161–162, 170, 173–174
Content (Be) 140
Contentment 132, 136–141
Correct breathing exercise 146
Counselling Method - Cleavages, Integration. 84
Covetousness 121, 132
Creative imagination 134
Creative Thread 8
Crowley, Aleister 45
Crown Chakra 11–12, 15, 24, 100, 102–103, 159, 169, 170

Cyber-bullying 90
Cycle of Necessity 5

D

Dali, Salvador 39
Dangers of Pranayama 146
Darwin, Charles 41
Debilitation 75
Debussy, Claude 39
Delirium problem 107
Delusion problem 78, 106–107
Depression 39, 43, 56, 58, 65, 77, 80, 96–97, 158
    glamour of 97
Desire 3, 7, 11–14, 18–21, 23, 32, 34, 36, 38, 40, 42–44, 49, 56, 66–68, 78, 80–82, 84–85, 88, 90, 95–96, 100, 102–103, 114–115, 117–118, 120–121, 125–126, 129, 137, 138, 148–149, 177
    body - the astral body 12
    for objects of pleasure 121
    nature 23, 68, 80, 130, 148
    uncontrollable 67
Detachment exercises 150–154
Detachment - see Pratyahara 13
Devitalisation problem 106
Dharana 112, 131, 155, 157
DHYANA - Meditation 131, 157–170
Dhyan Chohans 181, 183
Disciple - Disciples 9, 12, 17, 21–28, 33, 35, 37–41, 43, 45, 47, 56–61, 63, 81, 84, 95, 97, 99, 100, 102–103, 105, 107, 120, 137, 145, 149, 157, 172, 181
    defined 181
    problems of 99
Discipleship consciousness 22
Discrimination 76, 91–92, 104, 128, 129–130
Dispassion 115–117, 129, 148
Divine Trinity 31, 128
Djwhal Khul - see Master Djwhal Khul iv
Do not accept any of my words on faith 119
Dostoyevsky, Fyodor 39
Doubt 130
Drake, Sir Francis 45
Dreams 95–96
Duncan, Isadora 39
Dweller on the Threshold 24

E

Eating disorders 78

Edison, Thomas 41
Ego defined 14, 181
Egoic Lotus 7, 15–16, 180–181
Egoism 28, 43, 120
Eight Means to Yoga 131–172
Einstein, Albert 37
Electric fire 8, 32
Elementals 181
Eliot, T. S. 149
Emotional - Astral
    bias, glamour 43, 91
    body - nature 15, 153
    plane 16, 96
    r1 emotional 33, 60–61
    r2 emotional 35, 47–49, 60–61
    r3 emotional 37
    r4 emotional 39
    r5 emotional 41
    r6 emotional 43, 47–49, 56, 58–60, 75, 77–78, 83, 90
    r7 emotional 45
    ray emotional 48–49, 57–58, 60–61
Energy 10–11, 23–24, 34, 60, 82–83, 181, 183
    depletion 158
    fields of 70
    imbalance 73
    inter-relation of 70
Energy follows thought 117–118, 138, 153
Enlightenment 66
    defined 181
Epilepsy 75
Erroneous perception 115, 118
Esoteric 181
Esoteric Healing iii, 102
Esotericist 27
Esoteric Psychology - see Psychology 63
Etheric Body - Web 33, 35–36, 39, 41, 43, 45, 181
    defined 10
Euthanasia 76
Evolution
    of Consciousness 1–22, 1–28
Exercise in Spiritual Reading 141
Extroverts 88

F

Fainting fits 75
Falsehood 132, 135
Falwell, Jerry 43

Fear 12, 49, 62, 76–77, 92, 100, 112, 120–121, 133, 153, 166
Feuerstein, Georg. 152
Fire
    by friction, of matter 8, 36, 182
    electric 32
    of mind 8, 34, 122
    solar fire 8, 183
Five pm Mantram 172
Five Tibetan Rites 144
Flower meditation method 161
Fonda, Jane 43
Four Noble Truths 12
Franklin, Benjamin 45
Freud, Sigmund 35, 56, 65
Full Moon meditations 163–167

G

Galileo 41
Gandhi, Mahatma 33–34
Garden Meditation 170
Gautama Buddha 14, 69, 95, 119, 123, 131, 175, 180
Gayatri 172
Generosity, spirit of 138
Germanotta, Stefani 97
Glamour 84–85, 91–92, 94, 177, 181–182
    defined 91
    Dissipation Formula 94
Glamours associated with the Rays 92–93
God defined 3, 182
Golden bowl 10
Gorbachev, Mikhail 33
Graham, Billy 43–44
Great Invocation 156, 162, 165
Group - Groups 22–23, 28–29, 53, 71, 81
    ashramic 25
    bonding 172
    conscious 51
    criticism problem 108
    formation 27
    fusion 164
    gift to 62
    New Group of World Servers 165, 182
    problems of 108
    service 21
    soul 6, 18
    spiritual 180
Guidance problem 95
Gunas 109, 124–125, 127–129
Guru 27, 181
Gurudev 152

H

Hall of Ignorance 18
Hall of Learning 18, 19, 20
Hall of Wisdom 21, 22, 26
Halls of Spiritual Training 17–27
Harmfulness 132, 135
Harmlessness 28, 132–135, 153, 172, 182
Hate 12, 49, 108–109, 120–121
Hatha Yoga 110, 143–144, 159
Healing exercise for hate 121
Heart Chakra 9, 11–12, 15, 23, 28, 35, 100–103, 117–119, 137, 159, 170–171
Hepburn, Audrey 45
Hercules 33
Hierarchies 181, 183
    defined 181
Hindrances 120, 123, 141, 151
    remedy to overcome 122
Hitler, Adolf 33, 87
Hodson, Geoffrey 142, 168
Huffington Ariana 159
Human Constitution 5–16
    the lower nature 9–16
    the spiritual nature 5–8
Human Kingdom 4, 6–7, 18, 26, 38, 104, 110, 119, 174
    birth of 18
Human Soul 6, 18, 69, 120

I

I am pure gnosis 153
I am the owner of my actions 123
I Assert the Fact 33
Ida 8, 147
Ignorance 4, 12, 69, 120, 132, 138, 175
    mother-breeder" of all the hindrances 120
Illumination 22, 66, 115, 126, 130, 131, 157, 162, 173
    Raja Yoga meditation 162
Illusion 22, 24, 91–92, 112, 117, 182
Impairment of senses 158
Inclusiveness 33, 133
    material 59
Incontinence 132, 137

Individualisation 18
   defined 183
Initiate - Initiates 8, 12, 23, 25–26, 32, 55,
   102–103, 110, 155, 160, 166, 181
   consciousness 25
   defined 181
Initiation 179
Initiations 11–12, 17–27, 55, 69, 99, 103, 180,
   180–182, 183
   1st initiation 7, 11, 17, 20–21, 101
   2nd initiation 7, 11, 17, 21–23, 102–103
   3rd initiation 7, 12, 17, 22–25, 55, 102–103, 181
   4th initiation 7, 12, 17, 23, 26, 180–181, 183
      Arhat 180
      Solar Angel leaves 183
   5th initiation 17, 26
   6th initiation 17, 26, 180
   7th initiation 17, 26
   8th, 9th initiations 17
   defined 17, 182
   in our solar system 17
   path of 182
Insanity 107
   3 forms 67–68
INTEGRATION Problem 73–75, 78, 82–84
   an over-inflated sense of power 82
   major internal conflicts 83
   over-developed sense of direction 82
   tendency to over-emphasise 82
Integration words 33, 35, 37, 39, 41, 43, 45, 57
Intuitive mind 39
Invoke the power of the soul 96
I See the Greatest Light 35
Ishvara 119, 139, 142–143
Iyengar, B.K.S. 131

J

Jackson, Jesse 43
Jefferson, Thomas 45
Jesus Christ 21, 23, 43, 71, 95, 106–107, 135–136,
   139, 142, 175, 181
Jewel in the lotus 7, 102, 146, 171
Joan of Arc 43
Jones, Jim 87
Jung, Carl 35, 65
   ray chart 56, 58

K

Kaczynski, Theodore 86
Kama-manas mind 14
Karma 27, 70, 123, 132, 135
   defined 123, 182
   Yoga 119
Karmic
   experiences 71
   retribution 123–124
Khomeini, Ayotollah 43
Khrushchev, Nikita 33
Khul - see Master Djwhal Khul iv
Kim Jong-un 33
Kind (being) 3, 10, 51, 53, 100, 108, 116, 128,
   153, 155
Kindness 53, 133, 153
King, Martin Luther Jr 43–44
Kitchener, General 33
Kumaras 182
Kundalini 8, 11–12, 103, 110, 146, 159–160, 182
   danger 159
   defined 182
Kurukshetra 61

L

Lack of dispassion 115
Lady Gaga 97
Law of Karma 70, 120, 123–124, 140
Law of Rebirth 63, 70
Law of Repulse 25, 81
Law of Sacrifice 25, 81
Laws of the Soul 81
Laziness 115, 117
Lemuria - Lemurian 18, 110, 119, 182, 183
   Race 18, 119, 183
Lesser builders, devas 181
Life-thread 8, 16, 75
Light
   defined 182
   forerunner of the 36
   I see the greatest 35
   Make of yourself a light 174
   Shining forth of the light 174
   You are the Light of the World 174
Logoic plane 15
Logos
   1st 32
   2nd 34
   3rd 36
   beloved of 40

Lord's Prayer 156

M

Machiavelli 37
Macrocosm 182–183
Maitreya, the Christ 180
Major depressive disorder 77
Manas 5, 14, 128, 148
Manifesting Breath Technique 147
Manson, Charles 87
Mantram of the New Group of World Servers 172
Marchese, Maria 90
Maslow, Abraham 35
Master Djwhal Khul iii, iv, 9, 14, 58–61, 73, 76, 83–84, 89, 95, 97, 142, 163, 170, 174–175, 177
Master Koot Hoomi 26
Master Morya 26
Master-Pupil Relationship 26
Masters 17, 21, 26–28, 28, 38, 95, 141, 162, 165, 175, 180, 182
    and service 27–28
Maya 85, 91, 91–92, 182
Meditation 9, 11, 27, 70–71, 86, 95–97, 102, 110, 114–118, 120, 122, 131, 137, 141–146, 147, 153, 155, 156–172
    basic alignment 161
    benefits 158
    dangers 11, 158
    goal of 102
    inspiration 162
    preparation 160
    Raja Yoga Means VII 157–170
    selection of a seed thought 160
    without seed 157
    with seed 157
Meditations - Exercises - Affirmations
    Affirmation of a disciple 172
    Affirmation of service. 172
    Align with one's Spiritual Nature 170
    Alternate nostril breathing 147
    Be "in the now" 114, 135
    Brahma in the crown chakra 117
    Breathing with God 171
    Concentration exercises 155–156
    Correct breathing 146
    Detach from the mental nature 152–153
    Detach from the Personality 153
    Detach from the senses 150
    Detachment from desire-thoughts 117
    Detachment Meditation (simple) 153
    Do not accept any of my words on faith 119
    Emotional cleansing exercise 139–140
    Emotional observing exercise 140
    Evening review on harmlessness 133
    Five pm mantram 172
    Five Tibetan Rites 144
    Flower method 161
    Full Moon 163
    Full Moon meditations 163–167
    Garden meditation 97, 170
    Gautama Buddha 169
    Gayatri 172
    Great Invocation 162, 165
    Group Bonding 172
    Healing exercise for hate 121
    I am the owner of my actions 123
    I ask a blessing holy child of God 121, 141
    I give thanks for all the blessings in my life 141
    I have a body but I am not my body 153
    I invoke light and love of the soul 96
    I must to my own Self be true 136
    Invoke the power of the soul 96
    I wash myself through with love and light of the soul 96
    Make of yourself a light 174
    Manifesting Breath Technique 147
    Mantram of the New Group of World Servers 172
    Mindfulness in Breathing 147
    New Group of World Servers 172
    Noon mantram 172
    OM Mane Padme Hum 171
    Open the Heart 171
    Peace be still 139
    Practise of Dispassion 140
    Pranayama breathing technique 145
    Pure mind 152
    Purifying with white light 96
    Restraining exercises 150
    Rules of the Road 175
    Salute to the Sun exercise. 143
    Scorpio Full Moon 163
    Sequential Thinking 156
    Silence 170
    Solar Meditation at the Scorpio Full Moon period 163
    Spiritual Reading 141
    Standing on the bridge exercise 140, 151

There is only one Source of Life and Light 120
Think an opposite thought 117, 122, 134
Thinking during Pranayama 146
Think of something you own 121
Thou God seest me 160
Triangle Technique 122
Using a mantra to time the breath 146
Visualisation for inner strength 151
Visualise yourself stepping into the heart of God 121
Wash away the disturbance with Light 151
Yoga of Light 168
you are a spiritual Divine ray 122
You are the Light of the World 174

Memory 114

Mendel, Gregor 41

Mengele, Josef 41

Mental
- body - field 7, 13–14, 27, 58, 83, 153
- health 65–67
- inertia 115–116
- Plane 5–8, 10–11, 15–16, 18–20, 22, 25, 27, 40, 76, 80, 94, 103–104, 110–111, 119, 138, 144, 148, 158

Merlin the Magician 45

Mindfulness in Breathing 147

Mind - Manas 15
- bridging 39
- can make a man a Buddha or a beast 14
- chattering 111, 134
- cleavage 74, 80
- development of 19, 21, 104, 110
- fire of 34
- good mental health 66
- heavily influenced by the emotions 18
- higher 41
- ignorant 69
- illumined 20, 62
- illusion 181
- is a slave 11
- is the great Slayer of the Real 112
- light of 94
- lower 14, 16, 18–19, 25, 112, 119, 128, 173
- mind-stuff, chitta 111
- modifications
  - remedial action 114–115
- monkey-mind 111
- of God - Deity 5, 31, 36, 40, 51, 59, 152, 161–162, 165–166
- of the Logos 22
- powers of 21
- r1 mind 33, 47, 60–62
- r2 mind 35, 60–61
- r3 mind 37, 56, 58–59, 60–61, 83, 88
- r4 mind 39, 47, 60–61, 77
- r5 mind 41, 47, 59–61, 65, 87
- r6 mind 43
- r7 mind 45
- Raja-Yoga kingly science of 109
- ray mind 47–50, 53, 57, 60–62, 84
- ray of the mind 31
- synthesising 45
- training the 28
- ultimate function 14
- universal 157, 183
- unstable 73
- useless and inert 67
- versatile 88
- wisdom 70

Misplaced bodily activity 115

Moderation 43, 57

Monadic
- plane 15–16
- ray 25, 55

Monad - Monads 8, 12, 15–16, 24, 26, 89, 100, 103, 124, 168, 171, 180, 182–184
- defined 5, 182
- Father 25
- Triad, body of 5

Mood disorders 77

Morton, Andrew 78

Mother Teresa 35

Mozart, Wolfgang 39

Multiple personalities 75

Musco, Teresa 106–107

Mussolini, Benito 33

Mystical
- practices 75
- vision 95, 104
- vision problem 106–107

Mystics 20, 24, 27, 81, 84, 95, 99–100, 102, 105–107, 119, 168, 182
- defined 21, 24, 27, 95, 105
- practical 81
- problems 99

Mystics & Disciples Problems 99–108

N

Nadal, Rafael 77
Nadis 10
Napoleon 33
Narcissist 87
Nervous system 158
New Group of World Servers 182
Newton, Isaac 41
Nicholson, Jack 37
Nightingale, Florence 43
Nirvana 128
Niyama, the Rules 131, 139
Non-attachment 115–116, 129, 148, 149, 150
Noon Mantram 172

O

Obsessed 86–89, 106–107
Obsessive 77, 89–90
    fanatics 89
Obsessive-compulsive disorder (OCD) 77
Obstacles 20, 108–109, 115–118, 138
    when removed 118
Occult Meditation 9, 26–27, 161, 170
    basic method 161
Occult - Occultists 22, 27, 103, 183
    defined 183
Olivier, Lawrence 39
OM 160
    defined 183
OM Mane Padme Hum 171
Onassis, Jackie 45
Open the Heart Chakra 171
Oversoul 3, 118
Overstimulation
    1Problem Main 73, 85–91
    diseases of the Mystic 100
    emotional and sexual 159
    nervous system 158

P

Pain 115, 123
    driver of human evolution 6
Pairs of opposites 22, 61, 121, 144, 146
Paisley, Ian 89
Panic attacks 77
Paramahansa Yogananda 142, 159
Passivity 114
Pasteur, Louis 41
Patanjali 13, 79, 108, 110–111, 113, 115, 123, 132, 139, 155, 157, 173–175, 174–175
Path of Return 8
Path, the
    evolution 16
    spiritual development 16
Patton, General 33
Peace 6, 38, 118, 139, 147
    steadiness of the chitta 118
Pedophilia 68
Perception (pure) 128
Personality
    defined 14
    Profile Method 47
    r1 personality 33, 51–52, 61–62
    r2 personality 35, 51–53, 59, 61–62
    r3 personality 37, 51–52, 61–63
    r4 personality 39, 51–53, 56, 58, 61–62
    r5 personality 41, 51–52, 61–62
    r6 personality 43, 51–53, 61–62
    r7 personality 45, 51–53, 61–62
    ray personality 15, 47, 51–53, 57–59, 61–62, 79, 81
        can be any of the seven rays 47
        soul ray and the personality ray are always different 47
Personality Profile Method 47–56
Petals of the Egoic Lotus 7
Phobias 77
Physical-etheric 35, 60–61
    body 9–10, 15–16, 33, 35, 37, 39, 41, 43, 45, 181
    plane 15
    r1 physical-etheric 33, 58, 60–62
    r3 physical-etheric 37, 48, 56, 58, 60–61, 89
    r4 physical-etheric 39
    r5 physical-etheric 41
    r6 physical-etheric 43, 60–61
    r7 physical-etheric 45, 48, 60–61
    ray physical-etheric 48, 58–61
Physical plane 7, 92, 104, 181–182
Picasso, Pablo 39
Pingala 8
Plan
    Divine 27, 36, 44, 55
    for Humanity 70
    of God 25
    of Goodwill 27
    of Love and Light 162, 165
    soul's 75

Spiritual 22
Plant Kingdom 97
Plato 35
Pope Francis 43
Possession 75
Post, Emily 45
Post-traumatic stress disorder (PTSD) 77
Practise of Dispassion 140
Prakriti 124, 128
Prana 10, 146
   defined. 10
Pranayama, Breath Control 116, 131, 145–147
Pratyahara, Detachment 32, 60, 102, 115, 129, 131, 148–154
   right 102
Presented idea 128, 153
President Xi 33
Princess Diana 78
Psychic - Psychics 104–105
   defined 104
   higher, defined 104
   lower 105
      Aryan in consciousness 105
      Atlantean in consciousness 105
   lower, defined 104
   nature 111, 115, 148, 154
   powers 104
      mystical vision 106–107
      revelation of light 107
Psychoanalysis 70
Psychology - Esoteric 63–108
   clashing energies 66, 70
   disorders 73–103
   Esoteric Psychology 5
      goals of 70–71
      includes Eastern Wisdom 69
      is founded upon the Seven Rays 31
      points that distinguish 69
   explanation for ill health 66
   foundation of the new psychology 63
   includes Eastern Wisdom 69
   Problems of Mystics & Disciples 99–108
   Problems of the Masses 73–102
      3 forms of insanity that will not respond to counselling 67
      psychotic disorders 78
   psychologists 69
Psychometry 104

Psychopaths 37, 89–90
Purpose itself am I 37
Purusha 128, 129
Putin, Vladimir 33
Pythagoras 35

R

Rader, Dennis BTK 89
Rainbow Bridge 8
Rajas guna 111, 124–126
RAJA YOGA iii, 13, 23, 70, 79, 108–174, 109–172, 183
   7 Desires 130
   8 Means of Raja Yoga overview 131
   Book 1 111–118
   Book 2 119–154
   Book 3 155–174
   defined 110
   Impediment 1: four wrong ways we think 113–115
   Impediment 2: obstacles in our Bodies 115
   Impediment 3: the five hindrances 120–124
   Impediment 4: the Three Gunas 124
   two things that prevent Union 111
Ray 1 of Will & Power 31–33, 60–62, 87, 92
   glamours 92
   r1 emotional Ray 33
   r1 mind ray 33, 49–50, 62
   r1 monadic ray 55
   r1 personality ray 33, 51–52, 62, 87
   r1 physical-etheric ray 33, 58–59, 62, 83
   r1 soul ray 32, 53–55, 58–59, 62, 83
Ray 2 of Love & Wisdom 31, 34–35, 51, 60–62, 107
   glamours 92
   r2 emotional ray 35, 48–49, 62, 86
   r2 mind ray 35
   r2 mission 42
   r2 monadic ray 55
   r2 personality ray 35, 51–53, 59, 62
   r2 physical-etheric body 35
   r2 physical-etheric ray 59
   solar system 55
   soul ray 34, 53–56, 60, 62
   vocations 34, 54
Ray 3 of Intelligent Activity 31, 36–37, 88
   glamours 92–93
   r3 emotional ray 37
   r3 mind ray 37, 58–59, 83

r3 monadic ray 55
r3 personality ray 37, 51–52, 90
r3 physical-etheric ray 37, 45, 48, 56, 58–60, 89, 90
r3 soul ray 36, 53–54
vocations 36, 54
Ray 4 of Harmony through Conflict 31, 38–39, 60–62, 91, 96–97
   glamours 93
   r4 emotional ray 39
   r4 mind ray 39, 49–50, 60, 77
   r4 personality ray 39, 41, 51–53, 56, 58, 62, 83, 86
   r4 physical-etheric ray 39
   r4 soul ray 38, 53–55
   souls coming in 38
   vocations 38, 54
Ray 5 of Concrete Mind & Knowledge 31, 40–41, 60–62, 79, 85, 91, 166–167
   mental energy 79
   mental trouble 79, 85
   r5 emotional ray 41
   r5 mind ray 39, 41, 49, 49–50, 52, 59, 62, 65, 87
     humanity 65
   r5 personality ray 41, 51–52
   r5 physical-etheric ray 41
   r5 soul ray 40, 54–55
   vocations 40, 54
Ray 6 of Devotion & Idealism 31, 42–43, 60–62, 82, 88–89, 166–167
   glamours 93
   governs astral plane 76
   r6 emotional ray 43, 47–49, 56–59, 60, 62, 75, 77–78, 83, 90, 105
   r6 mind ray 43
   r6 personality ray 43, 51–53, 62, 86, 89
   r6 physical-etheric ray 43
   r6 soul ray 42, 47, 53–55, 54, 60, 62
   vocations 42, 54
Ray 7 of Ceremony, Order & Magic 31, 44–45, 60–62, 166–167
   glamours 93
   r7 emotional ray 45
   r7 mind ray 45
   r7 personality ray 45, 51–53
   r7 physical-etheric ray 45, 47–48, 60
   r7 soul ray 44, 53–54
   vocations 44, 54
Rays (Seven) 29–62

7 basic energies of the universe 31
assemble Ray Chart for Carl Jung 56
charts 47–62
   formulate Ray Chart 47–56
   reading ray charts 57–62
disciples can have any ray for any body 47
emotional - astral Ray 47–49, 57–58, 60, 80
for the average person 47
hard-line 31–32, 44, 53–54, 62
if the personality ray is evident 57
in most R6 is the problem ray 57
mind-line 31
mind - mental Ray 47, 49–50, 57, 61
monadic ray 25, 55
personality profile method 47–56
personality Ray 15, 47, 51–53, 57–58, 79, 81
physical-etheric Ray 47–48, 56
power-line 31
produce 7 psychological types 29
profile psychology chart 31
ray of Tibetan's disciples 60, 60–62
ray or spark of God, 5, 182
read Ray Chart 57–62
soft-line 31
soul and personality rays always different 47
Soul ray 27, 47, 52–58, 61–62
strengthen higher ray 57
validate ray selections 56
Razor-edged path 129
Reagan, Ronald 43
Re-orientation 45
Restraining exercises 150
Revelation of Light and Power 107
Rockefeller, John D. 37
Roosevelt, Franklin 33
Root Races defined 183
Rules of the Road 141, 175
Rules (the) - Niyama 139–142
Russel, Bertrand 37

S

Sacral Chakra 11–12, 15, 18–19, 21, 23, 68, 100–101, 103, 137
Sadat, Anwar 33
Sadistic - Sadism 85, 107
Salute to the Sun exercise. 143
Samadhi - Contemplation 118, 131, 155, 162
Sanat Kumara 183
Sankaracharya 175

Sannyasin 174
Sanyama 174
Sattva guna 111, 124–127, 131
Schizophrenia 78, 107–108
Schubert, Franz 39
Schweitzer, Albert 35
Sectarian fanatics 89
Seeger, Pete 43
Seer 128–129, 135, 138
Self-awareness 127
Self-control 132
Self-harm/ self-injury 77
Sequential Thinking 156
Service 15, 28, 95
   a life of 105
   a ray-type 57
   chosen field of 61
   commitments of the soul 43
   defined 28
   group 21, 81
   here on earth for 122
   in the world 25, 62
   mission 39
   plans 45
   practical life of 102
   scientific process 28
   selfish 92
   selfless 42, 54, 107
   selfless and compassionate 159
   some of the world's greatest servers 28
   soul's mission 41
   the ultimate goal 28
   to alleviate suffering 28
   to the teacher, leader or ideal 53
   world-service work 37
Seven Desires 130
Seven Rays & Psychology 29–62
Sex 11, 21, 68, 93, 96, 101, 103, 132, 137–138, 159
   abnormal 67
   frustration 96
   magic 93
Sexual responsibility 138
Shakespeare, William 39–40
Shamballa 17, 25, 183
Shankar, Ravi 173
Shylock 37
Silence 21, 112, 133–134, 142, 145, 152, 168, 170
   meditation on 170

practice of 108, 133
Silver Cord 8
Sir Galahad 43
Sizemore, Chris 75
Smothering in groups 108
Social anxiety disorder 77
Sociopaths 88–89
Solar Angel 7, 17–19, 24, 26, 183
   intervention 1 18
   intervention 2 19
   intervention 3 24
Solar Fire 8, 183
   meditation at the Scorpio full moon 163
   meditation method 163
Solar Logos 121, 182–184
Solar Meditation at the Scorpio Full Moon period 163
Solar plexus Chakra 11–12, 15, 23, 100–105, 140, 151, 171
Solar system 3, 15, 17, 26, 55, 183
Son of Mind 25
Soul 15
   animal soul 104
   defined 183
   find the Soul Ray 54
   human, defined 6
   Laws (7) 81
   r1 soul 32, 53–55, 58–59, 61–62, 83
   r2 soul 34, 53–55, 56, 58, 61–62
   r3 soul 36, 53, 61–62
   r4 soul 38, 53–55
   r5 soul 40, 54–55
   r6 soul 42, 53–55, 61–62
   r7 soul 44, 53–55, 61–62
   ray soul 27, 47, 52–55, 57–59, 61–62, 84
      can be any of the 7 rays 47, 53
   spiritual soul, defined. 6
   vocations 32, 34, 36, 38, 40, 42, 54
Spark of mind 18
Spirit, Soul and Body
   trilogy 6
Spiritual
   being 70
   hierarchy 81, 166
   mind 5, 16
   path iii, 4, 7, 13, 100, 167, 175
   plan 22
   triad 5, 7–8, 15–16, 24, 26
Split personality 75

Stalin, Josef 33
Stalking 90
Standing in spiritual being 70–71
Standing on the Bridge exercise 140
Steadfastness 39
Stealing 132, 136
Stillness 37
STIMULATION Problem 73, 83, 85–97
    1: Too intense thinkers 85–90
        megalomaniacs 87
        mental extroverts 88–90
        mentally introverted 86
    2: Illusion, Glamour, Maya 91–94
    3: Guidance and Dreams 95–97
Sudden Infant Death Syndrome 75–76
Sushumna 8
Sutratma 8, 16
Swami Sivananda 126

T

Tai Chi 78, 143, 159
Tamas guna 111
Thatcher, Margaret 33
Theft 88, 132, 136, 138
The goal of this book 4
The Great Invocation 162, 165
The Highest and Lowest meet 45
The Highest Light controls 43
There is only one Source of Life and Light. 120
Think an opposite thought 117, 134, 154
Thou God seest me 160
Thread of Continuity 8
Three Faces of Eve film 75
Three minds unite 41
Throat Chakra 8–9, 11, 15, 18–19, 21, 23, 100–103, 117–118, 138
Tibetan Master
    disciples 60–62
Tibetan Master (DK) 180
Touch of Acquiescence 19
Touch of Appropriation 18
Touch of Enlightenment 24
Transfiguration 24
Triad, Spiritual 5, 183
Triangle Technique 122
True servers 28, 172
Trump, Donald 33
Truth 20, 23, 27, 34, 39, 40, 42–43, 49, 53–55, 66, 70, 91, 97, 104, 107–108, 119, 130, 132, 135–136, 141, 149, 153, 168, 172, 180
Truthfulness 136
Two merge with One 39

U

Unabomber 86
Universal
    design 55
    love 11
    mind 3, 6, 157
    soul 6, 180
    soul, buddhi 180
    spirit 180

V

Van Gogh, Vincent 39
Vedanta teachings 3
Vinci, Leonardo da 39–40, 45
Vivekananda 111, 142–143, 154
Vocation 28, 71, 80, 82–83
    via the rays 32, 34, 36, 38, 40, 42, 44, 54, 56–58
Voice of Silence 112
Vrittis 79, 112, 114, 118
    defined 79

W

Wagner, Richard 39
Weak physical-etheric link 75–76
Wesak 163, 183
Wheel of Rebirth 13
Whitman, Charles Joseph 86
Whitman, Walt 33
Winehouse, Amy 77
Wisdom 3–4, 11, 17, 27–28, 34, 41, 53–56, 58–59, 67, 80, 87, 102, 109–111, 113, 122–123, 126–127, 131, 142, 157–158, 160–162, 169–170, 175, 180–182, 182, 183
Words of power 33, 35, 37, 39, 43, 45
Wright Brothers 41
Wrong questioning 115–116

Y

Yama, the Commandments 131–138
Yoga of Light Meditation 168

www.ingramcontent.com/pod-product-compliance
Lightning Source LLC
Chambersburg PA
CBHW060532010526
44107CB00059B/2624